POSTCARD HISTORY SERIES

Broward County

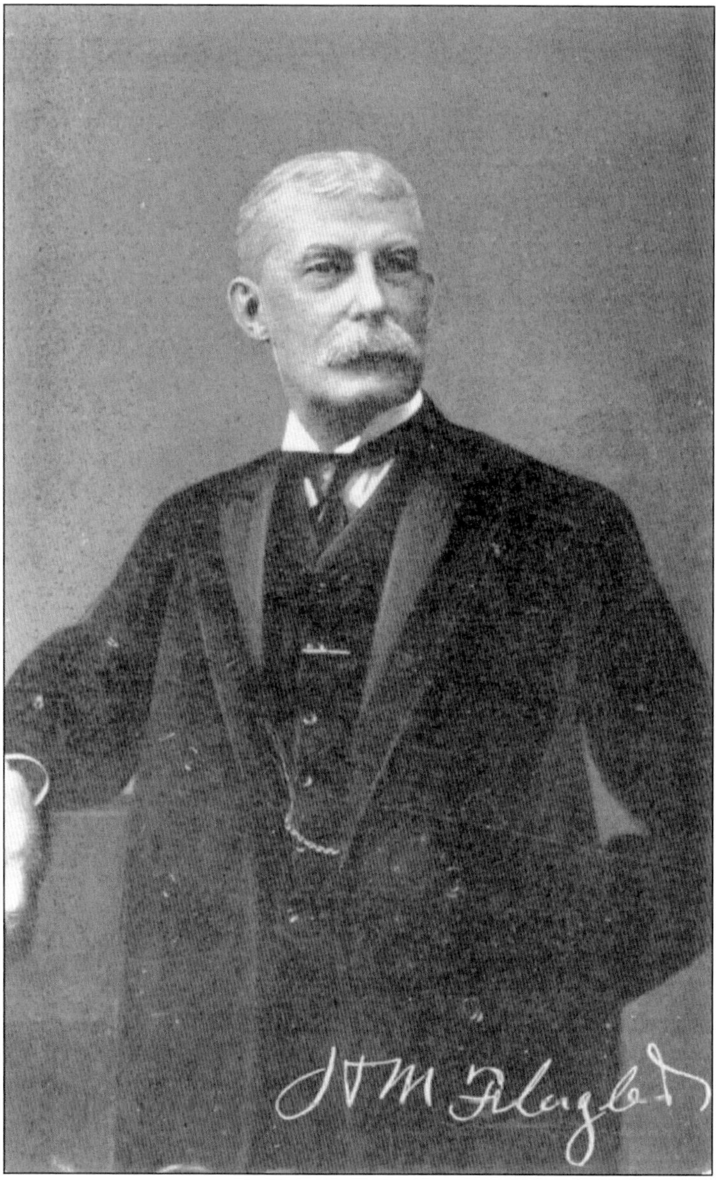

He was—and remains—the single most revered person in Florida history, and it was from the genius and vision of Henry M. Flagler that almost all of the east coast of Florida arose, including most of the eastern portion of Broward County. He is, unquestionably, "our founder." (Author's collection.)

On the Front Cover: A Seminole Indian family, most likely on or near the tribe's reservation on US Route 441 in Broward County (now the site of the Seminole Hard Rock Hotel and Casino), points to a passing National Airlines plane cruising over the reservation. (Author's collection.)

On the Back Cover: Although much busier, more hectic, and a good bit more fast-paced, most of Federal Highway in downtown Dania continues to offer visitors a friendly, small-town, at-home feeling similar to the one evinced on this postcard of that street in Dania around the late 1930s or possibly just after World War II. (Author's collection.)

POSTCARD HISTORY SERIES

Broward County

Seth H. Bramson
Foreword by Mayor Barbara Sharief

ARCADIA PUBLISHING

ISBN 978-1-4671-2722-6

Published by Arcadia Publishing
Charleston, South Carolina

Printed in the United States of America

Library of Congress Control Number: 2017937006

For all general information contact Arcadia Publishing at:
Telephone 843-853-2070
Fax 843-853-0044
E-mail sales@arcadiapublishing.com
For customer service and orders:
Toll-Free 1-888-313-2665

Visit us on the Internet at www.arcadiapublishing.com

Contents

FOREWORD

I am so honored to be a part of this Broward County postcard history book. My family and I certainly are a proud part of this local history. I was born in South Florida and raised as a teenager in Broward County, along with my seven brothers and sisters. Most of us still live in Broward and are raising our children here. My three daughters were born in Broward County and currently attend Broward County public schools. My father was a clothing manufacturer, my mother worked by his side, and as a child, I would travel with him throughout Broward County selling garments.

As an adult, I went on to start my own small business in Broward, and through much hard work and the grace of the good people who live here, it has grown and flourished over the past decade. As a business owner and active parent, I became very involved in community activities, which led to life in public service. I was elected to the Broward County Board of County Commissioners in 2012, and in 2014, I myself made history when I became the first African American woman to serve as the mayor of Broward County. In 2016, I was once again elected to serve as mayor and am honored to represent the residents of District 8, which is in the southwest portion of Broward County, including the cities of Pembroke Pines, Miramar, Hallandale Beach, Pembroke Park, and West Park. Prior to my election to the Broward County Board of County Commissioners, I served as vice mayor and city commissioner in Miramar.

I appreciate the multifaceted, multicultural history of Broward County and am honored to play a role in shaping our modern county—the second-most populous in the state and seventeenth-most populous in the nation—as it enjoys a thriving economy, an internationally diverse population, and being included among the top vacation destinations in the world!

It is my hope that our ancestors would be proud of the Broward County that we are today, and that we have paved the way for an exciting, prosperous Broward County in the future.

—Mayor Barbara Sharief, MSN, ARNP

Acknowledgments

The author extends warm thanks to Hollywood pioneer Robert A. Banks, whose family came to that city in 1923. Banks has spent a lifetime there and gave me a copy of the 2014 souvenir program of Broward County's 42nd annual Pioneer Days event. Much of the information herein was taken from that publication. Longtime friends Andrea and Jonathan Nelson loaned me the Hollywood Florida East Coast Railway station postcard shown on page 10.

A very special thank-you must also be extended to two dear friends: Bernard "Barney" Mayrsohn, veteran of the Battle of the Bulge in World War II, German prisoner of war, Stalag 4B survivor, and recipient of the Bronze Star and two Purple Hearts, and WLRN Radio's Ted Grossman, host of the *Night Train with Ted Grossman* program heard on South Florida public radio stations every Sunday night for 13 years, both of whom listened to my captions and offered warm thoughts and input throughout the writing of this book.

Finally (and I would write "it goes without saying," but I absolutely must say it), I could not have done it without my bride of now more than 40 years, Myrna, putting up with me, being my sounding board, encouraging me, and allowing me to vent my occasional annoyance at the gremlins creeping in.

Other than the aforementioned postcard loaned to the author by Andrea and Jonathan Nelson, all postcards in this book are from the collection of the author.

INTRODUCTION

The creation of Broward County is one of the most fascinating stories in the frenzied partitioning and naming of Florida counties that went on from the early years of the 20th century through the mid-1920s and even a bit later.

The county came into existence on October 1, 1915, and was named for Napoleon Bonaparte Broward, who served as governor of Florida from 1905 until 1909. Broward (April 19, 1857–October 1, 1910) was an American river pilot and captain. He later became a politician who, before becoming governor, served as the sheriff of Duval County, in which Jacksonville is located, and in the Florida House of Representatives. He was allied with the Straightouts, a group made up of the Populist-leaning elements of the Florida Democratic Party.

On January 3, 1905, Broward was elected as the 19th governor of Florida, with a term that lasted until January 5, 1909. He remains best known for his major project—"to drain the Everglades to recover land for agricultural cultivation and turn it into useful land." At the time, the idea of the state converting the swamp (now a major national park) into farmland was believed to be sound. Broward built alliances with the federal government to gain funds for the project, and many of the canals that run from south-central Florida to the east coast were either conceived of or begun as part of that project.

The county was originally intended to be named Everglades County, but then–speaker of the Florida House of Representatives Ion Farris amended the bill that established the county so that it would be named after Broward.

In 1915, Palm Beach County (which was created in 1909 by taking land from Dade County and which held approximately half of the land that would later become Broward County) and Dade County (which included most of what would become the southern half of Broward County) contributed nearly equal portions of land to create the new county. The term "contributed" is, of course, misleading, as the two counties had their lands removed from them by the state legislature in order to form the new county.

Broward County began a huge development boom after its incorporation, with the first "tourist hotel" opening in 1919 in Fort Lauderdale. A year later, developers began dredging wetlands in the county in order to create island communities.

By 1926, the great Florida boom of the early and mid-1920s was considered to have reached its peak, but the September 1926 hurricane, which devastated Dade and southern Broward Counties, caused an economic decline throughout South Florida; today, historians consider this a harbinger of the Great Depression yet to come in October 1929.

At its inception, Broward County was considered a leader in agricultural products and services within the state, with communities including Pompano Beach, Hallandale, Dania, and Fort Lauderdale becoming major farming centers.

Fort Lauderdale and Broward County were both founded in 1915, with both celebrating their centennials in 2015. Although Hollywood (created by the legendary Joseph Young) and Deerfield Beach (originally the Town of Deerfield, incorporated on June 11, 1925) were founded 10 years after Broward County came into existence, other towns and cities along the Intracoastal Waterway were incorporated a good bit earlier, including Dania Beach ("Broward's first city," founded in November 1904) and Pompano Beach (Town of Pompano, 1908), while Hallandale Beach (Town of Hallandale) became a municipality on May 14, 1927.

Interestingly, Dania Beach and Pompano Beach were founded in their original incarnations while those communities (as well as what would become Broward County) were still part of

Dade County. Had Broward County not been created, Dania Beach and the Town of Pompano would have been, respectively, the second and third incorporated municipalities in the county to the south. While Miami came into existence as a city in July 1896, it was not until 1913 that Homestead was created, so both the original Dania and the original Pompano are older than Miami-Dade County's second-oldest city.

As of 2016, the population of Broward County was approximately 1,800,000 people, making it the second most populous county in Florida and the 17th most populous in the United States. Broward County is considered part of the Miami metropolitan area, which, at the time of the 2015 census, was home to more than six million people.

As part of a major American metropolitan area, Broward County is home to several corporate headquarters, stunning condominiums, grand parks and recreational areas, innumerable homes and businesses, and a plethora of restaurant and club operations that run the gamut from fast food to ultra-elegant. The county has become, suffice it to say, a marvelous place in which to open and operate a business, raise a family, attend school, and enjoy cultural events and fine dining.

Florida International University, Nova Southeastern University, Broward College (formerly a community college; now a four-year school) and Florida Atlantic University all maintain campuses in the county. The Broward County Sheriff's Office, which encompasses Fire-Rescue, is one of the largest sheriff's departments in the country.

The city of Fort Lauderdale will host a station on All Aboard Florida's Brightline, the high-speed passenger train operation currently under construction, and the city and the county are now constructing the Wave, a new light rail operation that will connect destinations in and near downtown Fort Lauderdale and the arts and entertainment district. The suburbs contain upscale malls with a range of food and beverage and hospitality operations that can only be found in a metropolitan area as hip and attuned to quality and progress as Broward County.

Broward's history is both fascinating and intriguing, and in terms of the postcards related to that history, this book will present—for the first time—a new and unique look at the county. The reader should be aware that, while Arcadia Publishing has previously published postcard histories of both Fort Lauderdale and Hollywood, and while it is certainly necessary to include both of those cities in this book, not only are there no more than 18 postcard views presented for each of those two cities, but none of those postcards duplicate cards already seen in the previous two books.

A final—and very important—note regarding the importance of postcards as historical source material is in order here: readers are asked to note and recognize that, in many cases, the only visuals that exist of a given place (or of people) at a given point in time may often be the postcard or cards showing that scene or those people, and there are often no other comparable existing images. In this book, many of the scenes are one of a kind and may be the only record of a particular building, street, or locale.

Now, you are warmly and cordially invited to sit back, relax, peruse, and thoroughly enjoy the first-ever postcard history of Broward County, Florida.

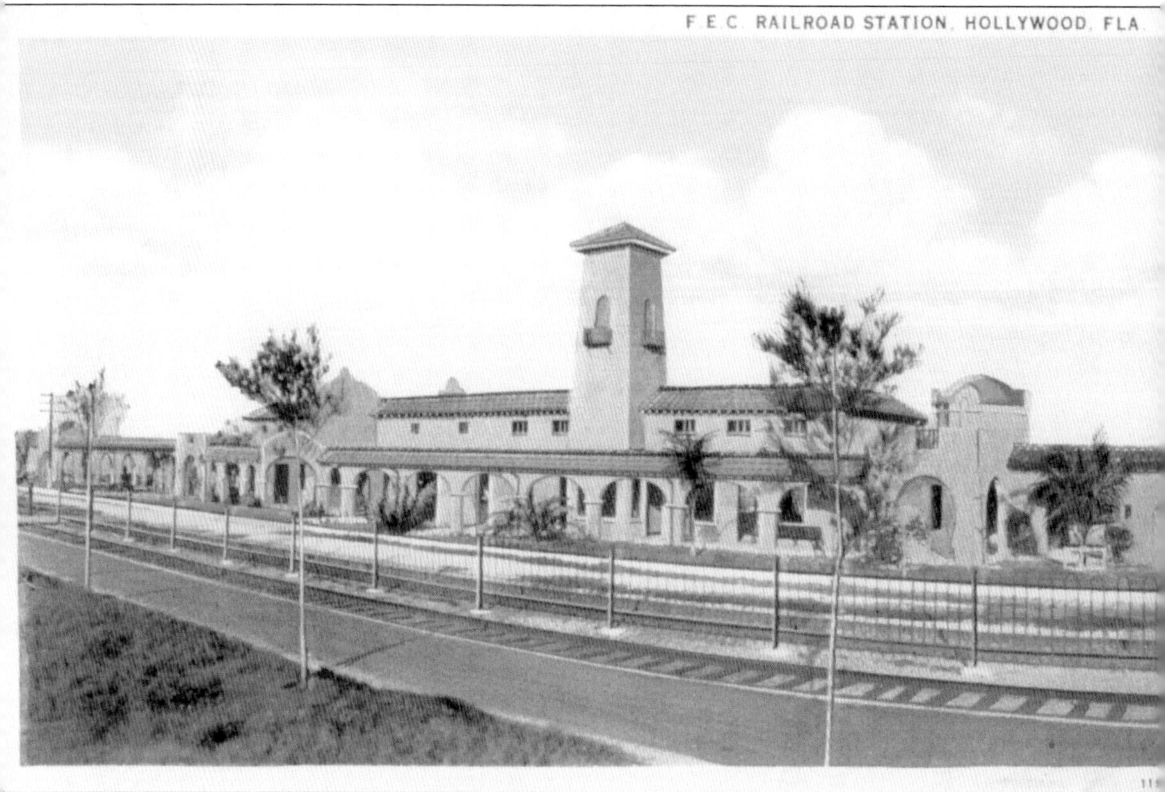

The Hollywood Florida East Coast Railway station was built by Joseph W. Young, founder of the city of Hollywood, so that those arriving in the area could see the beauty of Hollywood as soon as they got there. The city, committing one of the worst architectural crimes in the history of Florida, tore down this magnificent edifice sometime in the late 1960s—an act that would never be allowed today. (Courtesy Andrea and Jonathan Nelson.)

One

Hallandale Beach

Hallandale Beach, like most of Broward County, had no permanent population of European descendants until the end of the 19th century. Seminole Indians lived in settlements that lay inland of the Atlantic shore, hunted in the area, and gathered coontie roots to produce arrowroot starch.

According to *Hallandale Beach, Florida: For More Than 90 Years Broward County's City of Choice,* Henry Flagler's land commissioner, James Ingraham, recruited his brother-in-law Luther Halland to found a settlement south of the community of Dania. Halland and Swedish immigrant Olaf Zetterlund touted the frost-free climate and cheap land of the settlement (then named Halland, later changed to Hallandale) and constructed a small trading post.

By 1900, the community had slowly grown to include a dozen non-native families—seven of them Swedish, three of them English, and two of them of African descent. In 1904, the first school was built, and the first church followed two years later. Hallandale was primarily a farming community; the beach was undeveloped and used by residents only for recreational purposes.

Municipal records show that Hallandale was incorporated on May 14, 1927. By that time, it was a thriving community of 1,500 residents and had electricity and street lights. In 1947, Hallandale was reincorporated as a city, allowing it to expand its borders through annexation of nearby unincorporated land on the ocean side of the Intracoastal Waterway. In August 1999, the city's name was officially changed to Hallandale Beach. The city is home to two major pari-mutuel venues, Gulfstream Race Track and Casino and the Mardi Gras Casino, which includes the former Hollywood Dog Track.

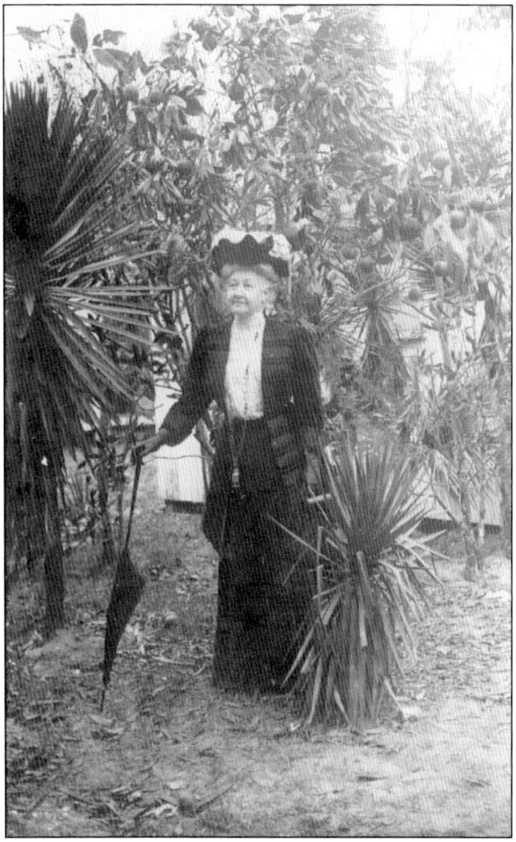

Almost from its beginning, Hallandale (later Hallandale Beach) was a town (later a city) with numerous tourist courts, trailer parks, and cabins for travelers en route to and from Miami and points south. In addition, it was farm country, and this 1910 original real-photo postcard shows "E.E.D." (her name was signed with initials) standing in front of an orange tree, likely at a private home.

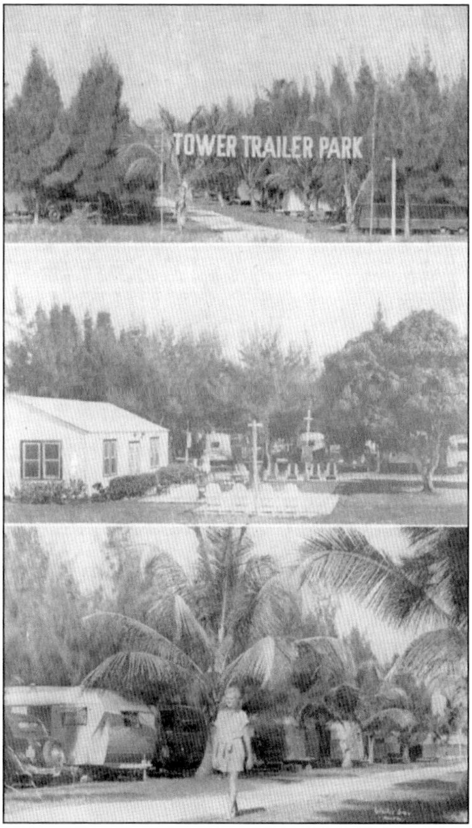

Tower Trailer Park was "1 1/2 miles south of Hollywood, two blocks west of Gulfstream Track," according to this postcard. It was complete with a clubhouse, "shuffleboards," large sanitary washrooms, and a "well stocked store."

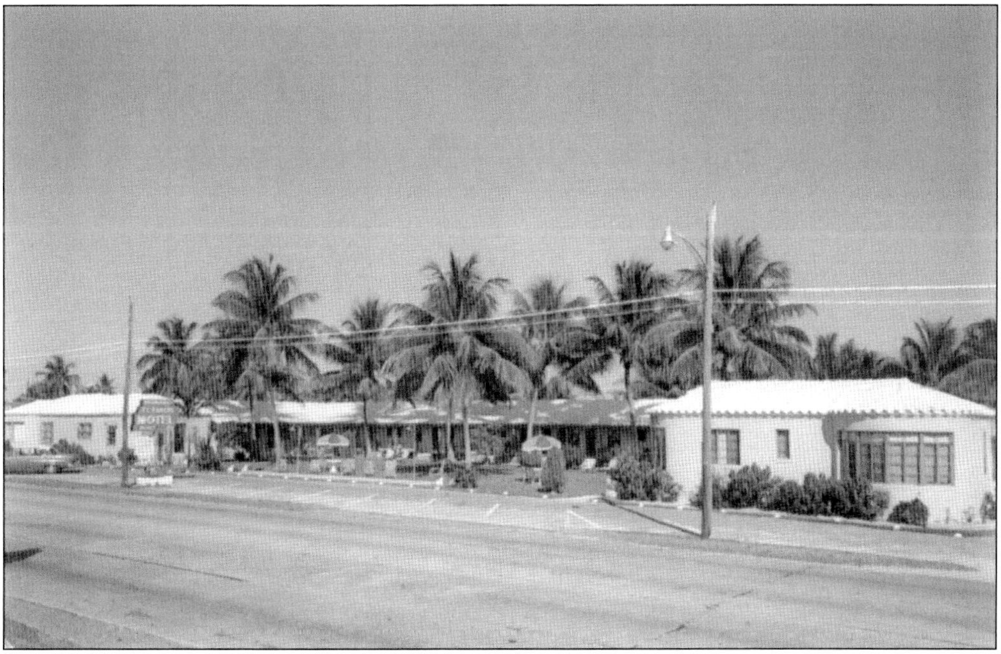

El Rancho Motel Court was at 426 North Federal Highway (US Route 1) and featured "modern hotel rooms, efficiencies and apartments." The time period depicted here is the early to mid-1950s.

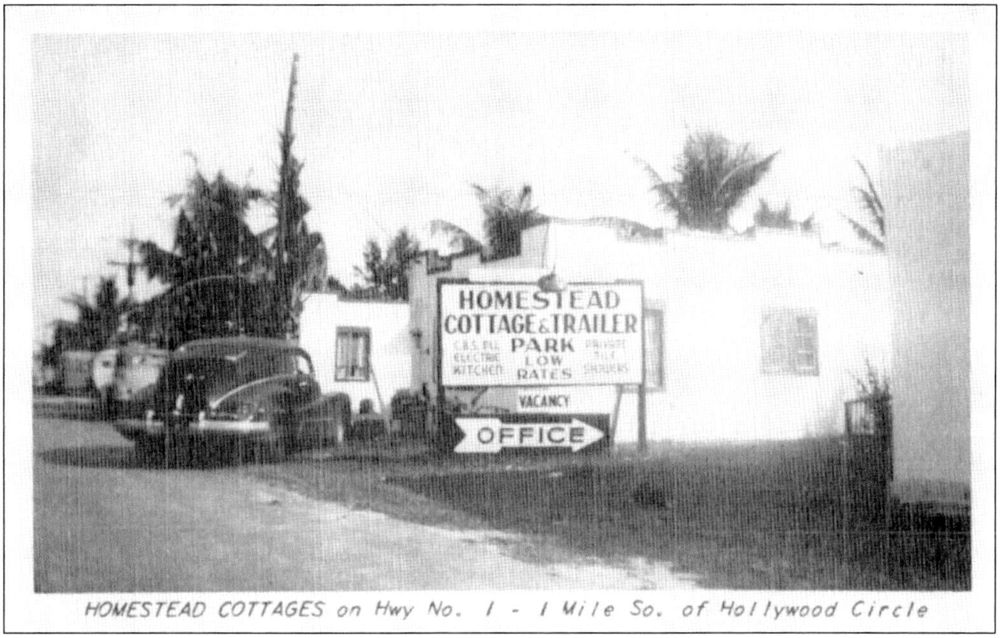

Homestead Cottage & Trailer Park, located one mile south of Hollywood Circle, offered the traveler CBS (concrete block structure), all-electric kitchens, and "private tile showers," which certainly would have been a welcome amenity for those in the know.

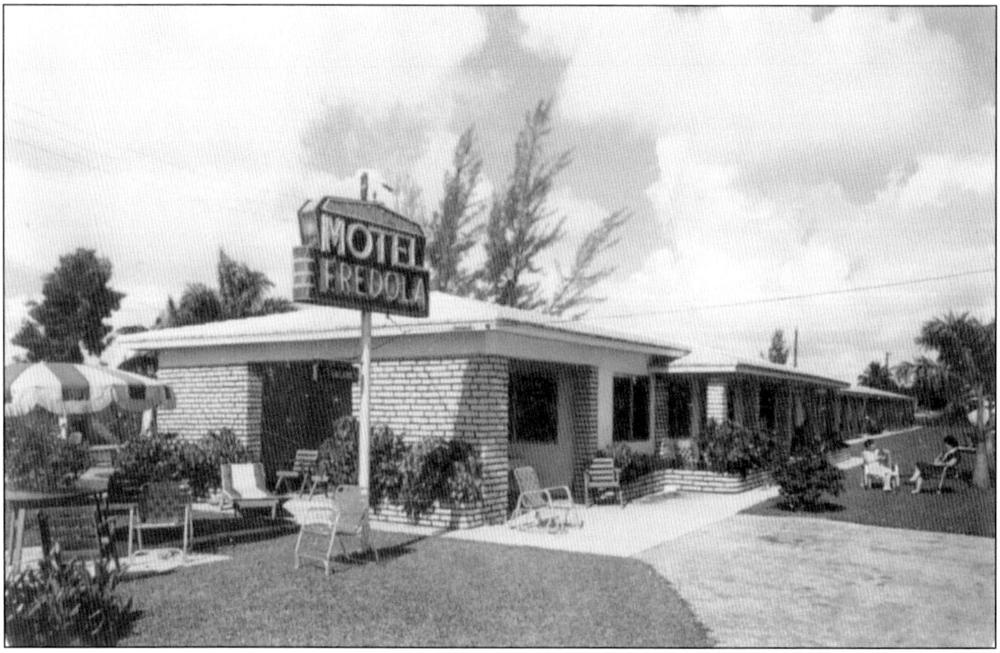

At 900 South Federal Highway, the Motel Fredola, operated by Mr. and Mrs. F.I. Biller, was directly across from the south entrance to Gulfstream Park. The Billers prided themselves on the Fredola's "clean, spacious rooms, hot water heat and tiled baths."

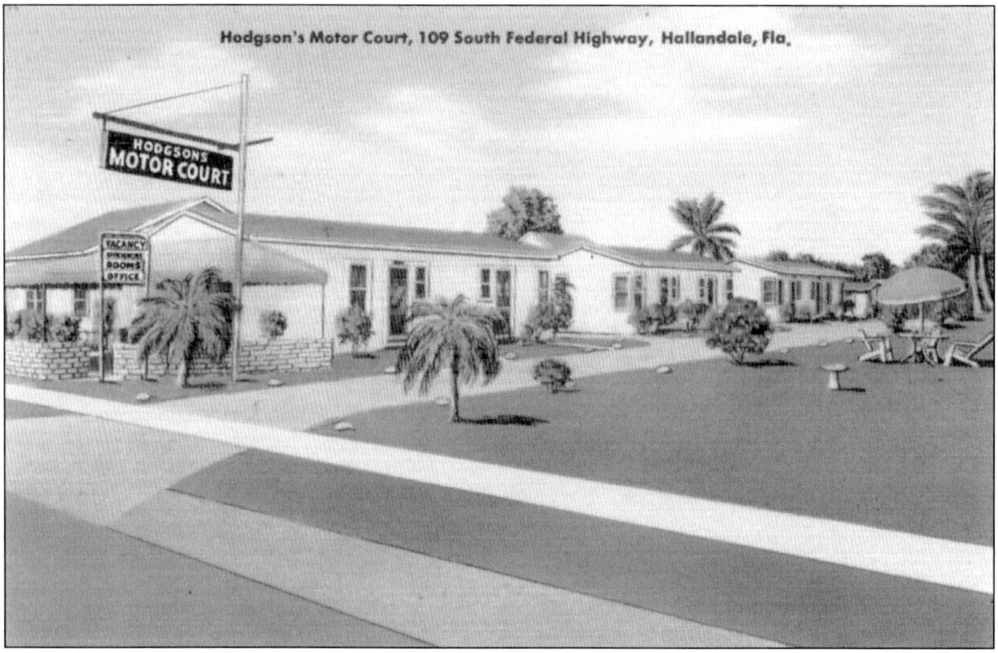

Hodgson's Motor Court, two miles south of the Hollywood Circle, was located at 109 South Federal Highway on the east side of the street just a block south of Hallandale Beach Boulevard. This card, with its linen finish, appears to have been published in the early 1940s.

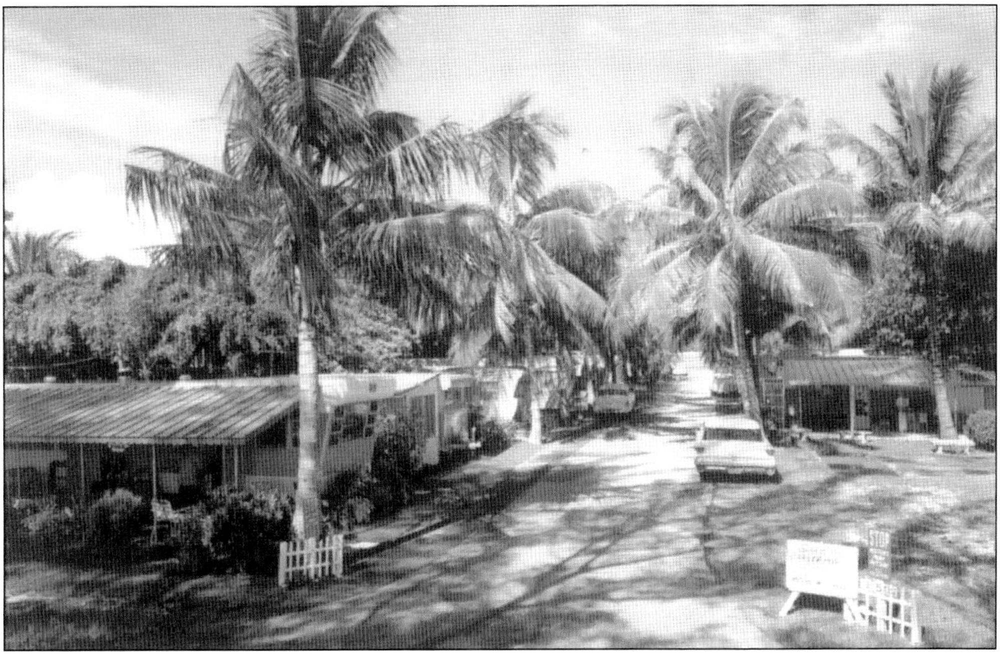

Sea Esta Trailer Court and Sales, located at 350 Northeast Seventh Street, was owned by Dorothy and Wayne Lagant. Apparently, a good number of the employees of the Hollywood Dog Track in Hallandale lived at Sea Esta during racing season, as the back of this card notes that the location was "1st Street South of Dog Track."

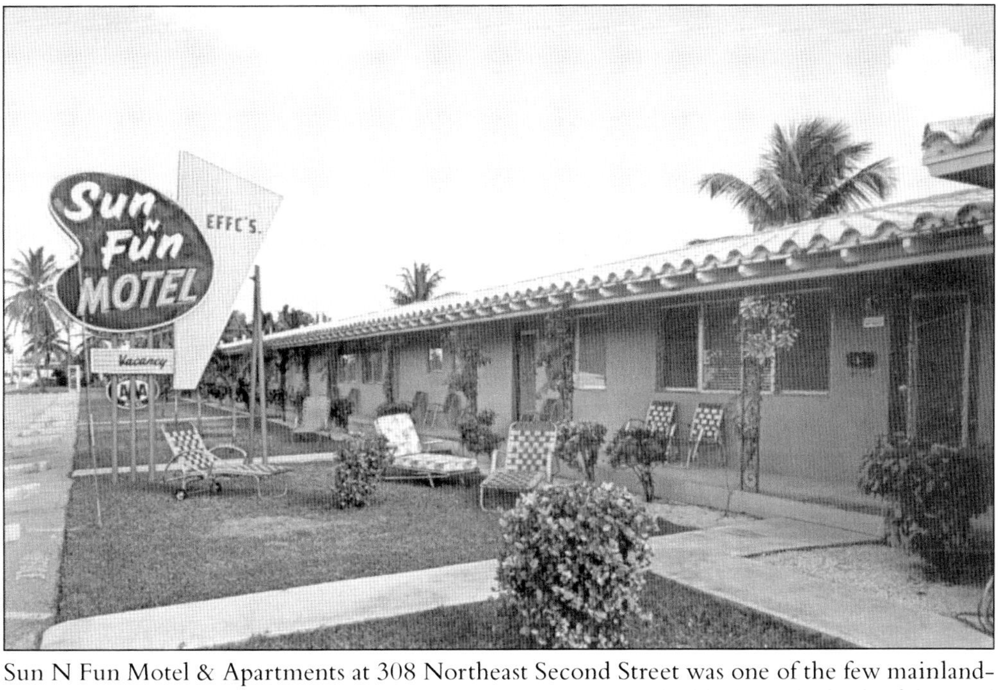

Sun N Fun Motel & Apartments at 308 Northeast Second Street was one of the few mainland-side inns to carefully note that it had air-conditioned rooms. The blurb on the back of this card states that it was "within walking distance of Gulfstream Park & Hollywood Dog Track."

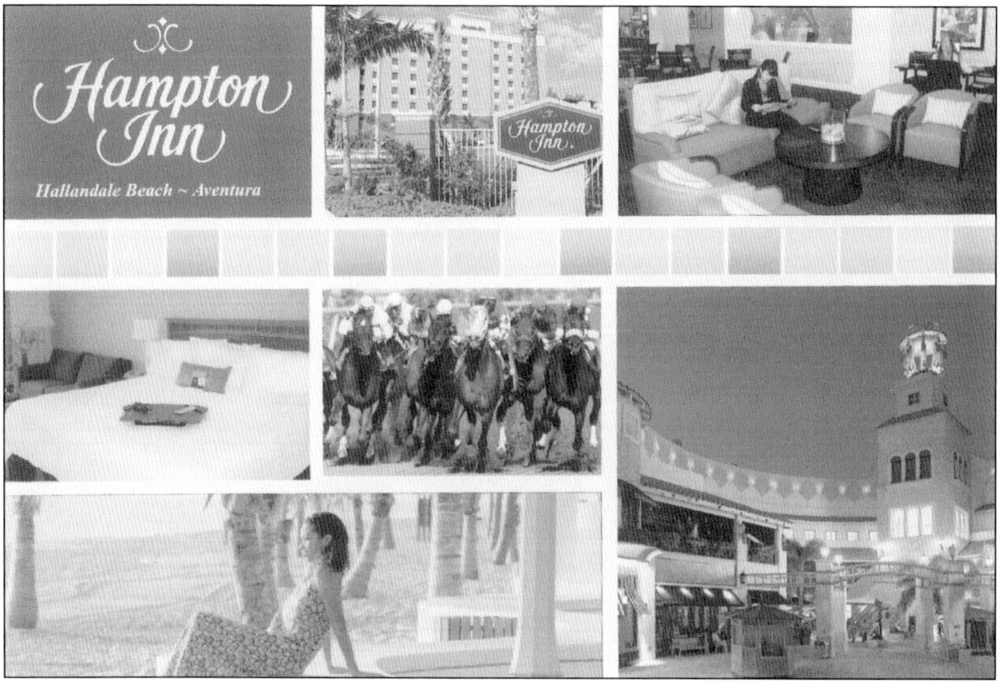

Modern Hallandale Beach has a relatively new Hampton Inn just north of the Miami-Dade–Broward line at 1000 South Federal Highway. With the amenities expected of an up-to-date hospitality venue, the Hampton Inn is a favored location for overnight or short stays near the Gulfstream Race Track and Casino.

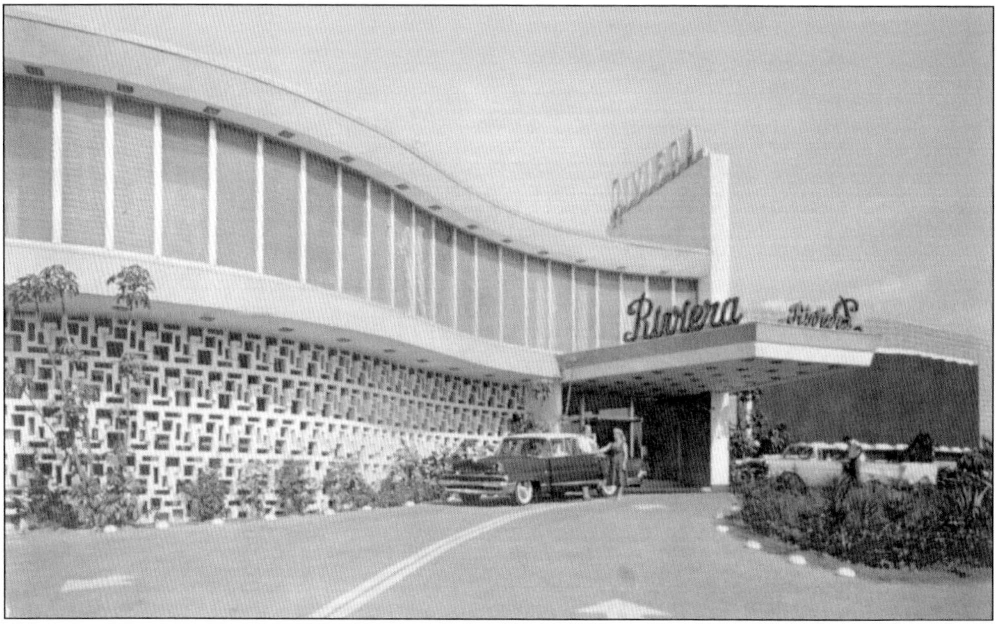

One of the motels on the ocean side of Hallandale Beach was the Gates Riviera at 2080 Ocean Boulevard. The back of this postcard stated it was "just north of Miami Beach," but in reality, Miami Beach was a good eight or nine miles south, with the traveler having to pass through Golden Beach, Sunny Isles Beach, Haulover Beach, Bal Harbour Village, and Surfside to reach it.

The Moongate Resort was also located on the ocean side at 1920 South Ocean Drive. This futuristic-looking property featured a swimming pool, coffee shop, and the Moonfleet Cocktail Lounge well before the USS *Enterprise* could "beam them up."

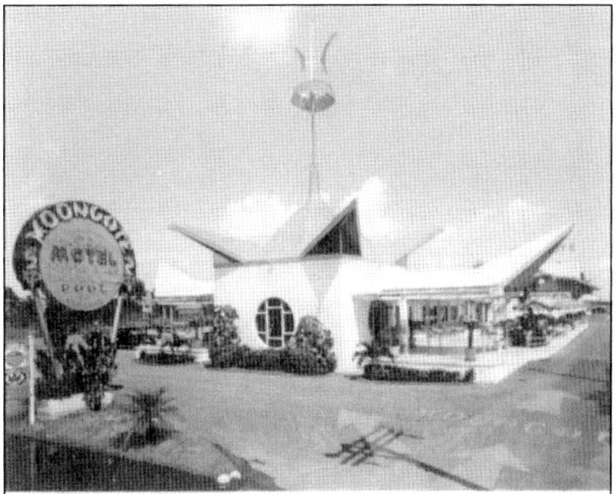

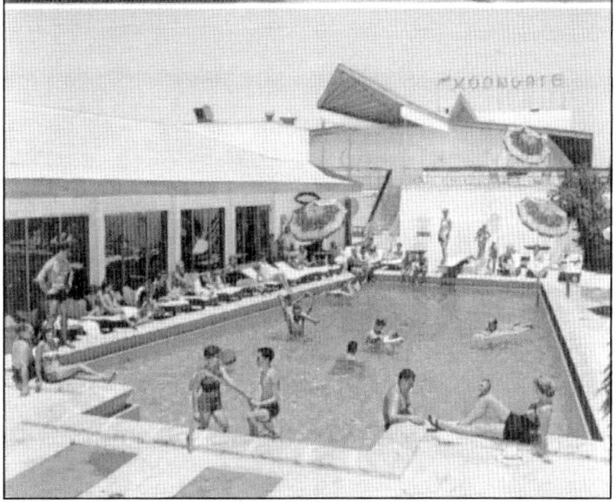

With this postcard making it appear as if there was nothing of note nearby, the Sea Banks advertised itself as "located in a secluded area just north of Miami Beach." Priding itself on its "carefully selected clientele," the motel was one of the few properties in Hallandale Beach that did not welcome Jewish guests.

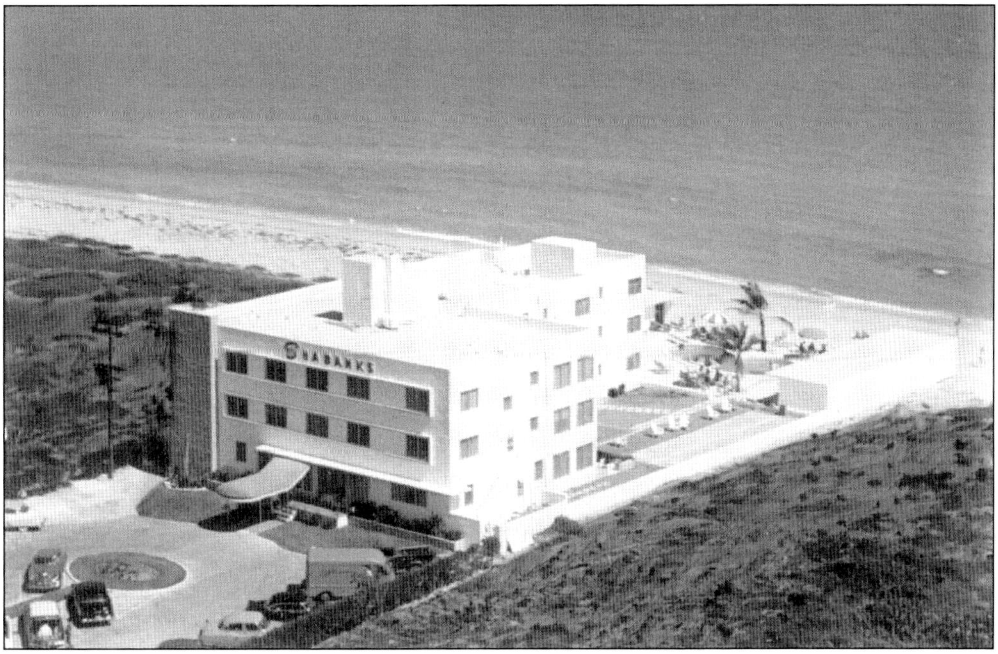

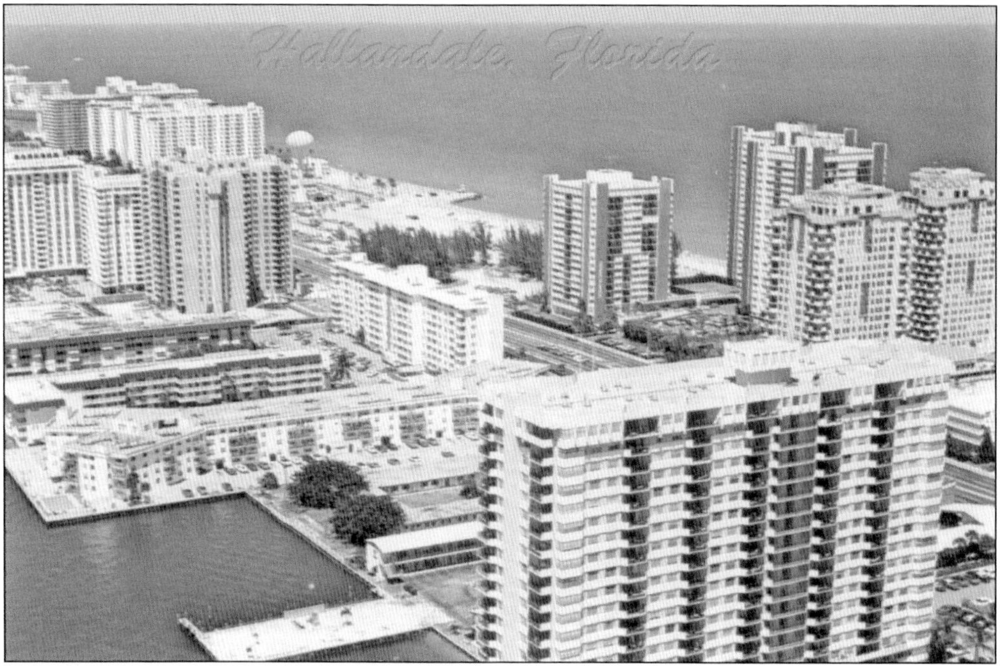

A later view of the ocean side of Hallandale Beach shows the city built up with high rises and condos and the small motels long gone from the scene. Here, the city's water tower is visible (upper left) at the intersection of Ocean Drive and Hallandale Beach Boulevard.

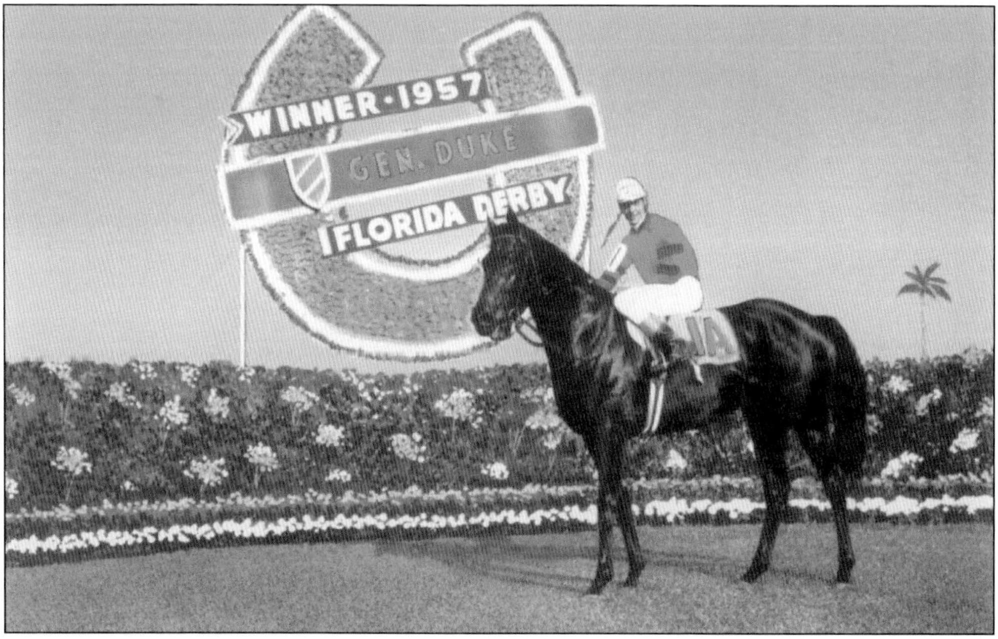

Gulfstream Park now features a major casino with numerous high-end shops, but until slot machines and unlimited poker were made legal through a state constitutional amendment, Gulfstream operated as a horse-racing track only during several winter months. The winner of the Florida Derby was generally one of the favorites to run in the Triple Crown of Thoroughbred Racing, and in 1957, Calumet Farm's General Duke, shown here, was that year's winner.

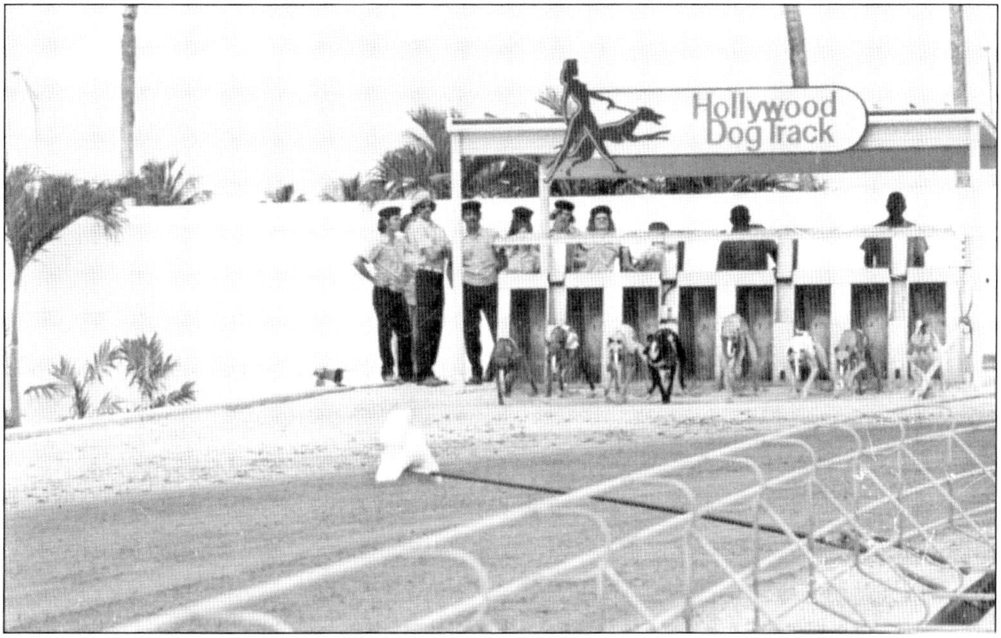

Hallandale Beach was the home of both Gulfstream and Hollywood Dog Track, with that pari-mutuel now renamed the Mardi Gras Casino. This view of the chutes, with the dogs leaping forward to chase the mechanical rabbit, is reminiscent of the pre-casino years.

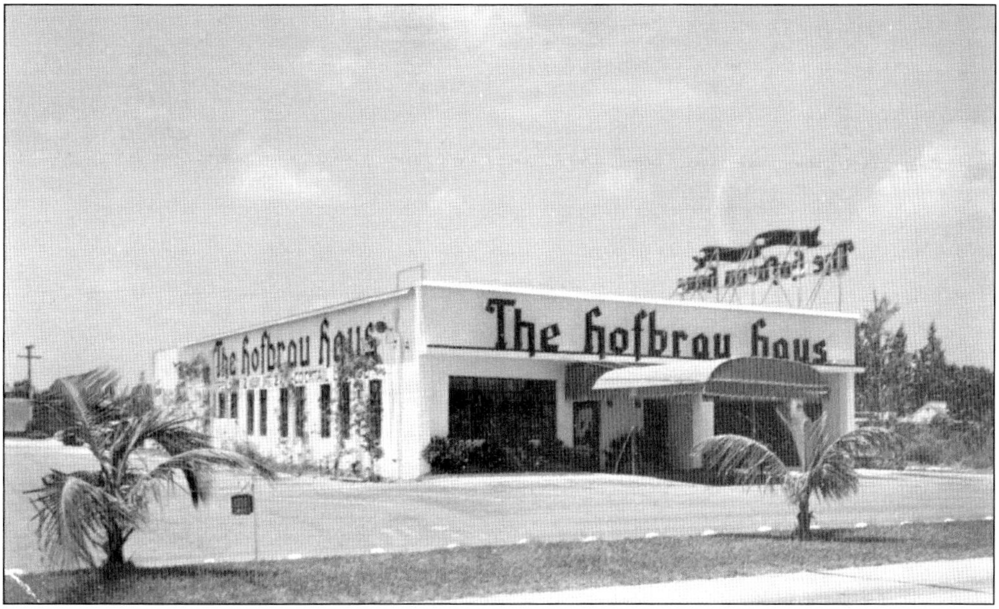

For many years, two German cuisine restaurants, Old Heidelberg and The Hofbrau Haus, were prime destinations for dining in South Broward County. The Hofbrau Haus is shown here in its original incarnation.

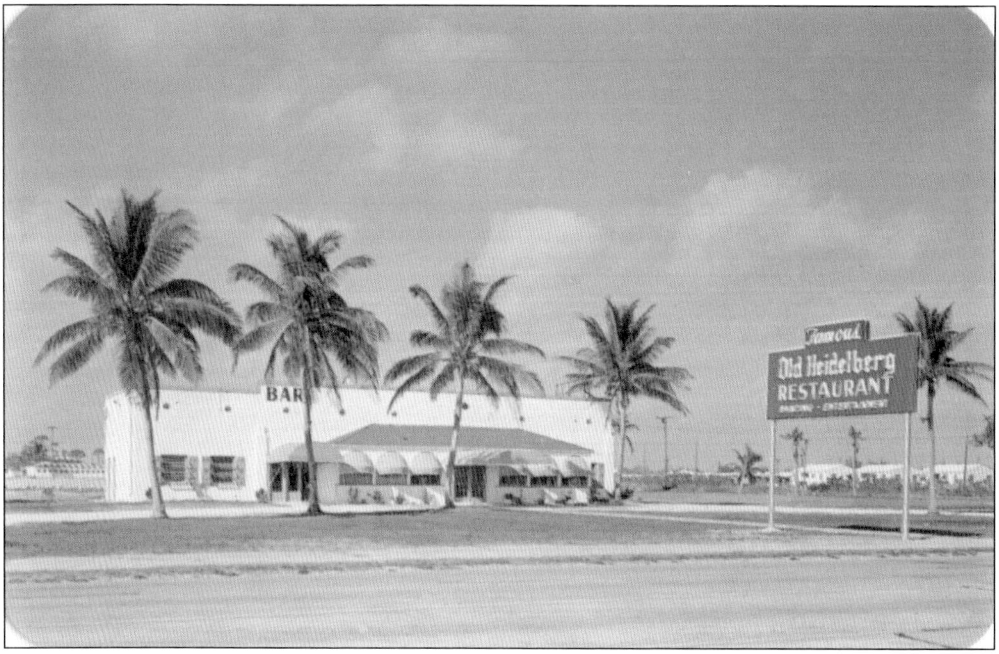

Another very popular German restaurant in Hallandale was Old Heidelberg, sometimes known simply as "Heidelberg." These two images show the original building on Federal Highway and the doubled-in-size remodeled facility.

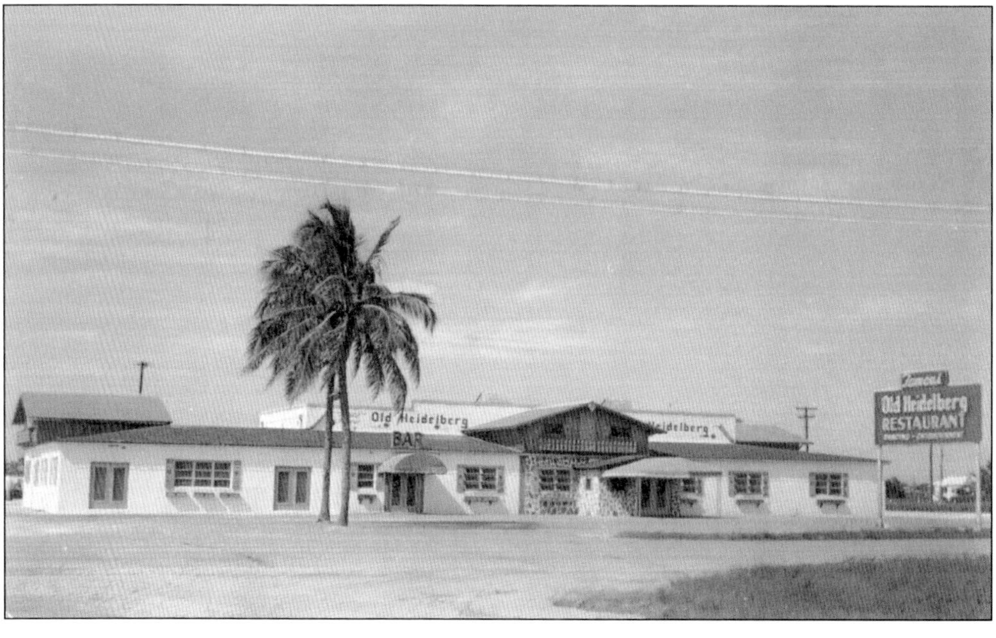

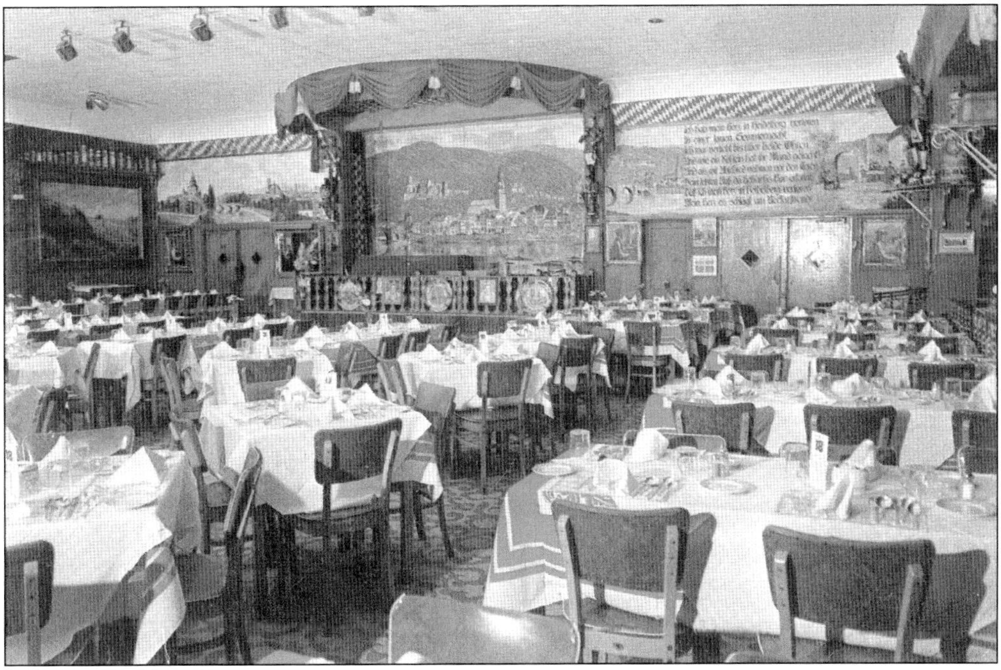

After it was rebuilt, Old Heidelberg, located next to the Hollywood Dog Track, was not only a fine dining spot but also a marvelous entertainment venue; the bandstand and stage are shown in the center background.

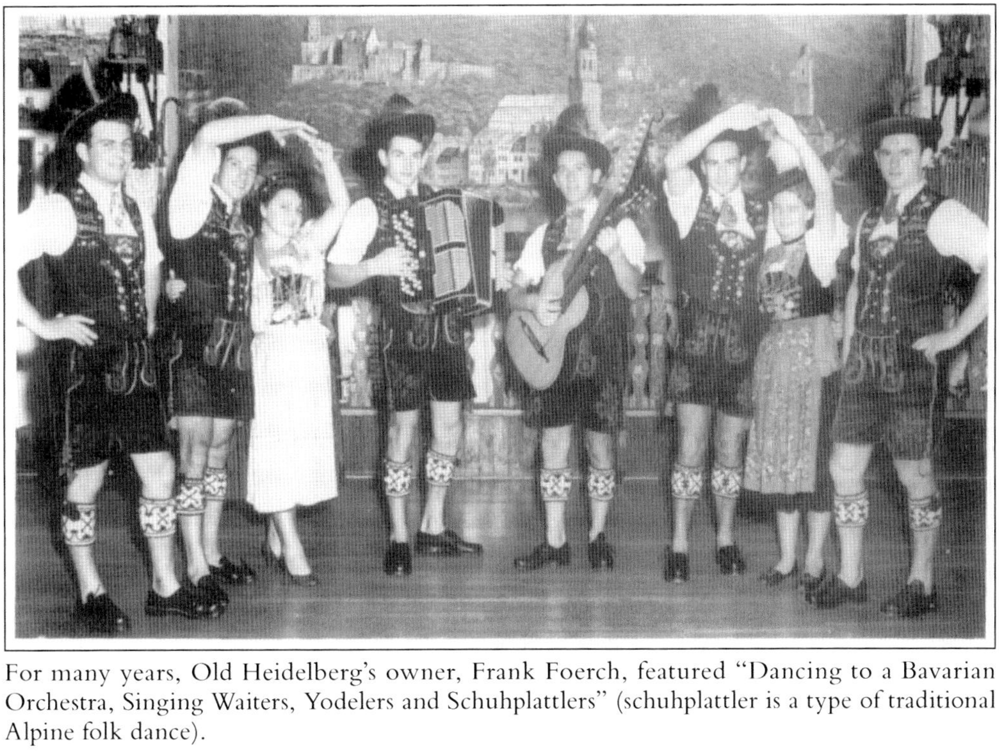

For many years, Old Heidelberg's owner, Frank Foerch, featured "Dancing to a Bavarian Orchestra, Singing Waiters, Yodelers and Schuhplattlers" (schuhplattler is a type of traditional Alpine folk dance).

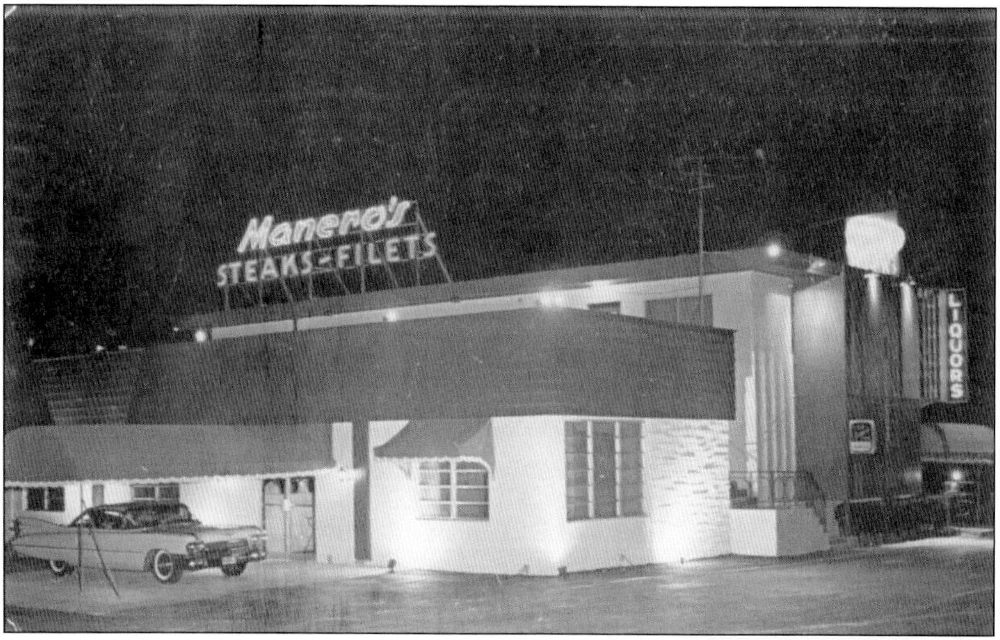

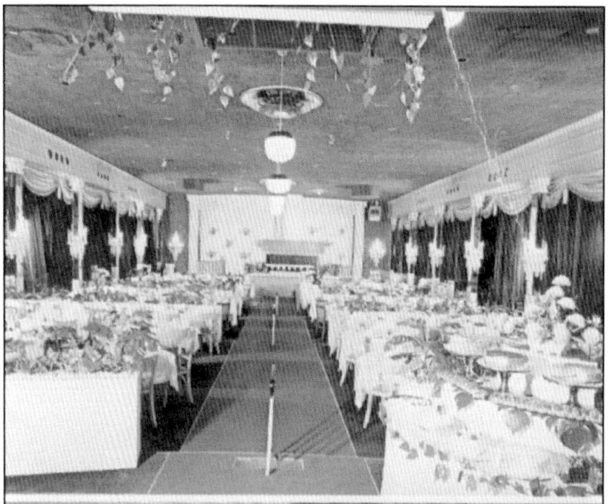

Numerous revered restaurants lured diners to Hallandale and Hallandale Beach. Manero's was on the south side of Hallandale Beach Boulevard just west of the Intracoastal Waterway Bridge. Famous for its steaks and filets, Manero's was the southernmost outpost of a chain of restaurants in Connecticut, New Jersey, and New York.

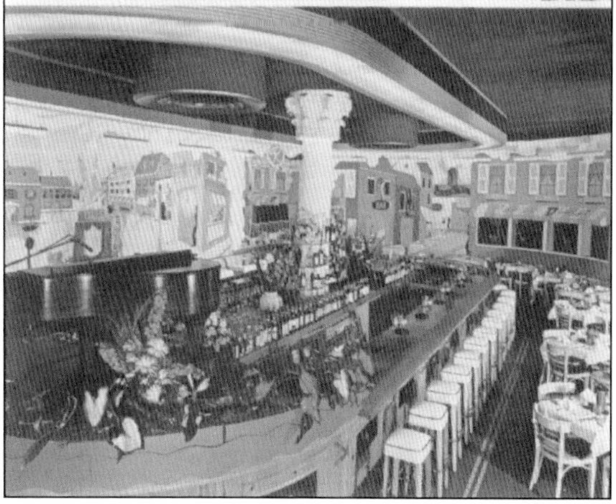

Dewey's was a steak and lobster house located next to Gulfstream at 935 South Federal Highway. It must have been enormous, as the back of this postcard states that it has a "Seating Capacity over One Thousand."

Appearing nightly at the Driftwood Lounge, located at 270 North Federal Highway, David Casson presented "the world's only three keyboard Hammond Organ in South Florida's first theater type installation." An asterisk notes that the claim of being "the world's only three keyboard . . . organ" is "To Our Knowledge"—apparently just in case it was not!

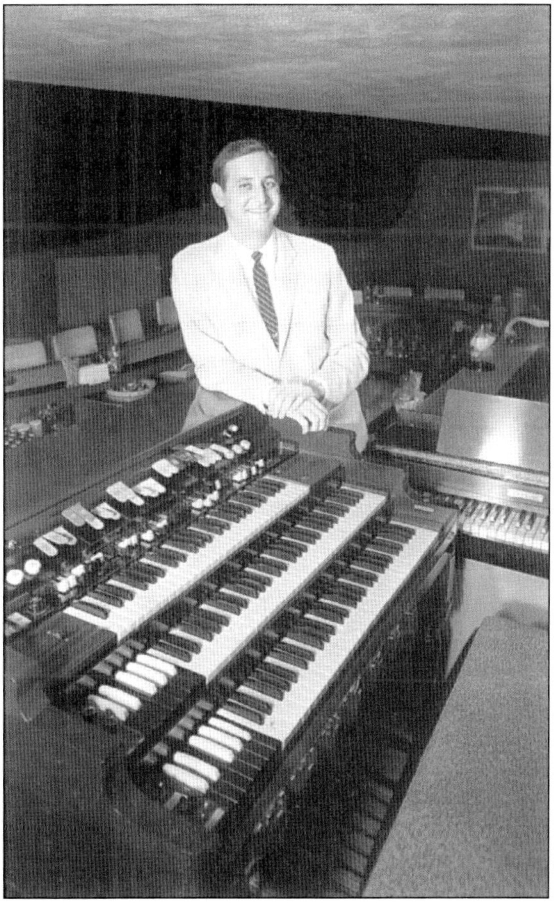

This absolutely astounding postcard shows a view of Hallandale Beach Boulevard looking east toward the ocean with "Hollywood, Florida" printed on the front of the card. The signs for the Gulfstream Drive-in and the Hallandale shopping center are on the right (south) side of the boulevard, while the Diplomat is visible in the distance at left. The back of the card correctly notes that the location is "Hallandale, Florida."

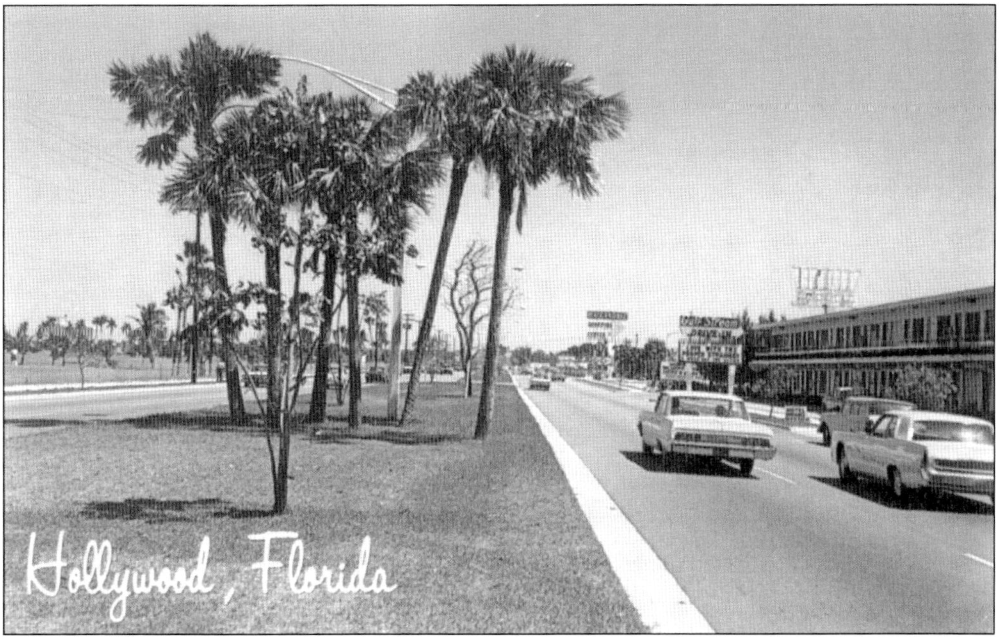

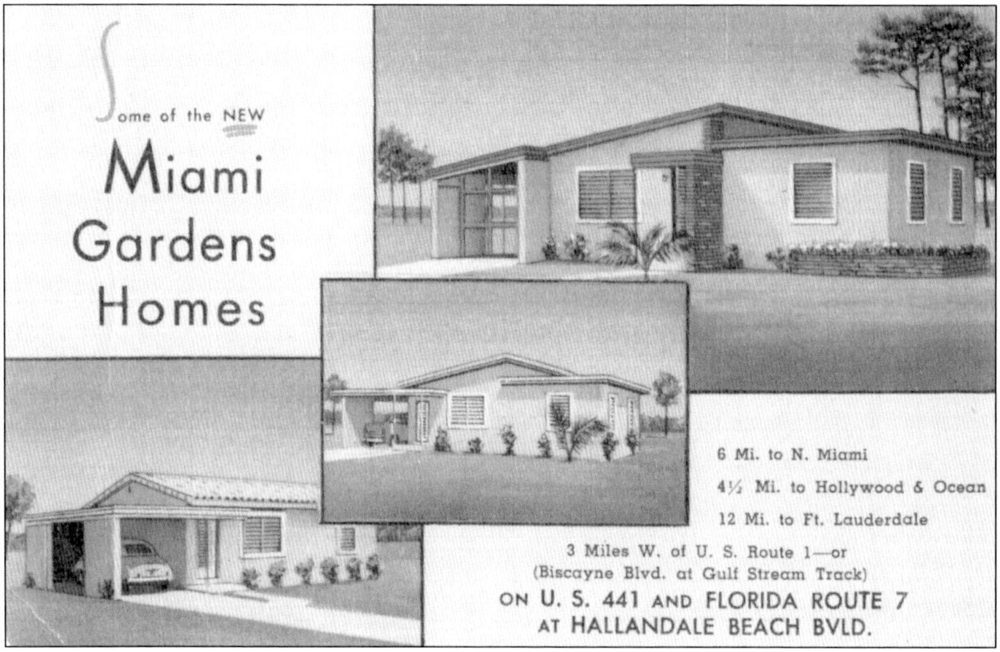

Miami Gardens Homes were not in Miami Gardens or even in Dade (later Miami-Dade) County, but rather on US Route 441 and Florida Route 7 at Hallandale Beach Boulevard. The moderately priced homes contained two or three bedrooms, with each home on a spacious lot.

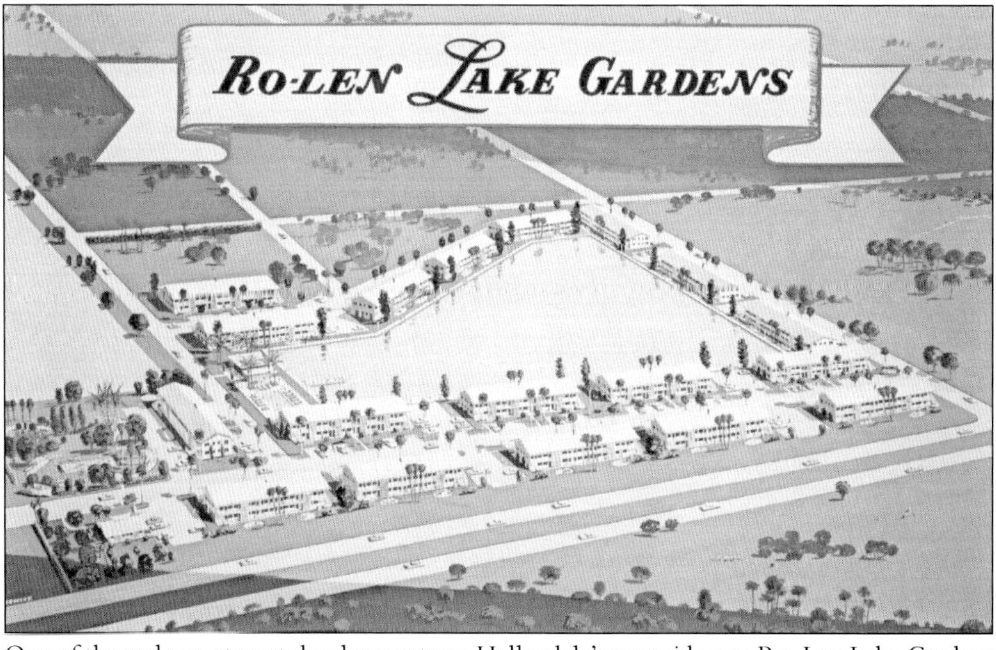

One of the early apartment developments on Hallandale's west side was Ro-Len Lake Gardens Co-Op at 714 Southwest 11th Avenue. Numerous amenities are shown, including air conditioning, weekly movies, and all-electric kitchens.

Two

Hollywood

Hollywood began as the glamorous and exuberant idea of Joseph W. Young, the man for whom Young Circle is named. Young came east from Washington State and California in 1920 at the age of 38, with the idea of building a wonderful city in the Florida sunshine.

According to information gleaned from numerous books on Hollywood's history, Young planned to sell acreage in the Miami area so that he would have the funds to build his dream city. Bonnie Wilpon noted in *Hollywood in Vintage Postcards* that Young's plans included "a wide boulevard from the ocean to the edge of the Everglades and two lakes, each with a turning basin for yachts." He intended Hollywood to be "a city for everyone, from the opulent at the tops of the industrial and social ladders to the most humble of working people."

Young's plans almost became reality, but the horrific hurricane that struck the area on September 17–18, 1926, killed more than 600 people, and like so many other South Florida developers, Young was essentially forced to withdraw, unable to meet his numerous financial obligations.

While the Hollywood story has been well told numerous times in both books and articles, two of the preeminent volumes are *Hollywood* in Arcadia Publishing's Images of America series, and *Hollywood in Vintage Postcards* in Arcadia's Postcard History Series. In both of those books and the hardcover volume published by the Hollywood Historical Society, the history of Young and Hollywood Inc. is related at length and in detail, allowing for a brief discussion to begin this chapter. Suffice it to say, although the two Arcadia books named above are must-haves for any Broward County or Hollywood historian, the postcard images in this book featuring Broward's second largest city are different from those in the other two books and will present another perspective of Hollywood.

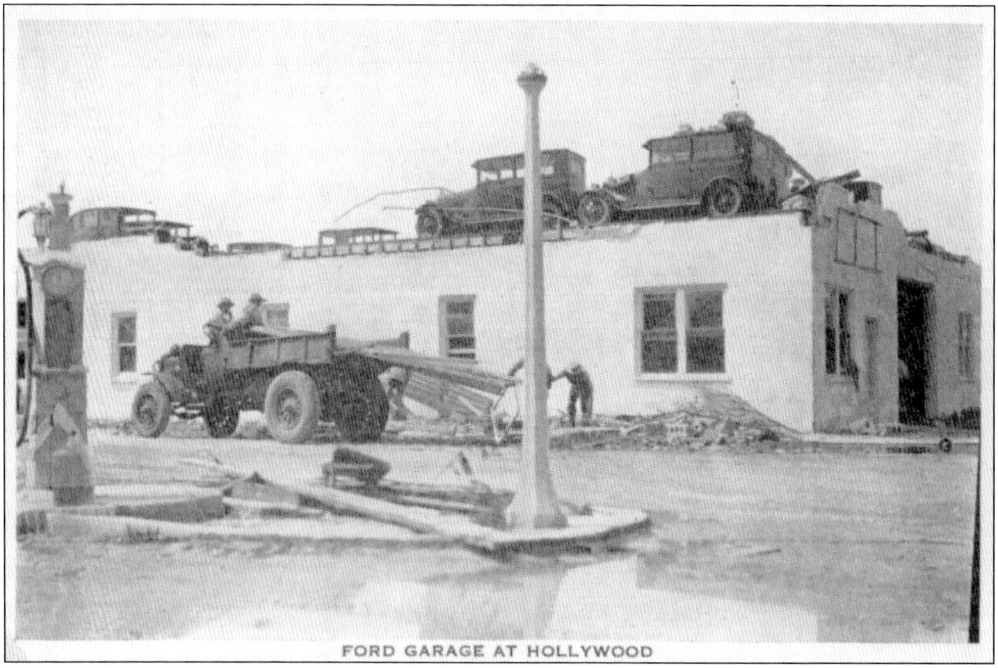

The horrifically brutal September 1926 hurricane devastated the region from Greater Miami to northernmost Broward County. This postcard, published by the H.H. Hamm Company of Toledo, Ohio, barely shows the depth and breadth of the damage caused by that storm. Shortly after the hurricane passed, cleanup efforts had already begun at the Hollywood Ford Garage.

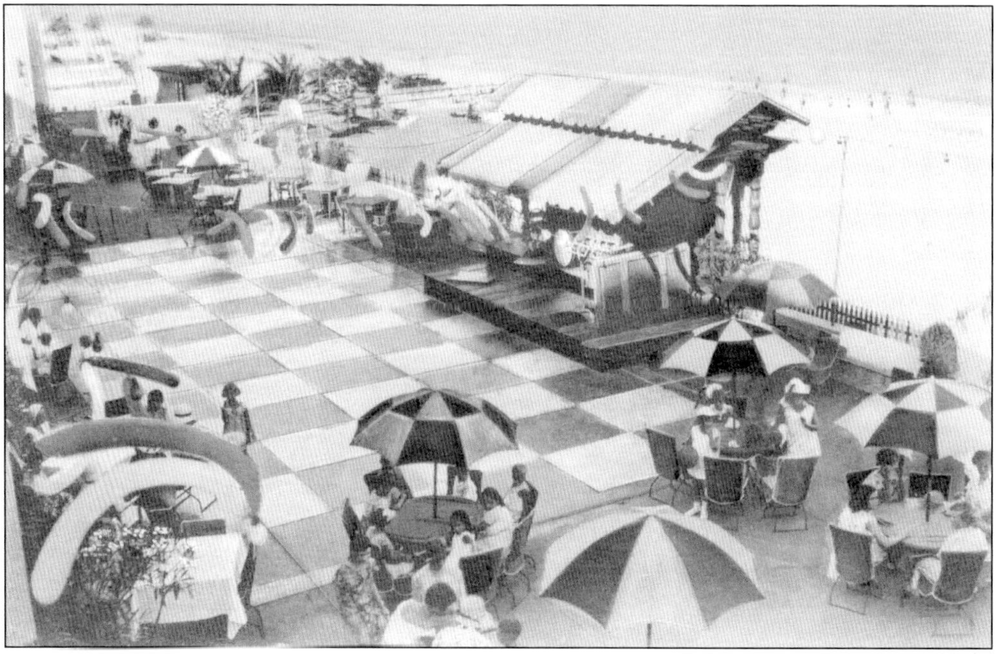

The glory and beauty of the Hollywood Beach Hotel are evident in this stunning view of the Children's Carnival on the Ocean Deck at the hotel. This type of card was published, along with a good many others, in order to publicize the hotel shortly after it opened in 1926.

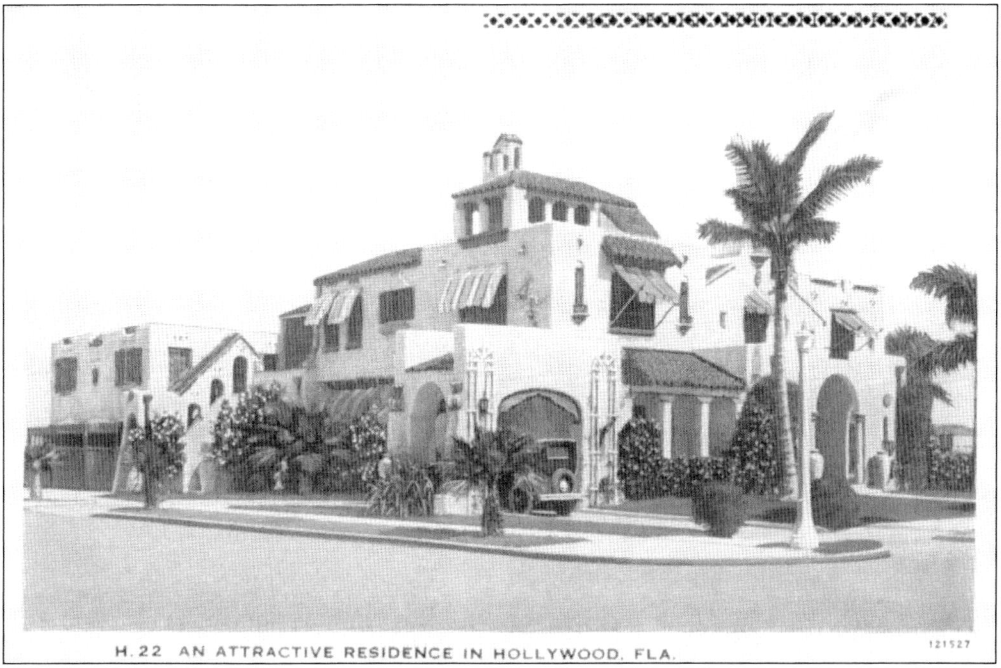

Titled "An Attractive Residence in Hollywood, Fla.," this postcard depicts one of the homes built by Joseph W. Young, likely on or close to North Lake. As with a number of early to mid-1920s Florida boom-era developments, including Fulford-by-the-Sea (North Miami Beach), the Shoreland Company (Miami Shores) and Coral Gables, the original developers built a number of homes as showcases for their projects.

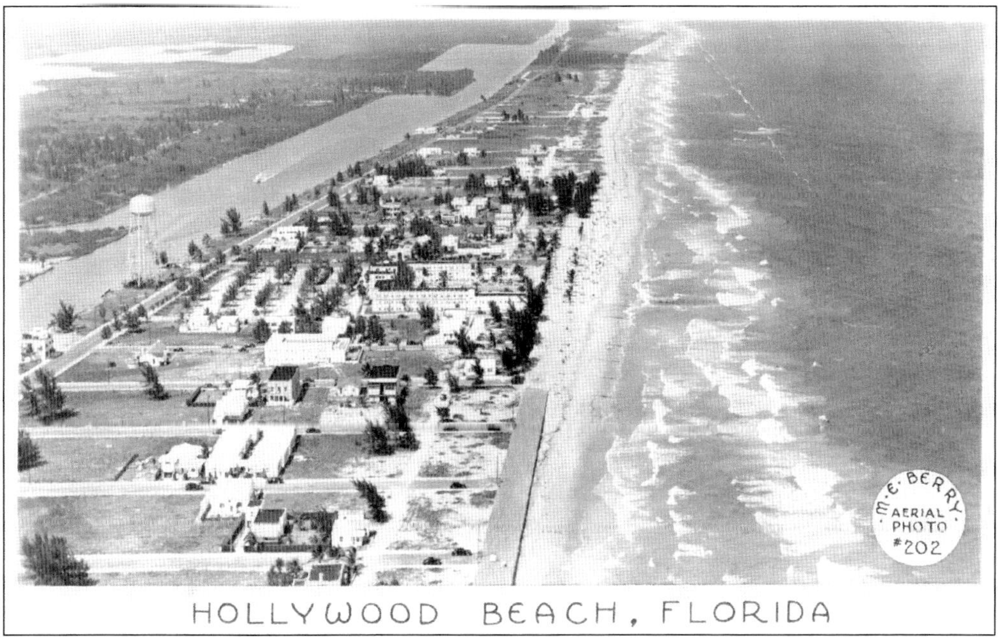

Postmarked November 17, 1944, this early 1940s aerial view of Hollywood Beach north of the Hollywood Beach Hotel is particularly evocative, because with the massive and unending development on the beach side of the city, few if any of the buildings shown are still in place.

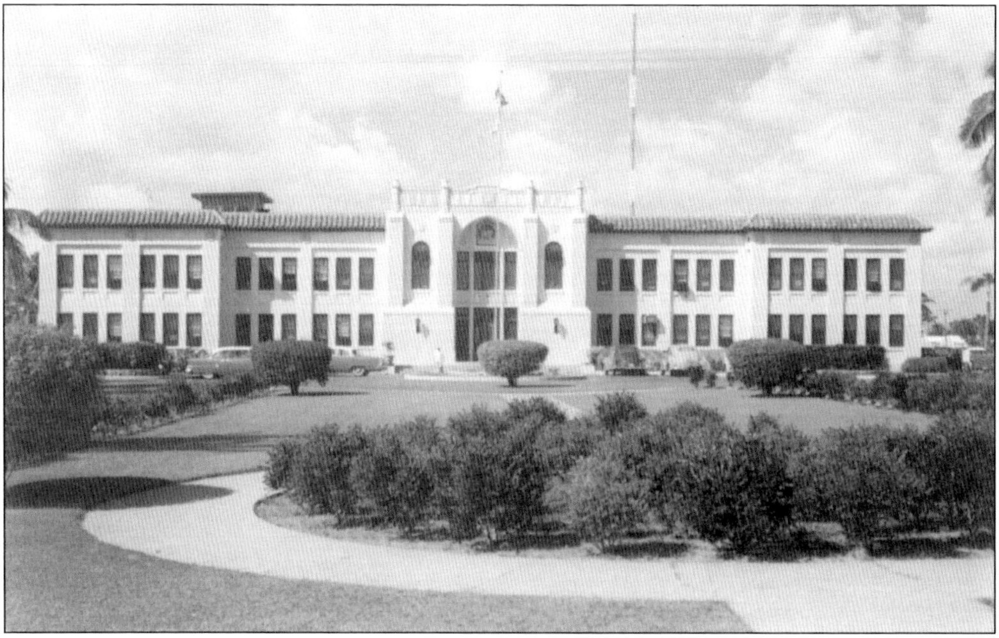

While this was not the first Hollywood City Hall, the 1950s-era version shown here was barely large enough for the growing city. Although it was replaced in the late 1970s, even the "new" city hall now has several annexes.

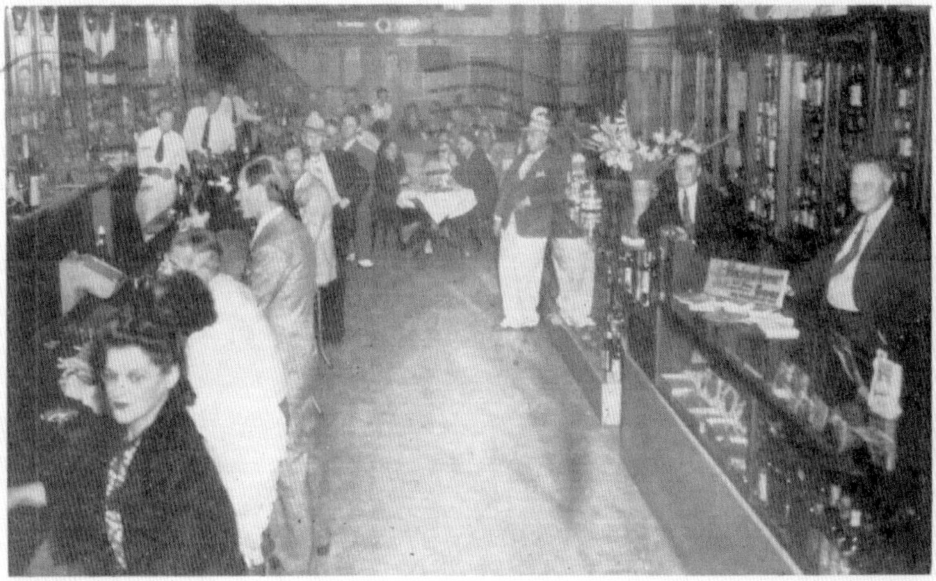

TITCOMB BAR AND GRILL 2011 HOLLYWOOD BOULEVARD HOLLYWOOD, FLORIDA

Shortly after Prohibition ended in 1933, L.B. and Elizabeth C. Titcomb opened their Titcomb Bar and Grill "right downtown" at 2011 Hollywood Boulevard. The interior shown here may give the reader an idea of the popularity of the Titcombs' food and beverage emporium.

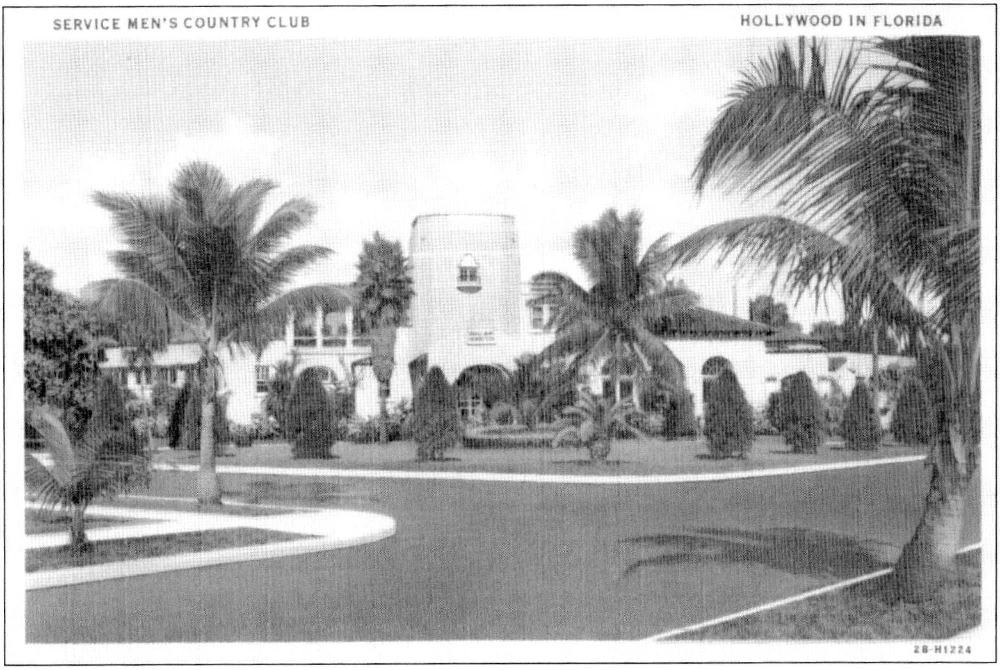

During World War II, the Hollywood Country Club became the Service Men's Country Club sponsored by the Chamber of Commerce, and likely operated as a USO club by that organization. An astute viewer will note the words "Hollywood in Florida" at top right.

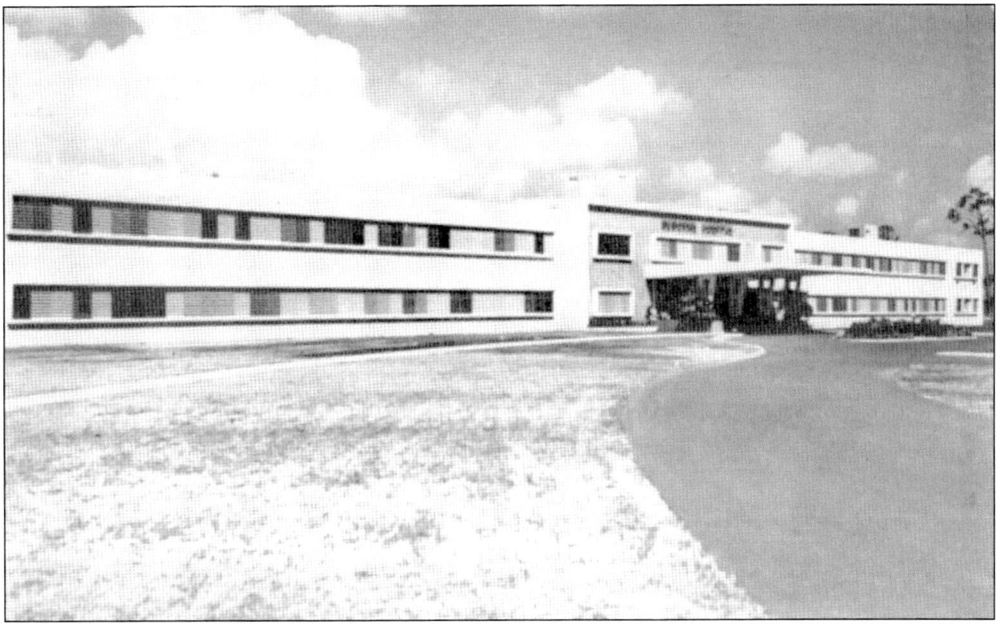

Owned and operated by the South Broward Hospital District, Hollywood Memorial Hospital, now one of Florida's premier health care facilities, opened in 1953 with 100 beds and 26 bassinets. When it opened, it was considered one of the most modern hospitals in the South.

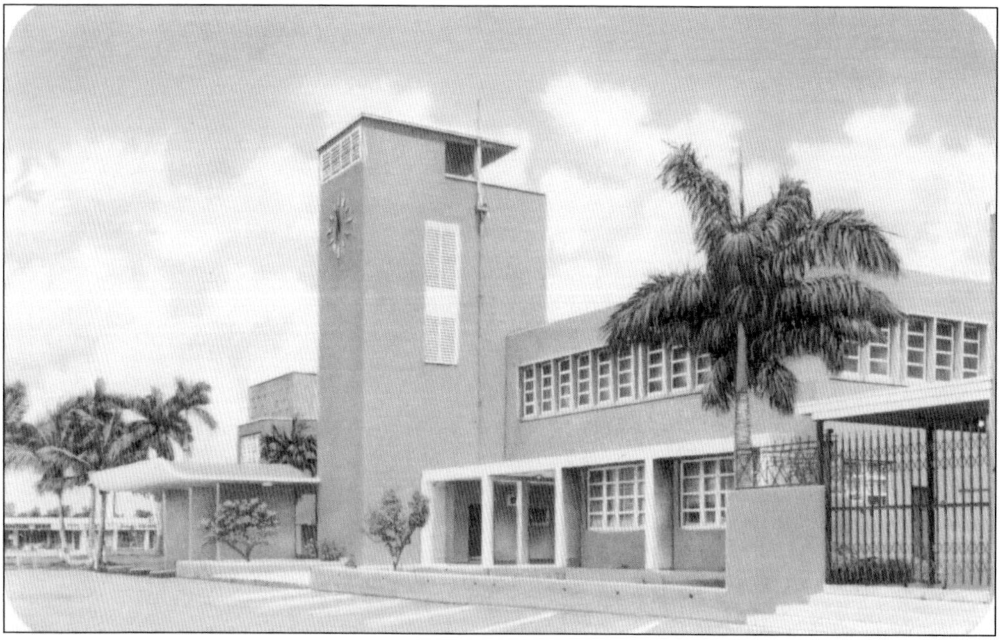

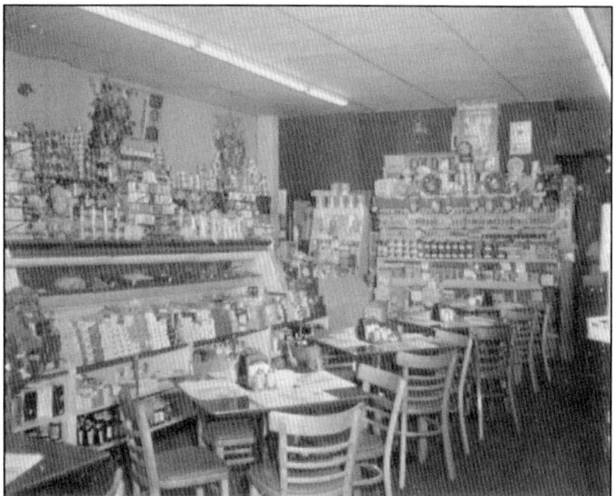

Because of the overflow of students at Fort Lauderdale High School, South Broward High School, located on US Route 1 south of the Hollywood Circle at Harding Street, opened in 1938 and relocated to a new facility (shown here) in 1949.

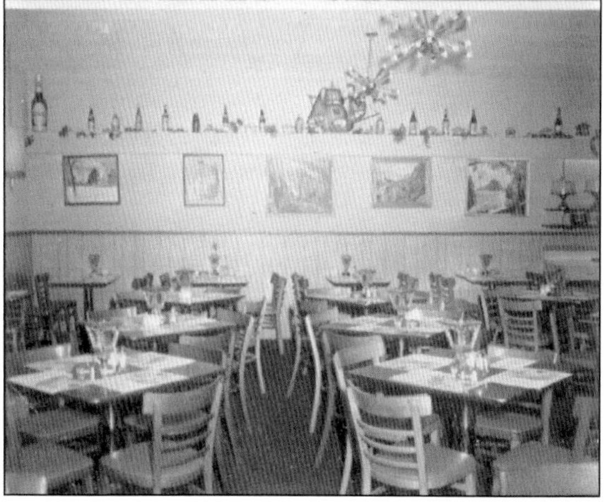

Both the Hollywood Mall, which opened in 1964 as Florida's first air-conditioned mall with a major department store as a tenant, and its various stores, have been gone since the mall closed in 2004. Located at US Route 441 and Hollywood Boulevard, one of the favored dining spots at the mall was John and Helen Larsen's Delicatessen (pictured).

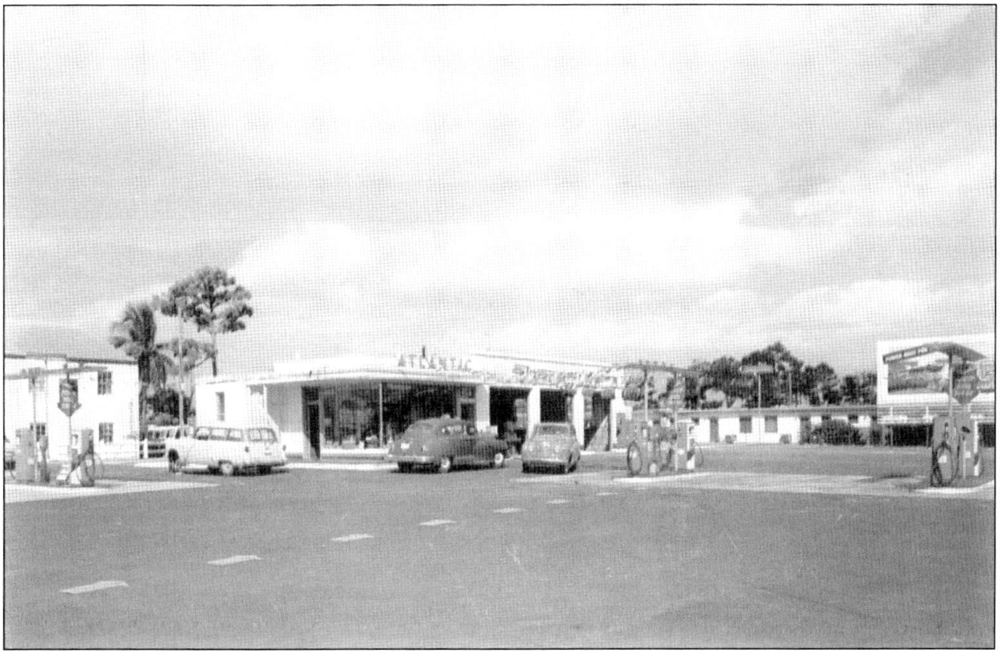

Also located on US Route 441 and Hollywood Boulevard, Steve Coar's Atlantic Corner Service Station advertised itself as "first of its kind in Southeastern Florida" without explaining what that meant. In any case, both the station and any memory of it appear to be long gone.

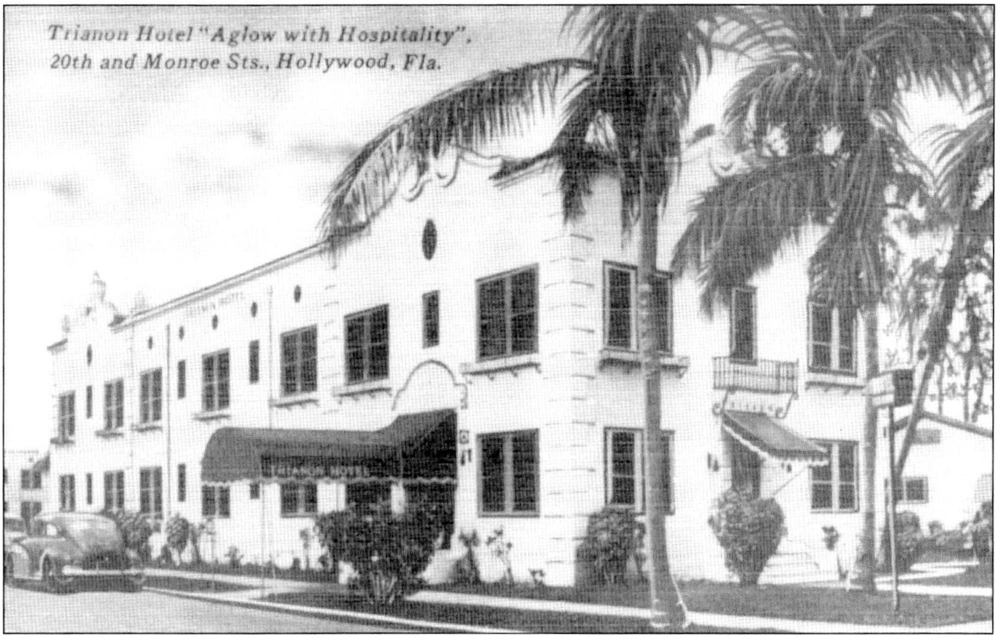

As shown on this 1940s postcard, H. Lee and Sally Merriman's Trianon Hotel at Twentieth and Monroe Streets was "Aglow with Hospitality!" The terminology was absolutely unique, and the author notes that, even with his massive collection of Florida hotel postcards, he has never seen it used elsewhere in brochures, booklets, or postcards.

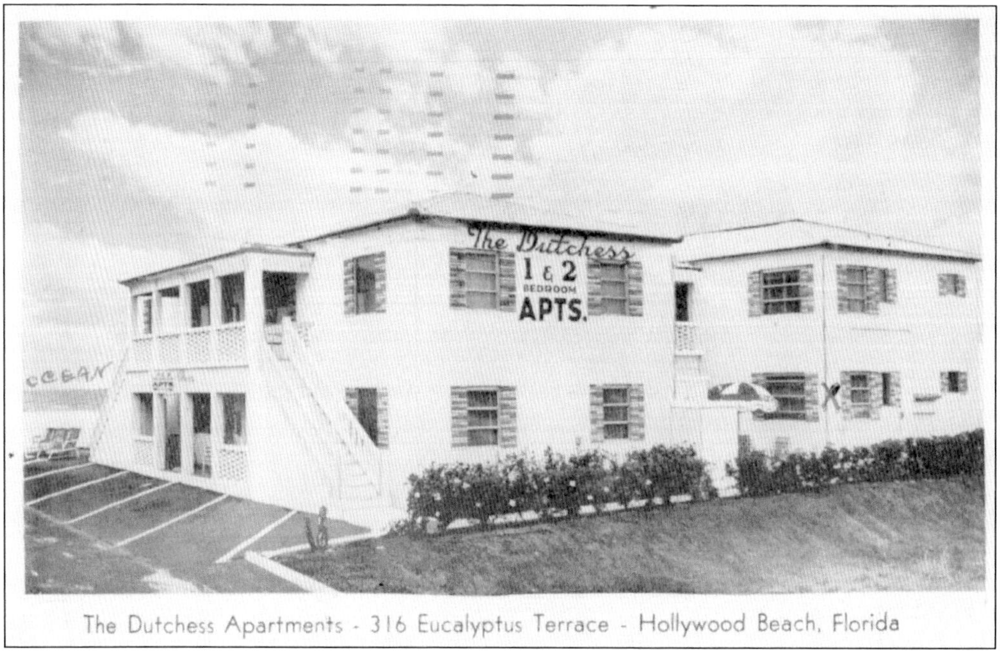

The Dutchess Apartments, "electrically heated and air-cooled" (which meant fans in the room, but no air conditioning), were located at 316 Eucalyptus Terrace, a half-mile south of the Hollywood Beach Hotel.

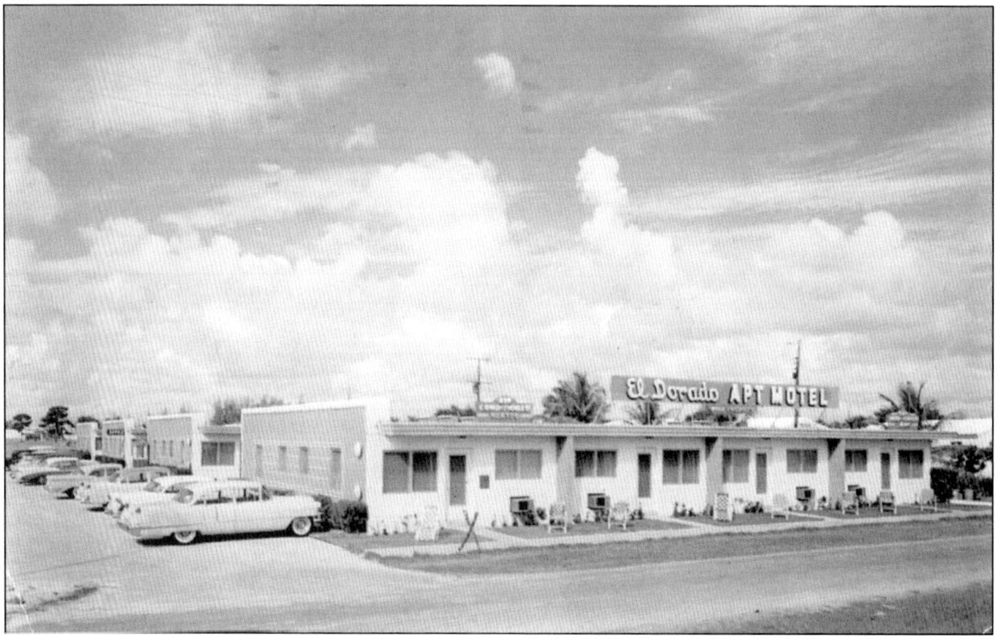

At 1841–1853 Moffett Street, the El Dorado Apartment Hotel was almost directly across the street from the Hollywood Dog Track (now the Mardi Gras Casino). The mid-1950s automobiles make it easy to date this postcard.

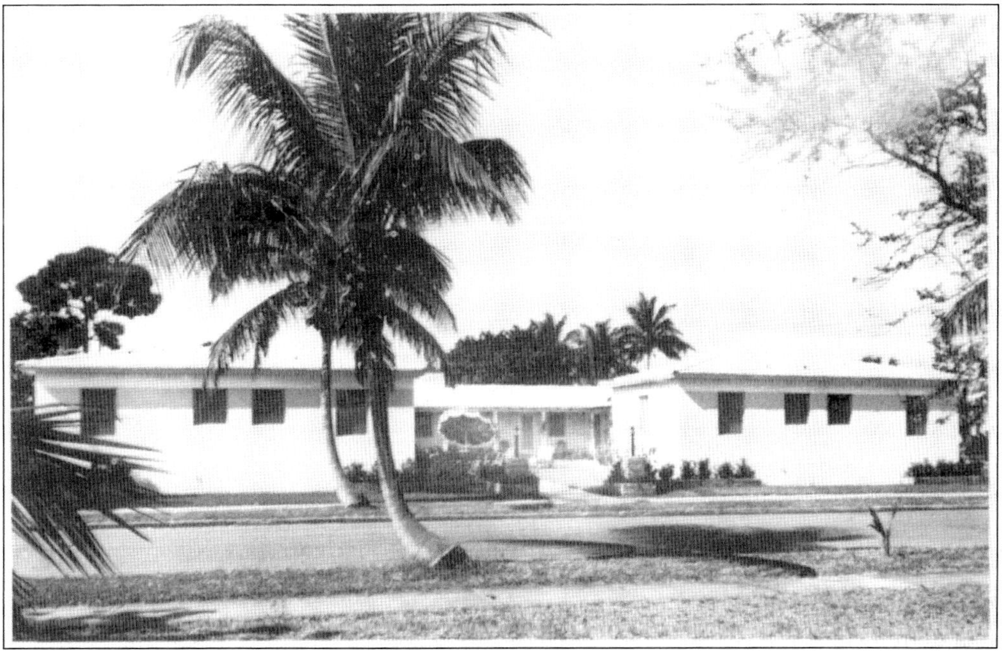

Illinois Courts, located at 2000 Washington Street (corner of Twentieth Avenue), was managed by C.O. Naumer and is shown here in 1955. The motel is long gone and has been replaced with a newer, more modern apartment building.

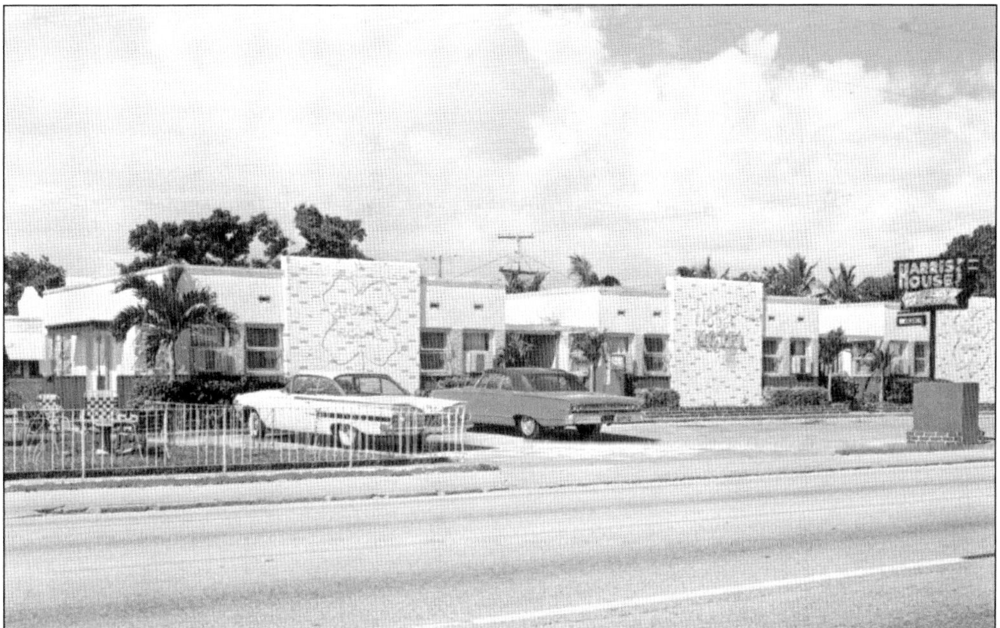

Harris House Motels, owned and operated by the Grant family, was at 410 North Federal Highway, two blocks north of the circle on US Route 1. This postcard, which was likely created in the early 1960s, was mailed in 1970.

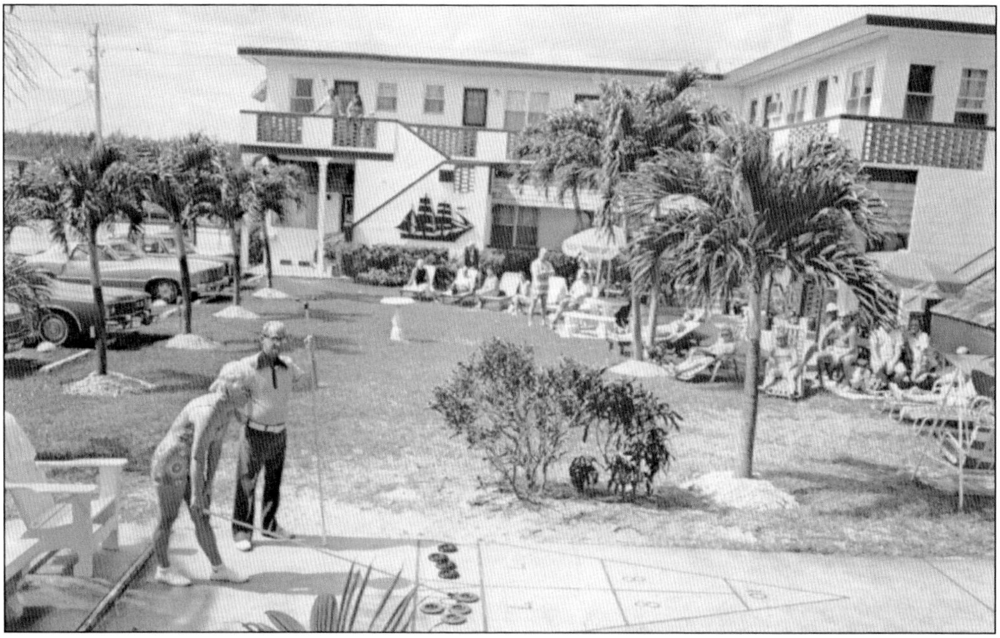

From the 1940s until the late 1960s, shuffleboard was a de rigueur accoutrement for any hotel built in South Florida. Although it is generally no longer played, the game was a major draw for prospective guests. The court shown here was at the Cape Cod Motel at 3001 North Ocean Drive.

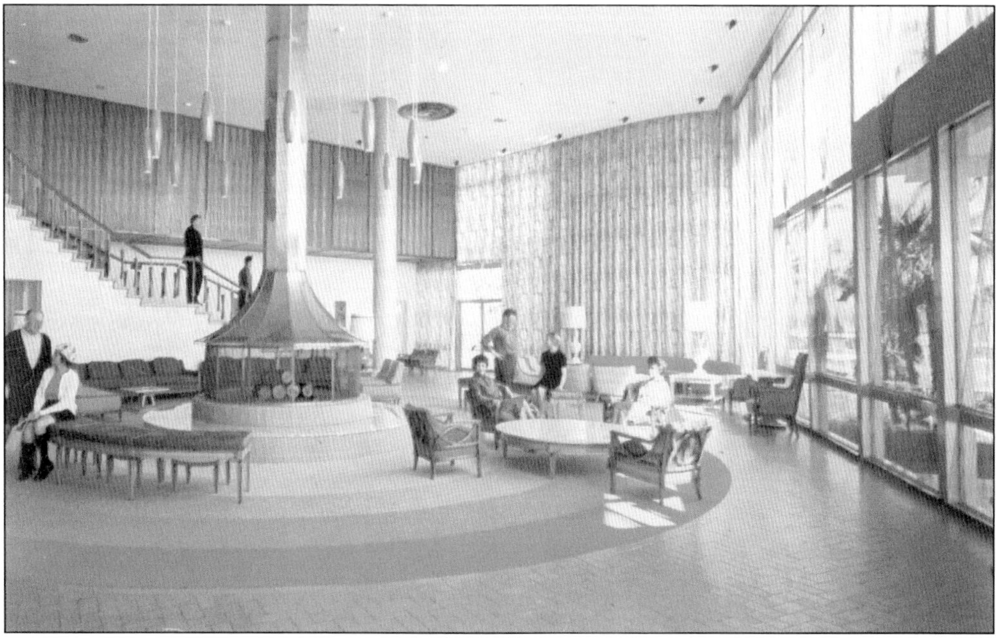

While the Diplomat by the Sea was, for many years, Hollywood's premier resort hotel, the Diplomat Inn and Country Club, with its private golf course on the mainland side, was a magnet for local golfers, tennis players, and sports enthusiasts. The Diplomat Inn's lobby was a regular rendezvous spot for hotel guests and club members.

Three

DANIA BEACH

In the late 19th century, through the efforts of Henry M. Flagler, Dania Beach began as a neighborhood called Modello with many of the new settlers emigrating from Denmark. In November 1904, the area was incorporated as the town of Dania, honoring that Danish ancestry. On January 4, 1926, Dania voted to annex itself to the City of Hollywood.

After the September 1926 South Florida hurricane decimated Hollywood's fortunes, most of Dania seceded from that city and reincorporated as a separate municipality, again taking the name Dania. The areas that chose to remain part of Hollywood caused Dania's current somewhat-less-than-contiguous boundaries.

In November 1998, the city formally changed its name to Dania Beach in order to capitalize on its oceanfront property on the east side of the Intracoastal Waterway that had long been part of the city. Today, though, the name Dania is still often used to refer to the city.

In 2001, the city annexed several unincorporated areas of Broward County, increasing its population by about 3,600 people and giving it a current population of approximately 30,000 residents.

At one time, Dania was known as the "Tomato Capital of the World." However, sometime in the mid- to late 1960s, with the housing boom taking over many growing areas in South Florida, the city transitioned from a farming settlement to becoming part of the South Florida megalopolis, and soon took on the name "The Antique Capital of the South," with numerous antique shops and jewelry stores in downtown Dania Beach, especially in the area along Federal Highway known as "Antique Row."

Although a number of those shops remain, even that area is changing. New restaurants and the metamorphosis of Dania Jai-alai, located on Dania Beach Boulevard, from a pari-mutuel venue to a major casino with slot machines and card rooms, as well as seasonal jai alai, has signaled yet another transformation of the city.

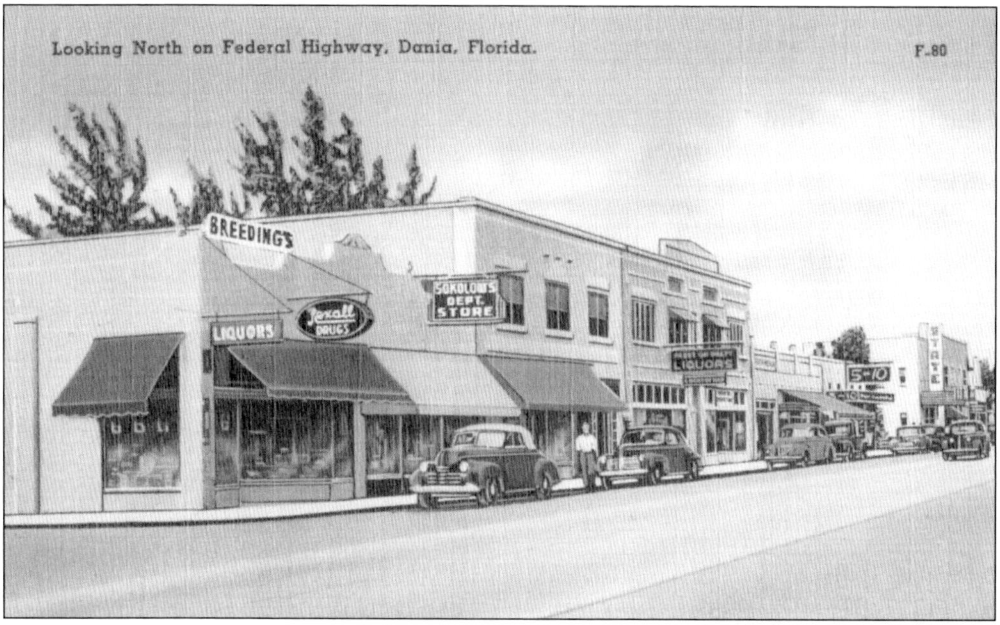

This view, from a linen postcard, looks north on Federal Highway (US Route 1) sometime in the late 1930s or early 1940s.

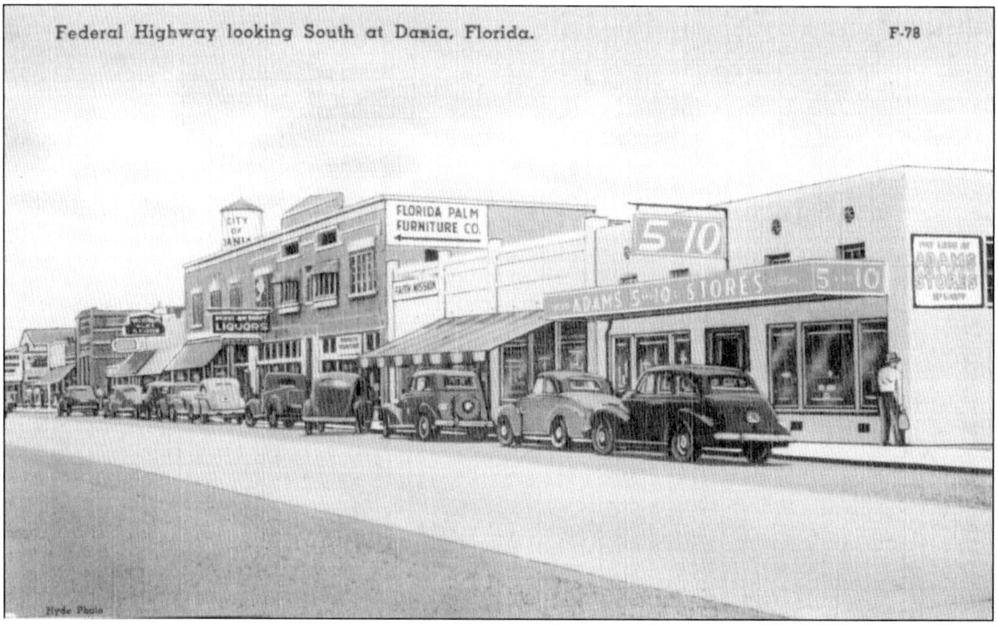

At approximately the same time as the previous view looking north was captured, the photographer turned the camera in the opposite direction and captured this view looking south on Federal Highway.

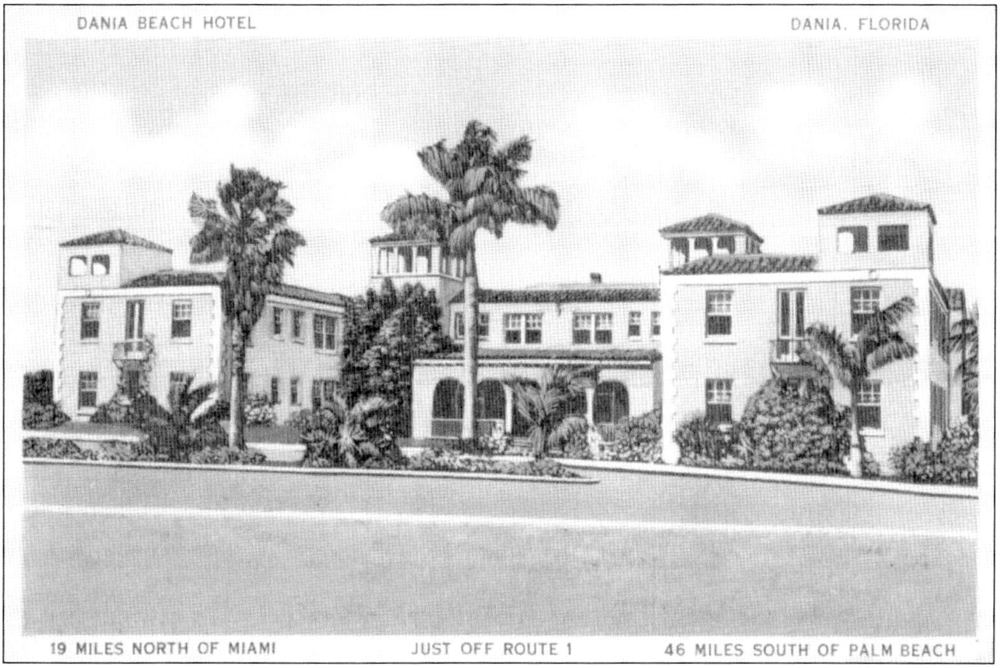

The Dania Beach Hotel was for many years "the place to stay between Hollywood and Fort Lauderdale." Located just east of Federal Highway on Dania Beach Boulevard, in the 1940s it featured rates of $2.50 per night for rooms "with private bath or shower."

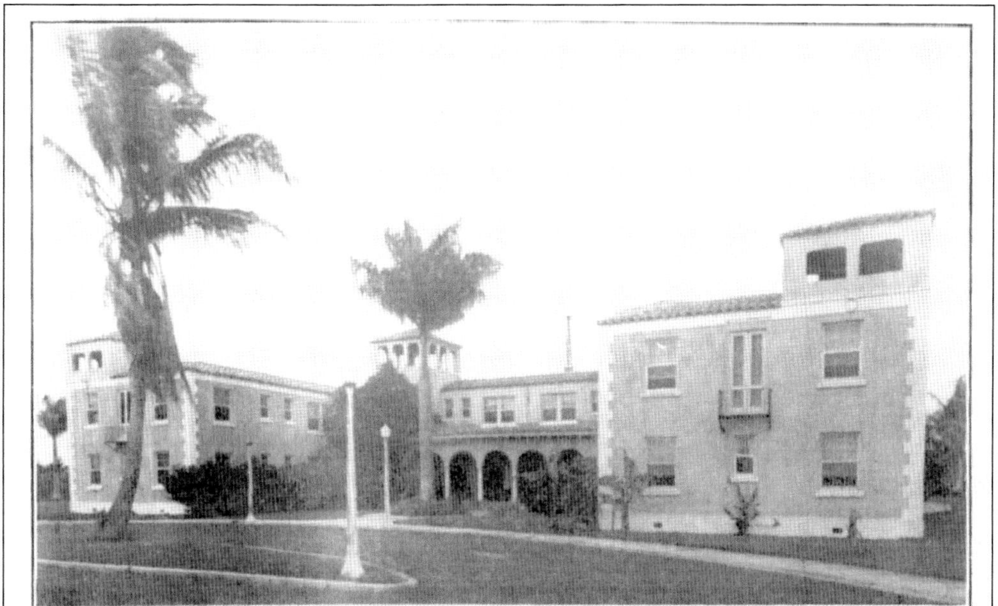

This green-tinted postcard is actually a fold-out that shows the hotel from a different angle. At the time this card was published around 1925, the hotel had a New York office at 233 West Ninety-Ninth Street.

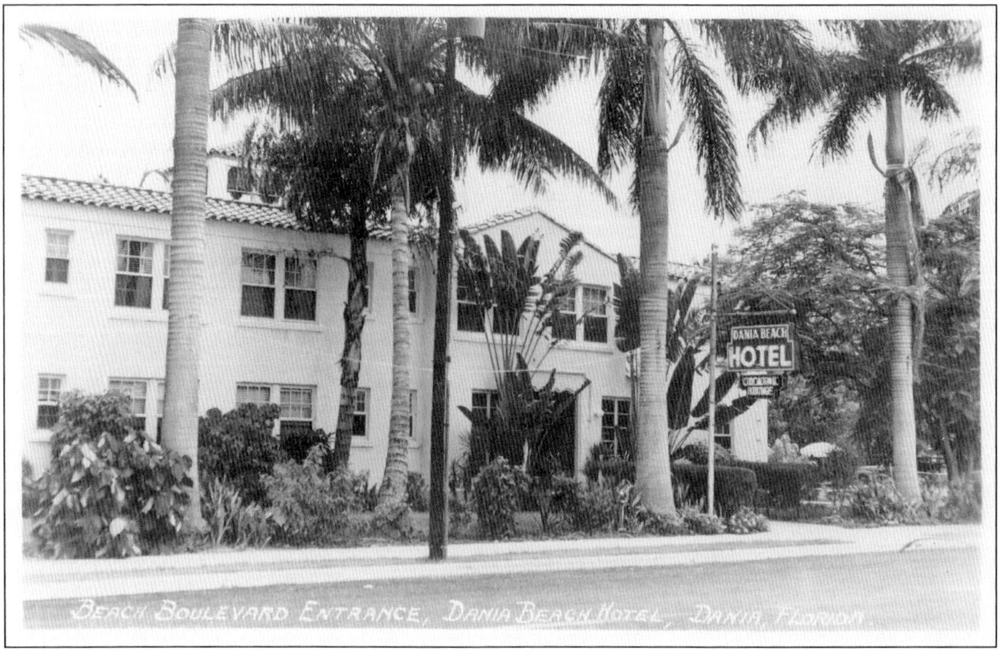

This black-and-white, white-bordered postcard view shows the Dania Beach Hotel's entrance on Dania Beach Boulevard, complete with a neon pole sign highlighting the hotel's cocktail lounge.

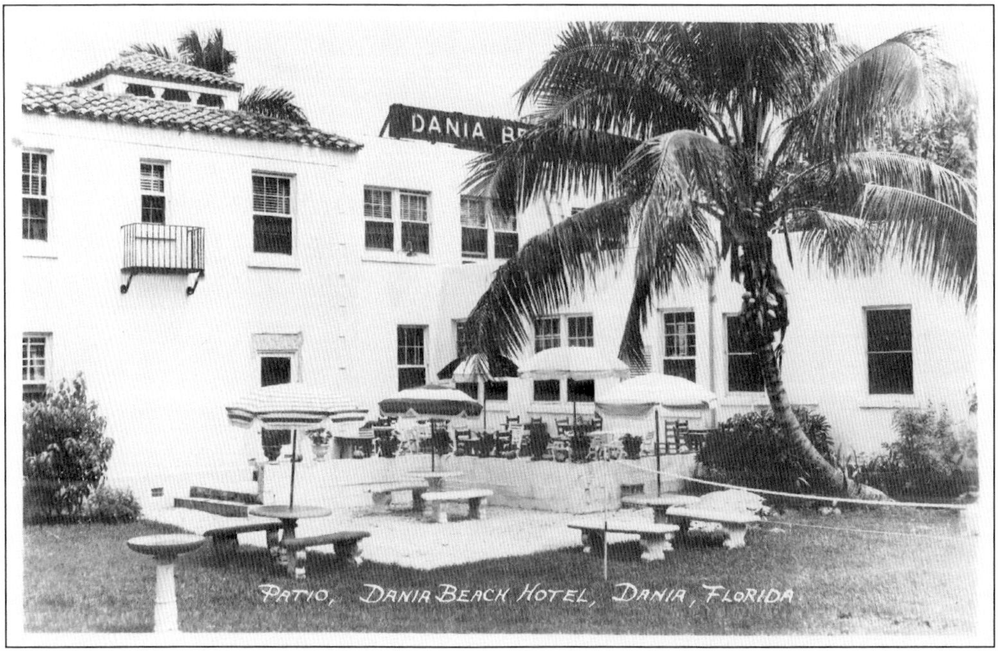

Another white-bordered, black-and-white postcard shows the Dania Beach Hotel's patio. Note the badminton net on the right.

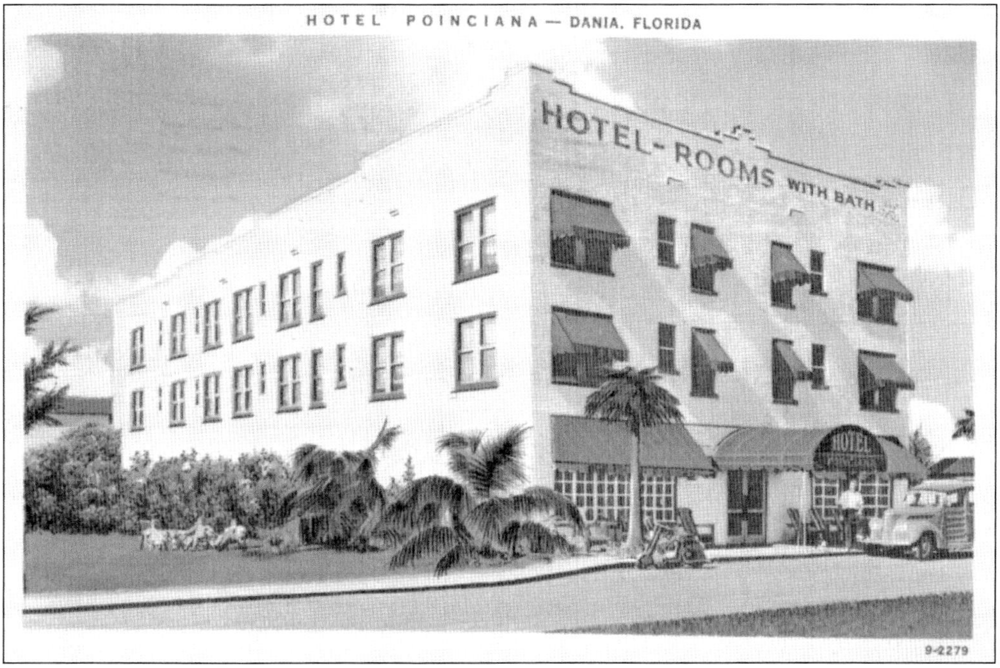

This late 1930s postcard is postmarked February 25, 1941. The card from the Hotel Poinciana notes "Rooms With Bath" on the front of the building, a somewhat unique bit of signage. The verbiage on the back noted "Free Station Wagon to the Beach."

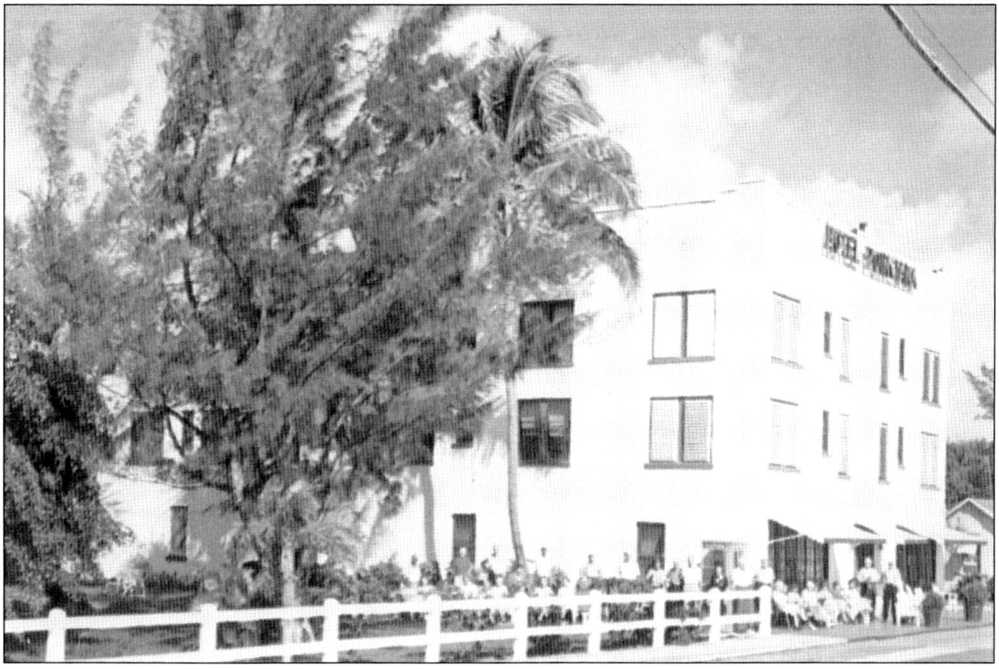

A later, chrome-finish postcard for the Hotel Poinciana shows a different sign on the front featuring just the full name of the hotel. A fence is in place, trees have grown tall on the side of the hotel, and a large crowd is enjoying the South Florida sunshine.

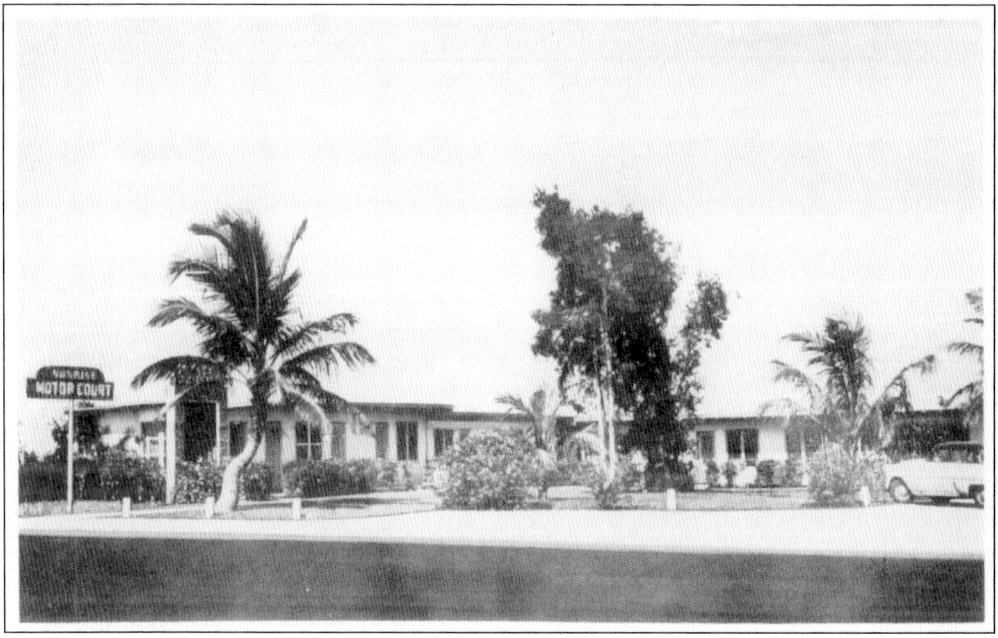

Sunrise Motor Court was located at 2432 North Federal Highway on property that is now part of Fort Lauderdale–Hollywood International Airport. The property was originally taken by the state through eminent domain in the early 1970s in order to widen US Route 1. In the early 2000s, that part of the road was placed in a tunnel so that the new runway could be built over it.

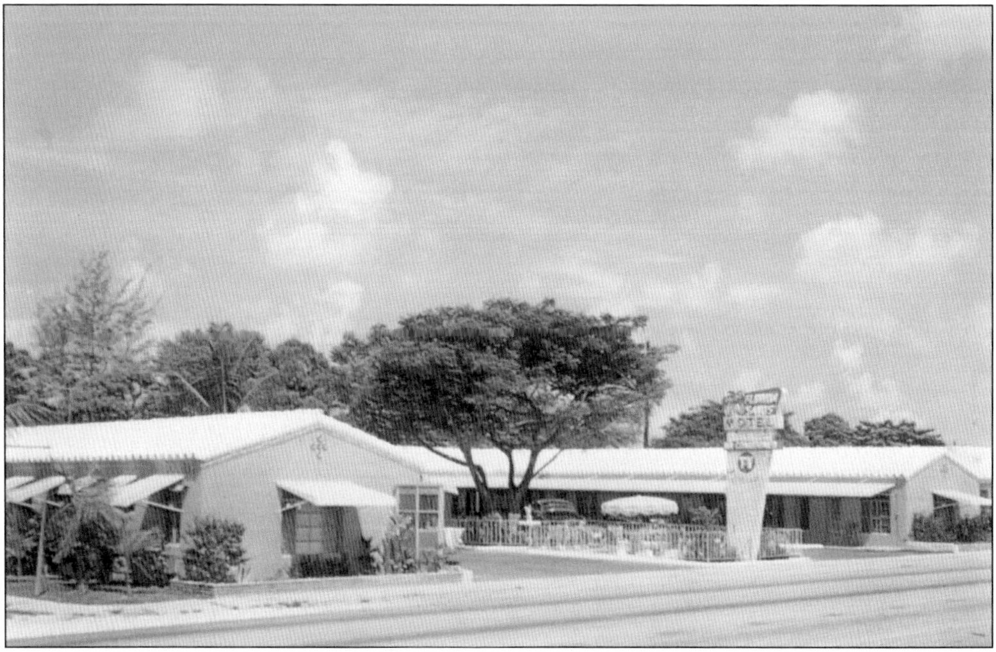

The Florida Sands Motel, located at 1290 South Federal Highway, featured air conditioning and "free TV." The back of the card had a blurb for "Sleeprite" mattresses. Like almost all of the small motels, motor courts, cabins, and tourist lodges in Dania Beach, the Florida Sands is now nothing but a memory.

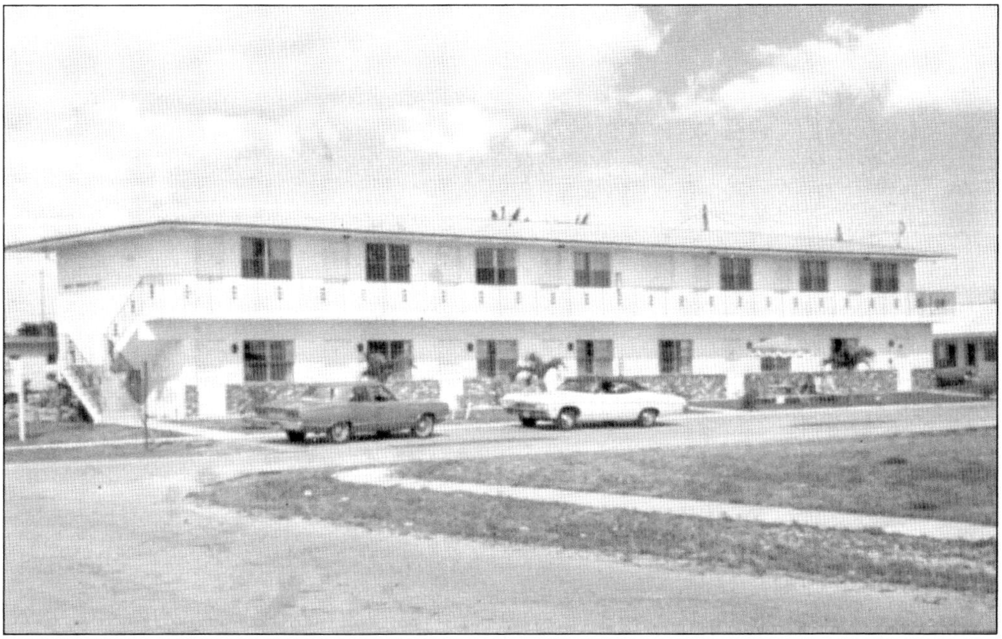

"Across from Jai-Alai," and with "Large-Clean-Complete-Apts.," Becky's Apartments was at 211 Southeast Park Street. Because of its convenient location, a number of jai alai fronton employees were residents there.

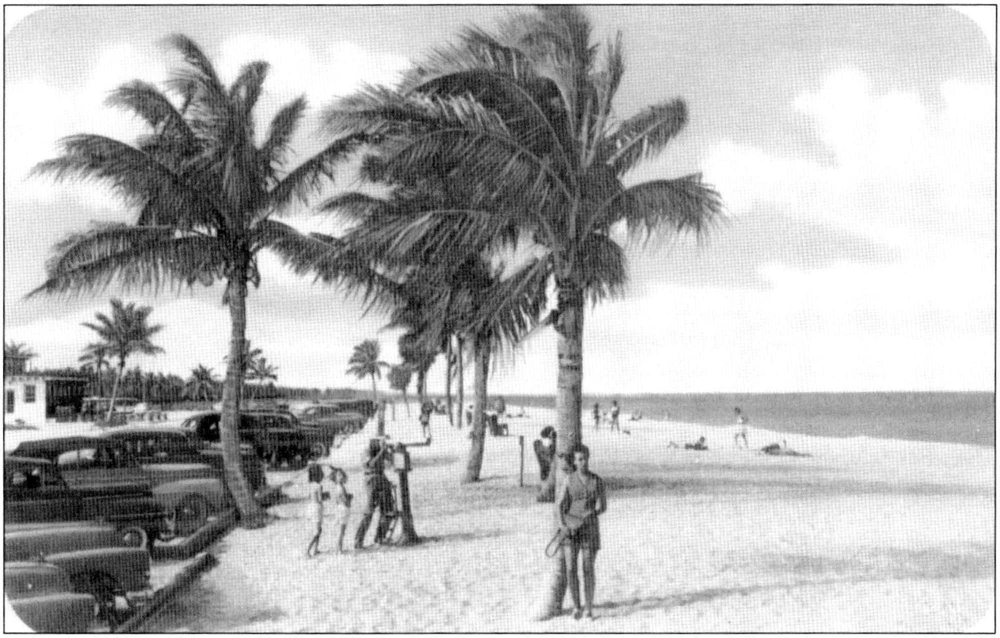

Though not as famous as Miami Beach, Hollywood Beach, or Fort Lauderdale Beach, Dania Beach was (and remains) an inviting spot for sunbathing and swimming.

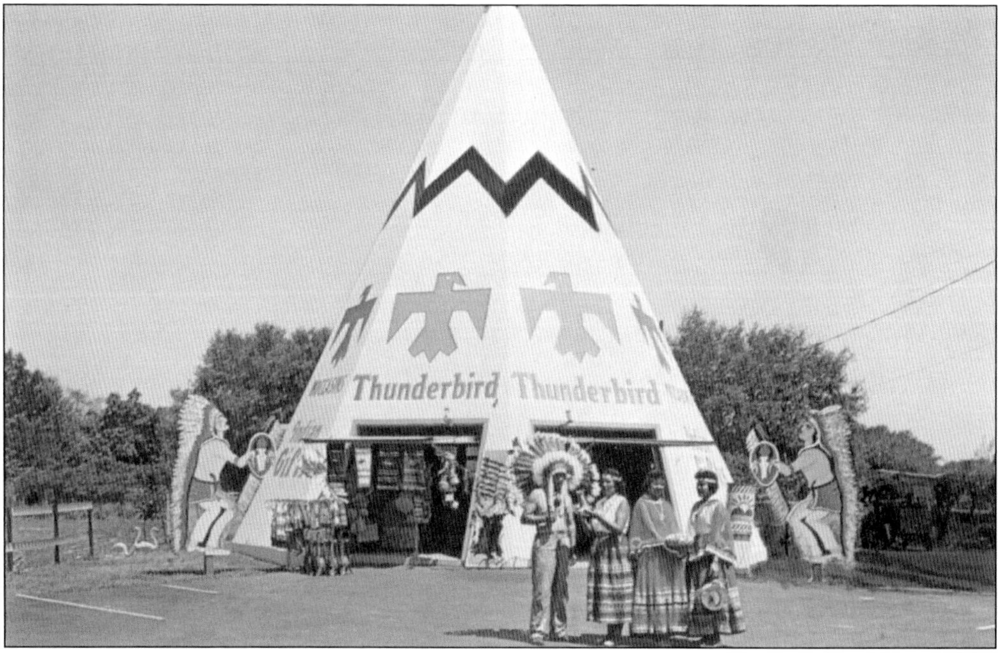

The Thunderbird Tepee at the Dania Seminole Indian Reservation on US Route 441 featured deerskin and buffalo moccasins as well as Indian handicrafts. This unique building (as well as the one shown on the following postcard) is now part of the Seminole Hard Rock Casino & Hotel in the same location.

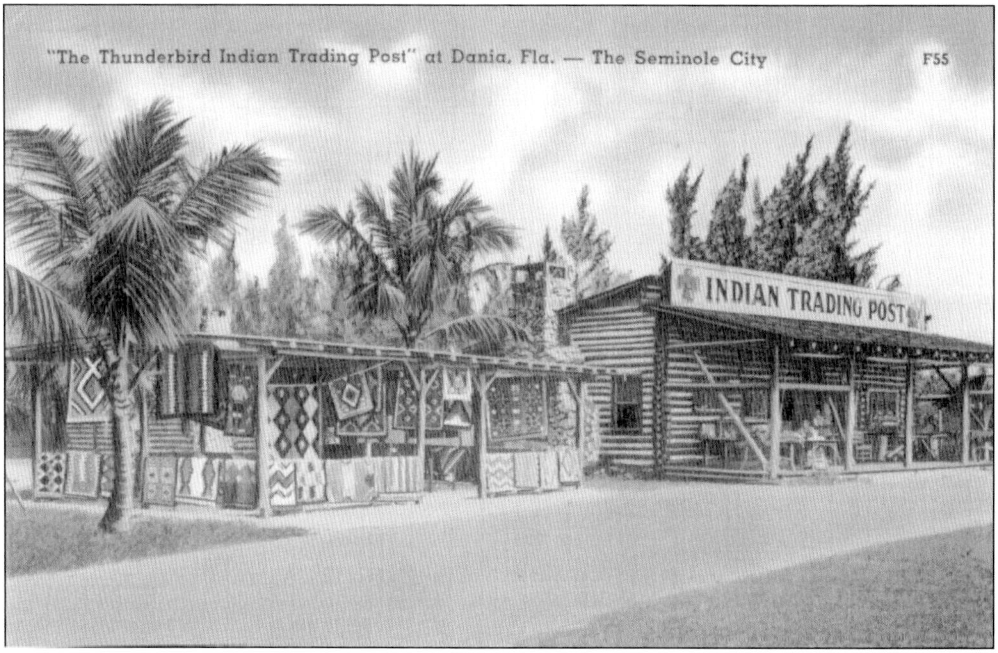

The Thunderbird Indian Trading Post, billing itself as "The Seminole City," was a mecca for Native American crafts, clothing, souvenirs, and even certain animal hides that could be purchased for use as blankets or rugs.

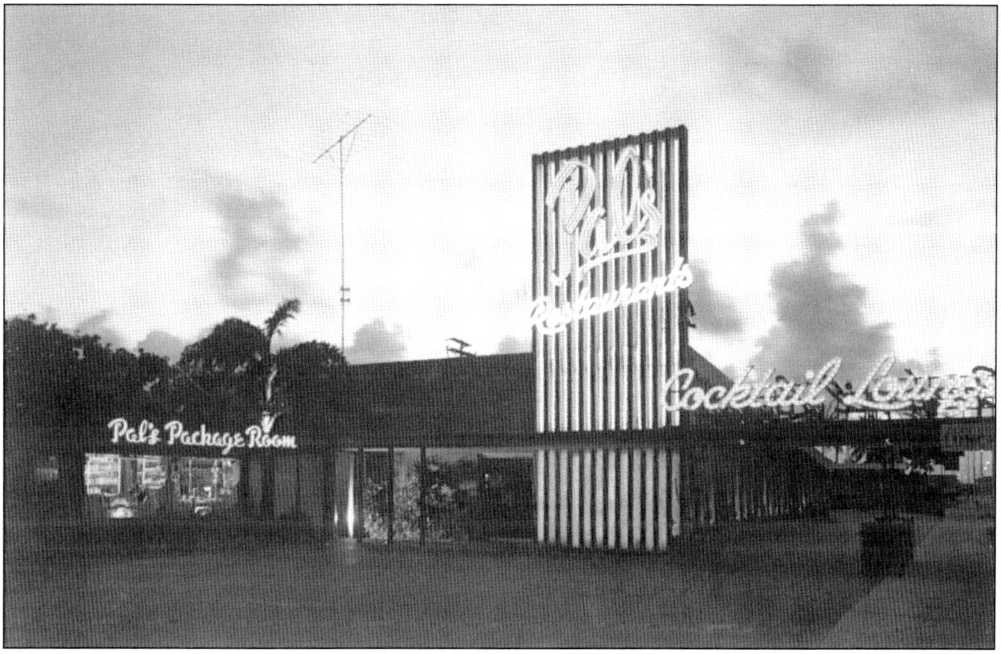

Hank Hagmann owned several Pal's Restaurants, including the Dania location shown here. All are now gone.

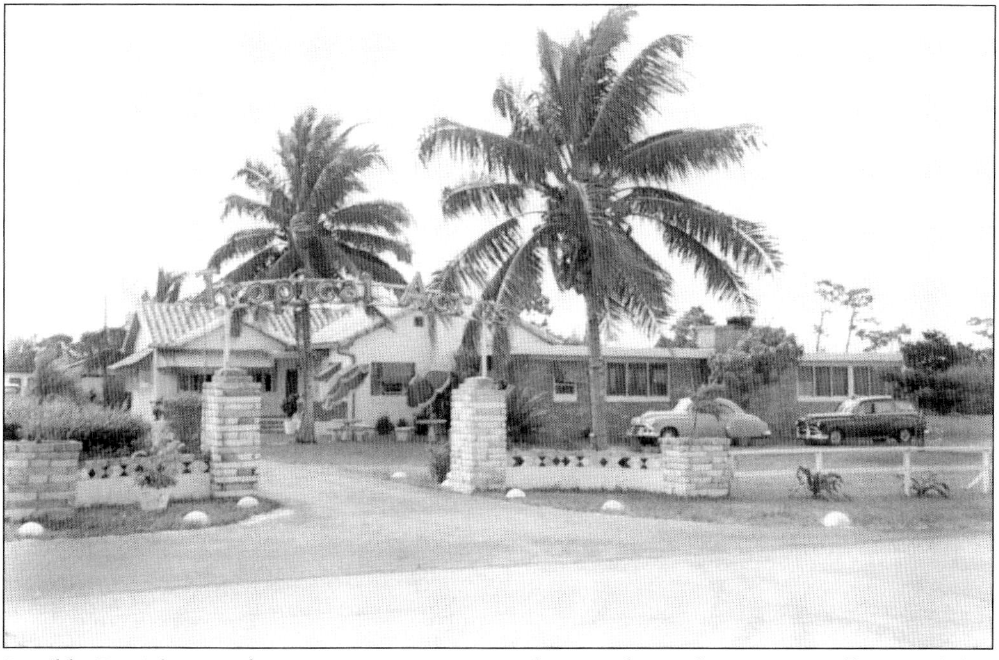

Possibly Dania's most famous restaurant, Tropical Acres, located at 2500 Griffin Road, has been in the same location in Dania/Dania Beach since 1949. This 1951 postcard shows the original building.

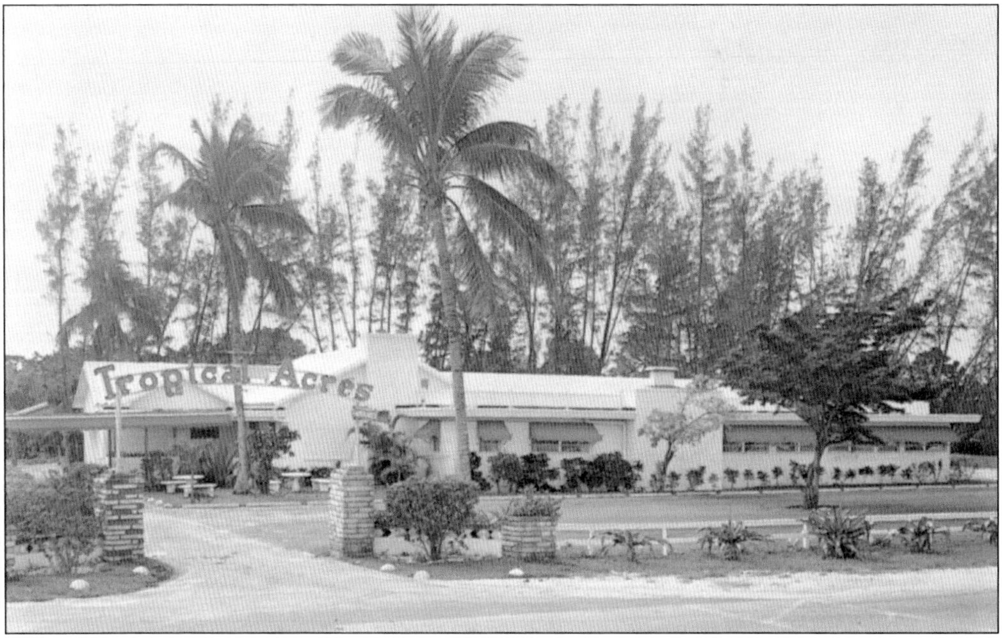

Great, high-quality food and terrific service brought more business to Tropical Acres, and by the late 1950s, the restaurant had enlarged and expanded, as shown here.

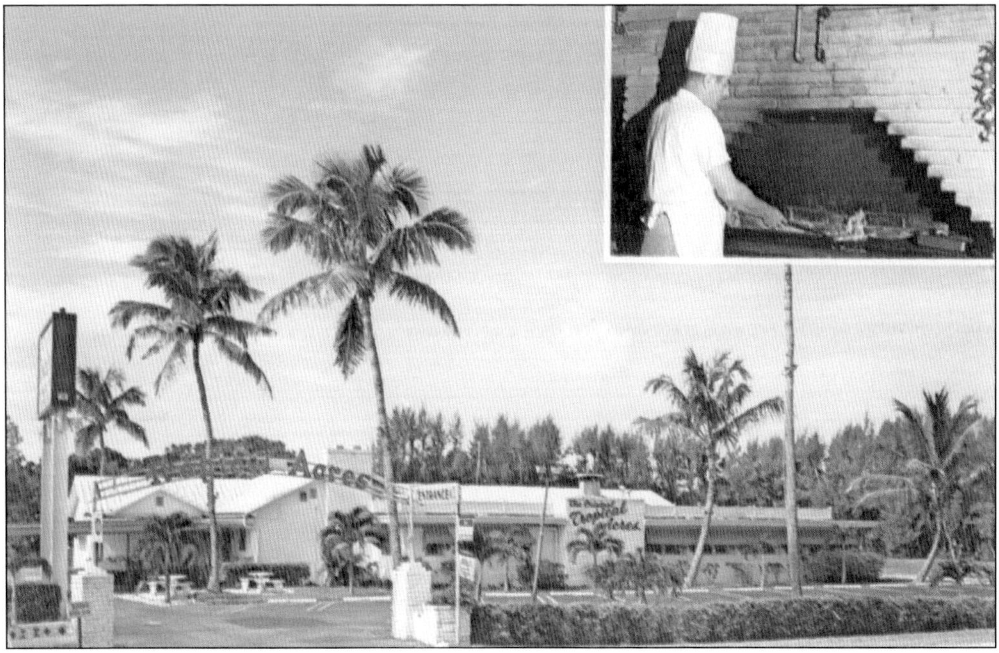

By the late 1970s (note that the restaurant's sign is on the building as well as the entrance arch), Tropical Acres, "Famous for Steaks," featured "Organ Music Nightly." The restaurant is still owned by the family of the founders and remains one of Broward's—and South Florida's—favored dining locales.

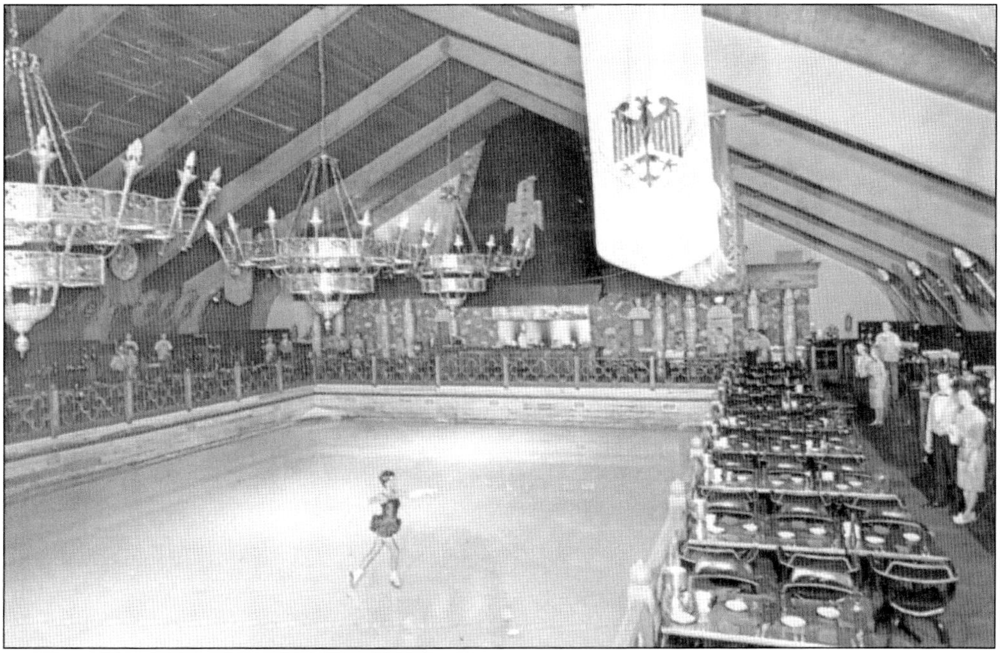

The Viking Restaurant and Lounge was at 1150 South Federal Highway. Its great claim to fame was the 50-by-100-foot ice-skating rink in the middle of the building, which featured "daily exhibitions for the enjoyment of the diners." Famed South Florida champion ice skater Turalura Lipschitz is shown going through her paces in the middle of the rink.

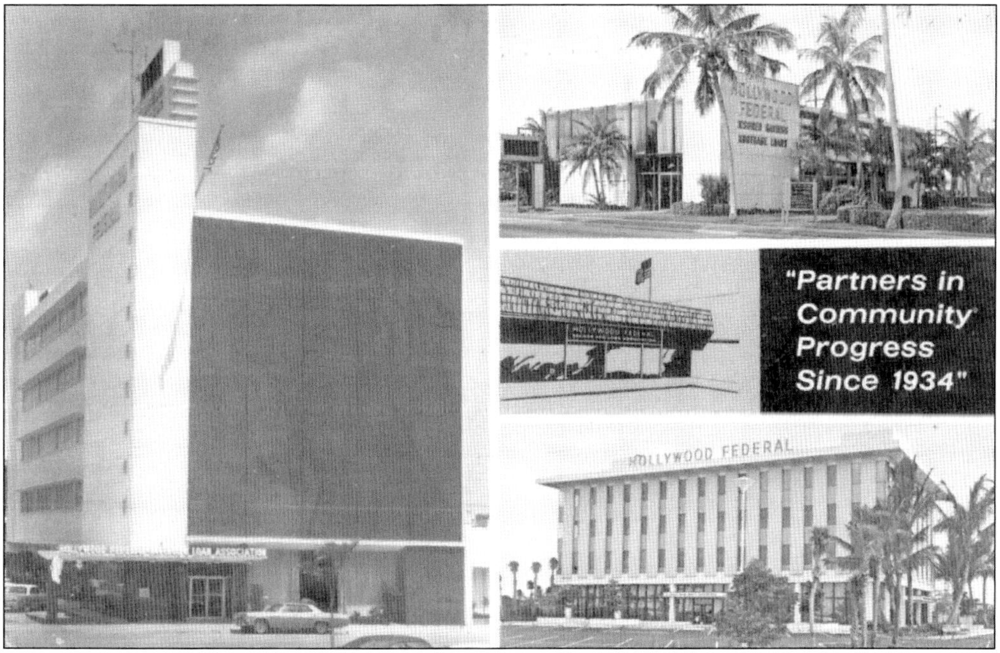

Hollywood Federal had a branch in Dania at 140 South Federal Highway, which is shown at upper right on this chrome postcard.

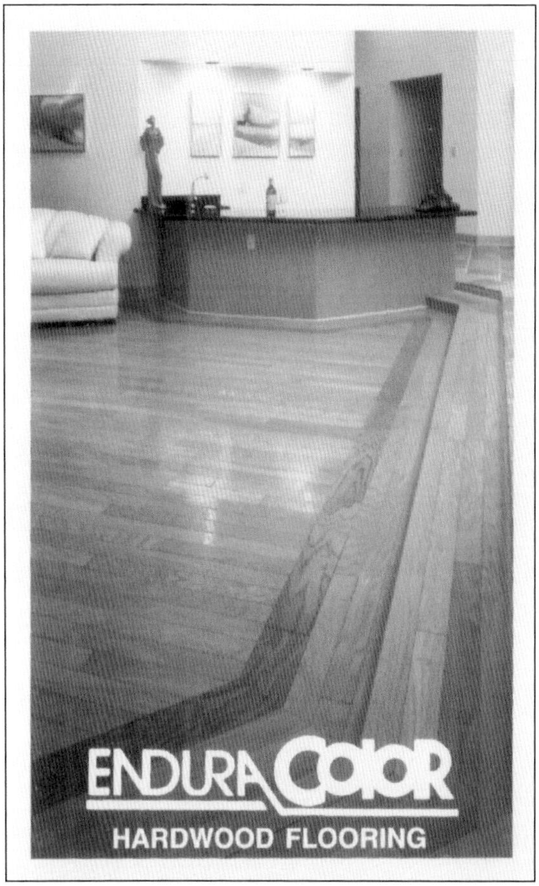

EnduraColor Hardwood Flooring maintained its Dania showroom at 1942 Tigertail Boulevard and featured "Broward County's Largest Selection of Wood Flooring" as well as installation, new construction, and remodeling.

This is the interior of Bishirjian's Dania Rug Company, importers of Oriental rugs at 234 South Federal Highway. This card is at least 30 years old, as the area code (which was changed to 954 sometime in the 1980s) is still shown as "305," which originally covered all of South Florida and is now only in use for Miami-Dade and Monroe (Florida Keys) Counties.

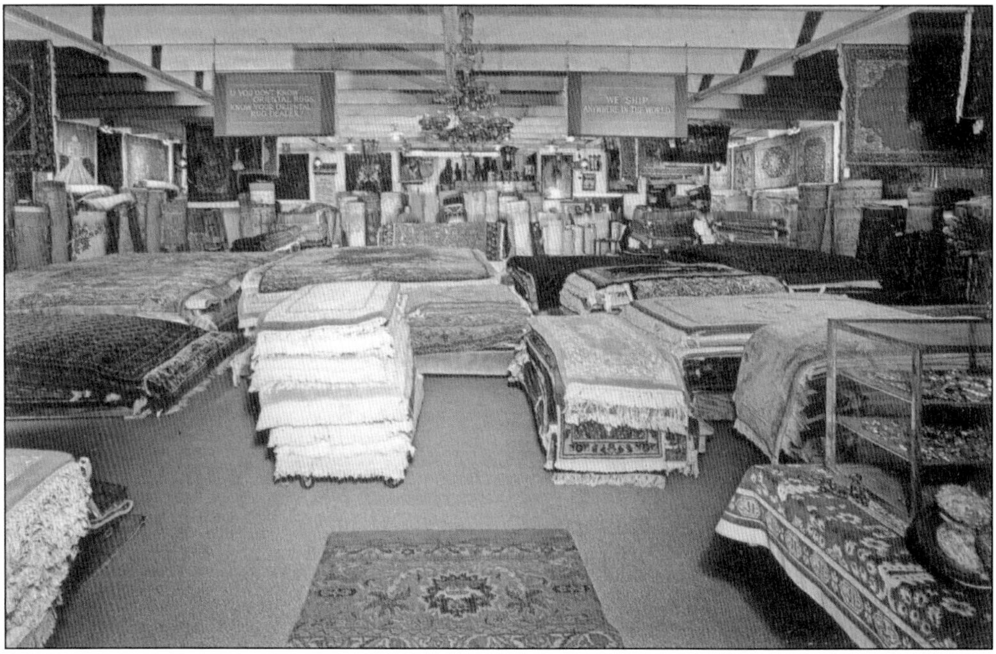

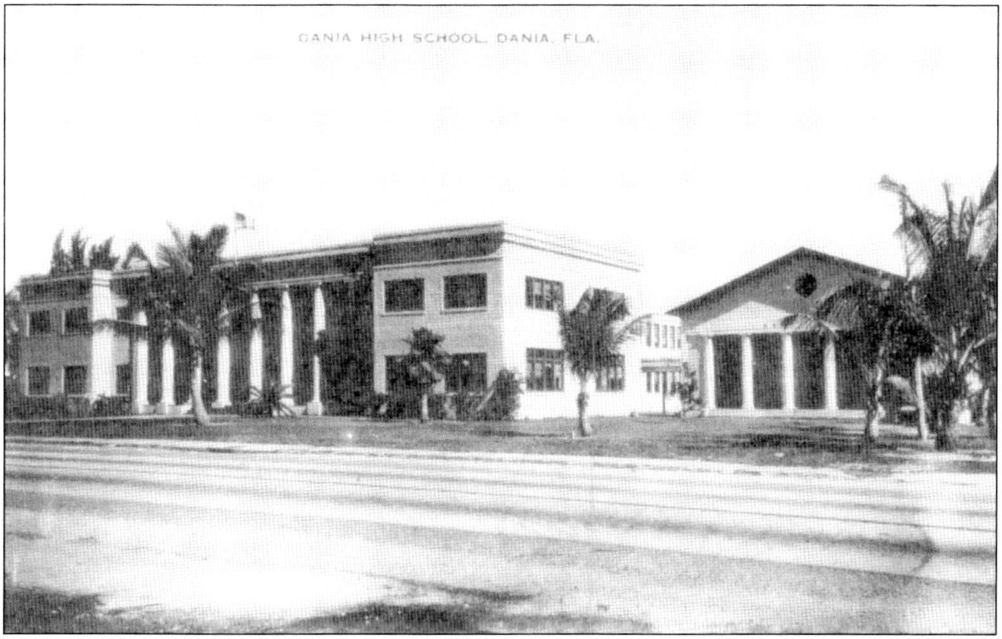

Dania High School was founded in 1913 by the Dade County School Board (Broward County was part of Dade County until 1915). This, the original Dania High School, was the second-oldest high school in what is now Broward County. Renamed South Broward High School in 1938, the school was moved to its current location two miles south, in Hollywood, in 1949. This location is now home to Dania Elementary School.

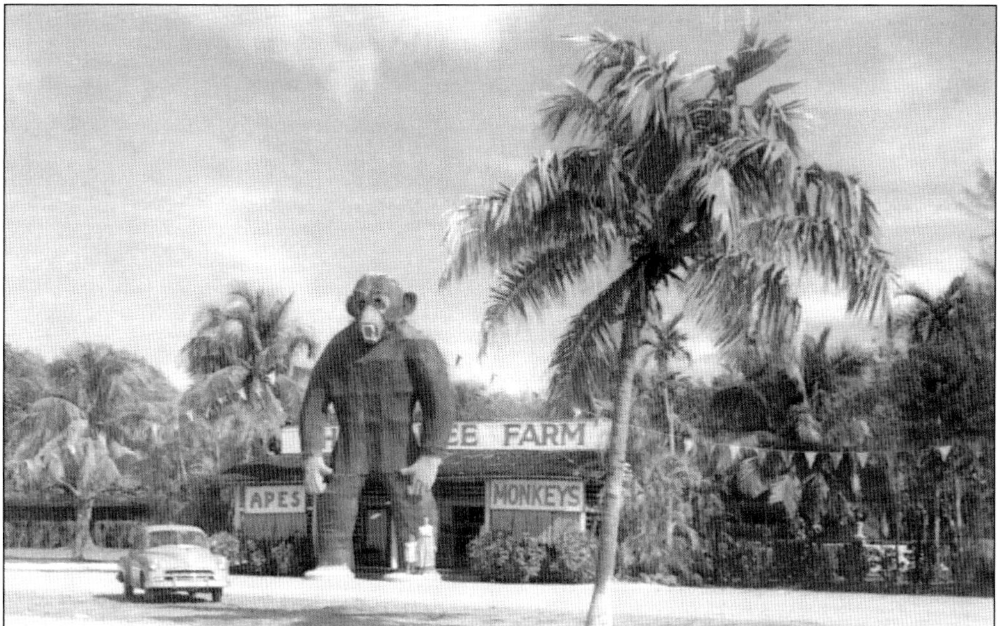

Among several tourist attractions in Dania was The Chimpanzee Farm (also known as "The Chimp Farm"), which not only featured this enormous chimp awaiting visitors at the entrance but claimed that "the world's largest apes" could be seen at this location.

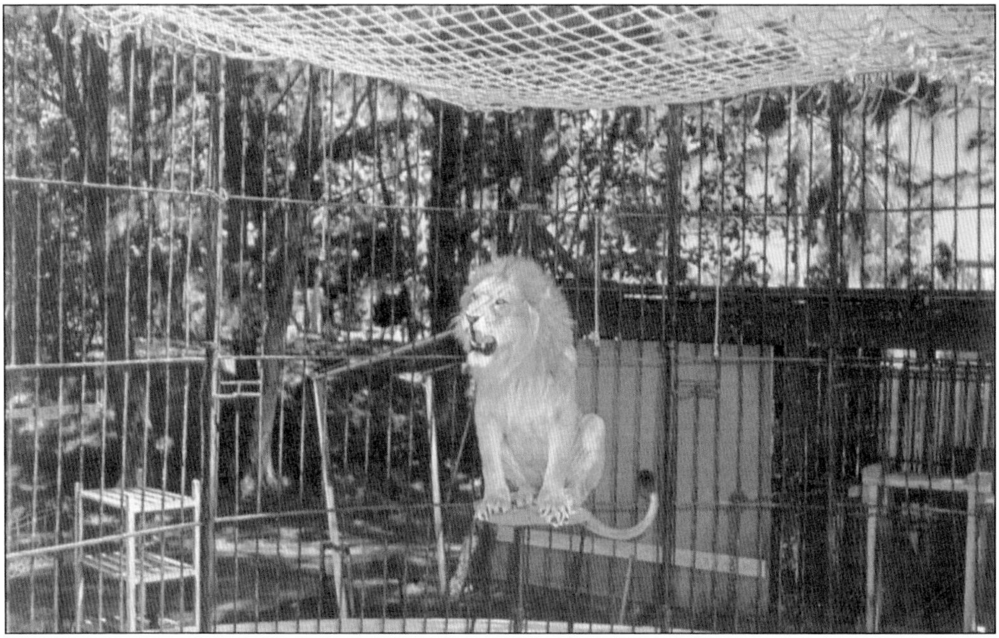

In addition to chimpanzees and other species of simians, including baboons and orangutans, The Chimp Farm also housed a variety of large cats, including this lion.

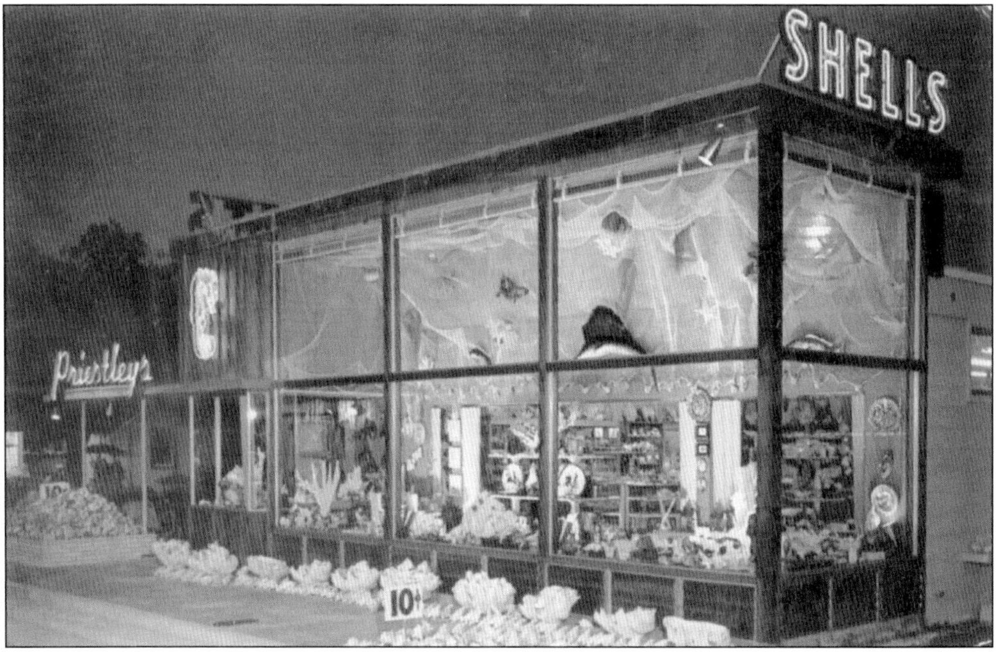

Priestley's featured shells, coral, and other marine and aquatic-themed gifts at this store at 222 North Federal Highway. A most unique and unusual night view of it is shown here.

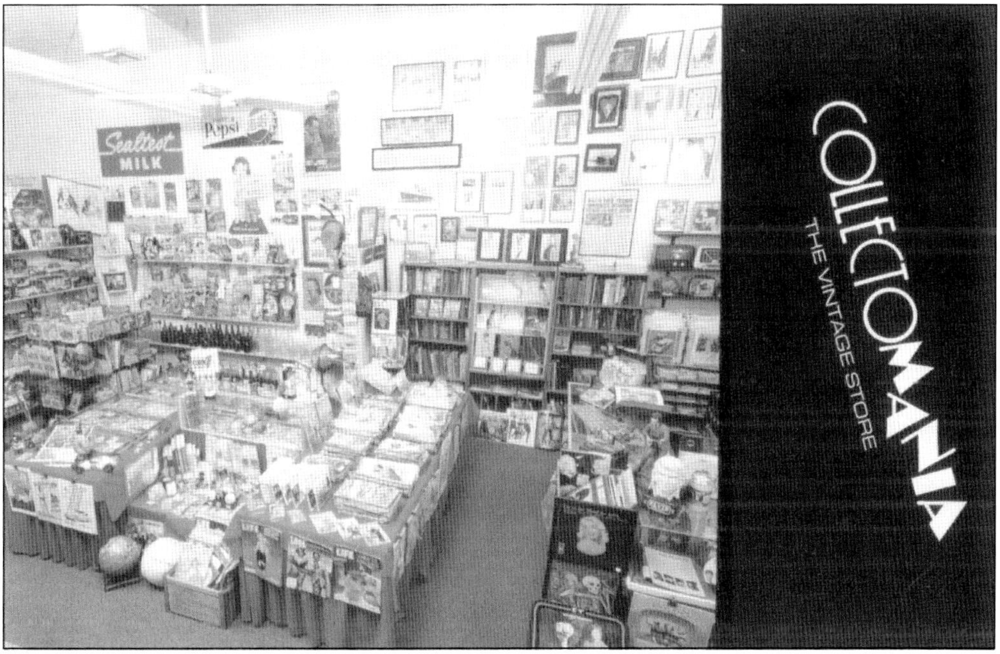

Collectomania, "The Vintage Store," located at No. 10 North Federal Highway, featured a wide variety of "20th Century Memorabilia," including records, comic books, baseball cards, postcards, and other items relating to the era. For some years, it was a regular haunt for local and out-of-town ephemera collectors, but with changing tastes, times, and availability of the same type of items via the Internet, the store closed at the end of the first decade of the 21st century.

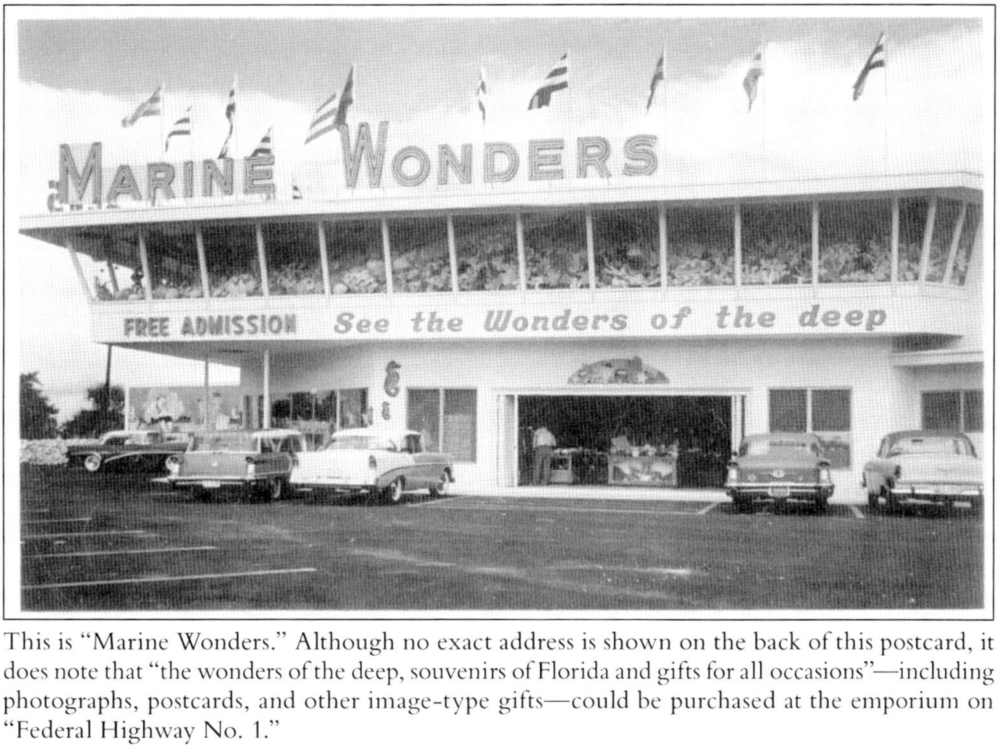

This is "Marine Wonders." Although no exact address is shown on the back of this postcard, it does note that "the wonders of the deep, souvenirs of Florida and gifts for all occasions"—including photographs, postcards, and other image-type gifts—could be purchased at the emporium on "Federal Highway No. 1."

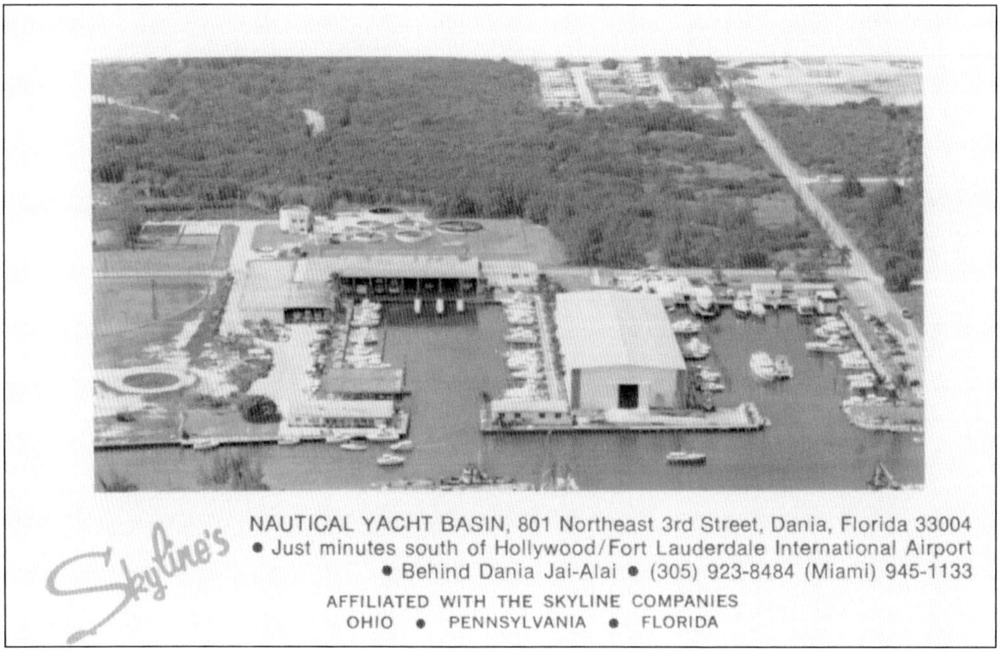

Skyline's Nautical Yacht Basin offered storage, painting, repairs, marine supplies, dock rental, food, and fuel for boaters. It was at 801 Northeast Third Street "behind Dania Jai-Alai."

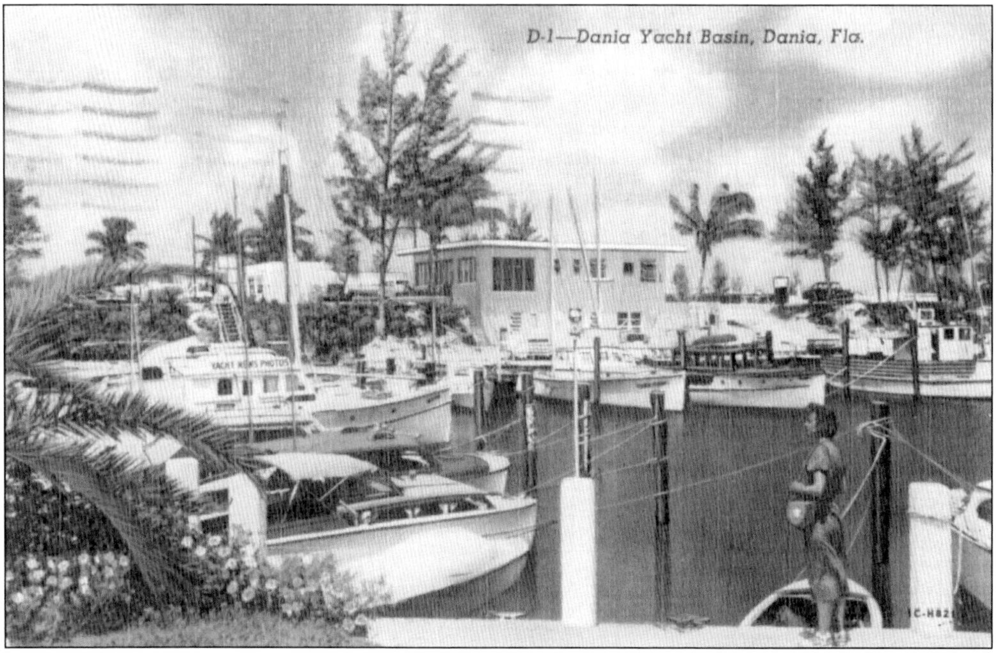

While there is no address shown on this linen postcard postmarked 1954, it is likely that the Dania Yacht Basin was in the same general area as Skyline's.

Four

By Train, Boat, Bus, and Plane

In the earliest years of the 20th century, access to what would become Broward County was possible by non-commercial vessels via either the Atlantic Ocean or the Florida Coast Line Canal and Transportation Company (later the Intracoastal Waterway), with passenger train service beginning on the Florida East Coast Railway in March 1896. Horse-drawn omnibus and buckboard service began just a few years later, while the first Seaboard Air Line Railway train came to the county in 1925.

Commercial air service did not begin until 1956, although a flying field named for Merle Fogg, a World War I fighter pilot who established a flying service in Broward County, came into existence on May 1, 1929. That airfield became Fort Lauderdale Naval Air Station (NAS) in 1942, with the US Navy constructing three main runways and building a control tower as a training facility during World War II.

In 1943, Ens. George H.W. Bush arrived at NAS Fort Lauderdale to train as a pilot. He would become the Navy's youngest pilot, and later, the nation's 41st president. In January 1948, Broward County assumed control of the facility, and in 1953, the county formally took ownership. Three years later, Mackey Airlines introduced the first scheduled airline service at Fort Lauderdale–Hollywood International Airport (FLL).

Today, FLL is the nation's 21st-busiest airport, while South Florida's Tri-Rail commuter service has numerous daily trains operating from Palm Beach County through Broward (with a stop at FLL) into the Miami International Airport. Amtrak runs two daily New York–Miami passenger trains, both of which stop in West Palm Beach, Deerfield Beach, Fort Lauderdale, and Hollywood. Greyhound buses operate along the East Coast throughout the day, while several express lines pick up or drop off passengers in Fort Lauderdale.

Port Everglades has become not only a major bulk freight and container port but a regular terminal for several cruise lines offering worldwide service.

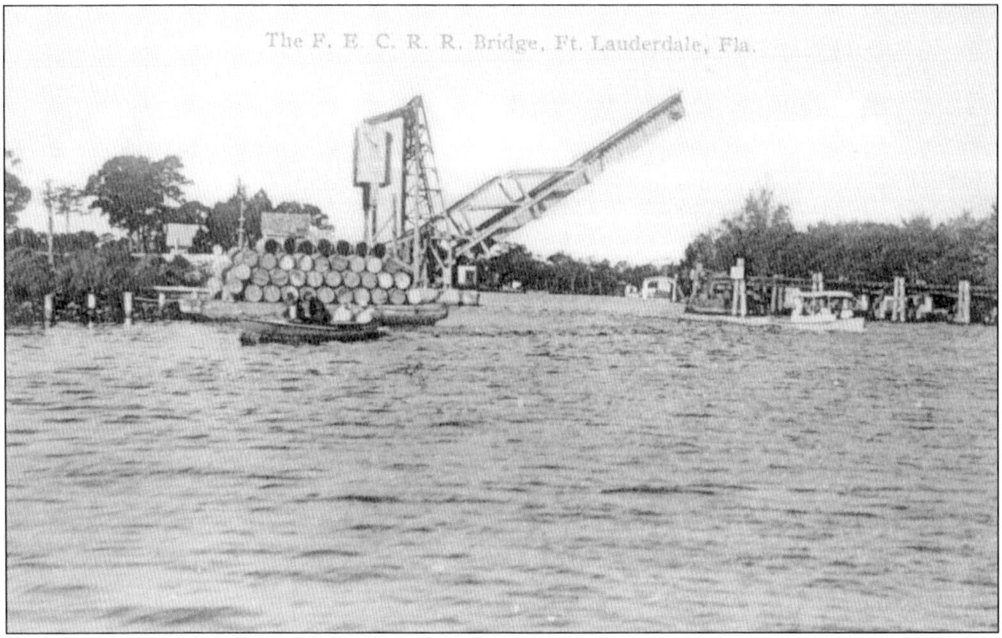

One of several waterways in Broward County that had to be crossed by the Florida East Coast Railway (FEC) en route south to Miami in early 1896 was the New River in Fort Lauderdale. The FEC's drawbridge is shown here around 1912.

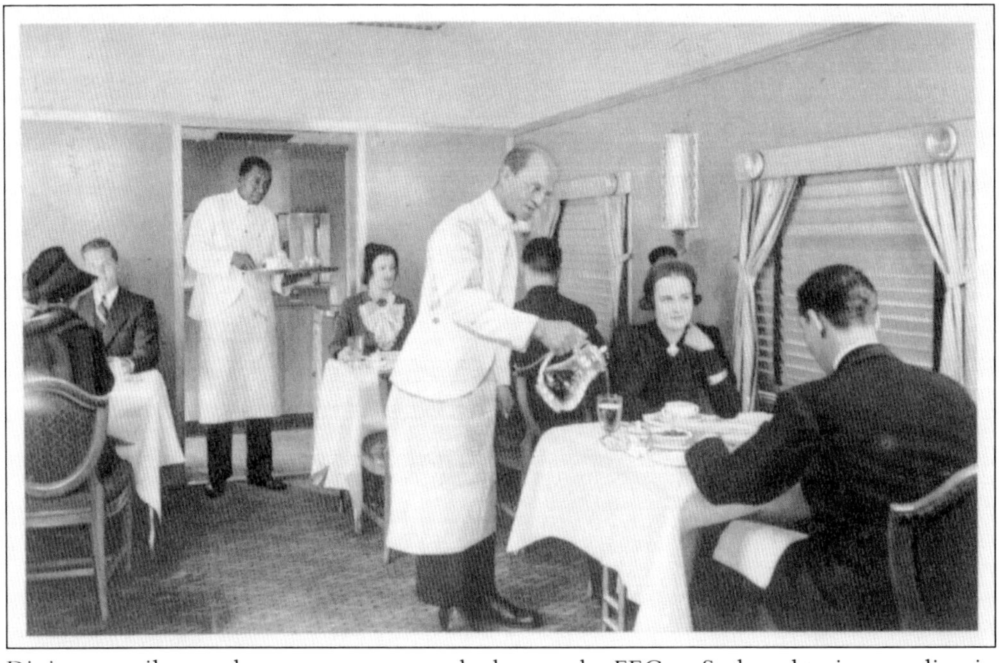

Dining on rails was always a great treat, whether on the FEC or Seaboard trains traveling in either direction through Broward County. A typical railroad dining car is shown here.

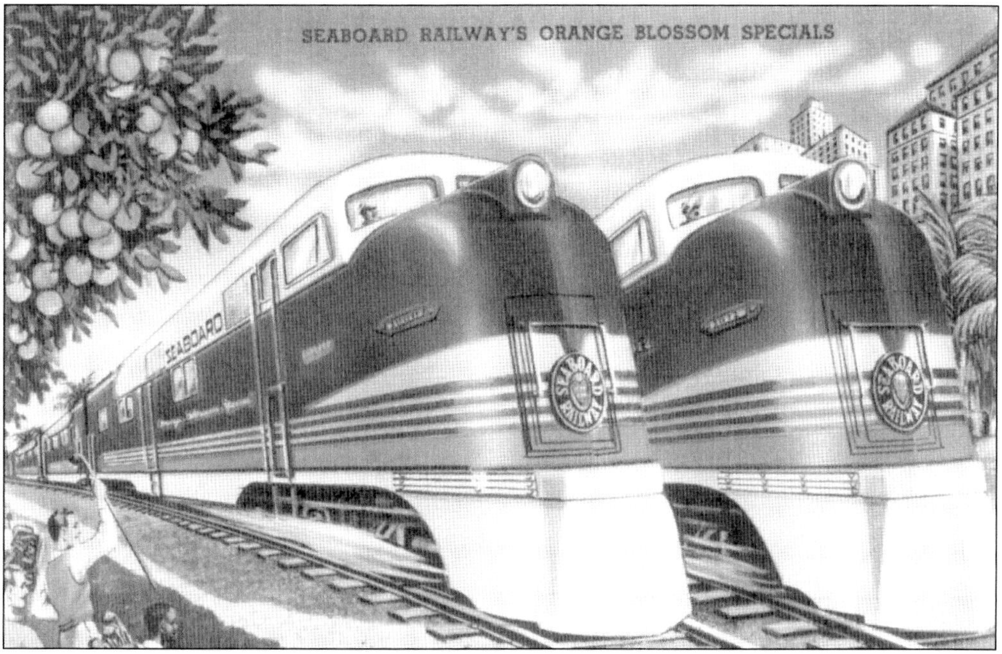

Inaugurated in 1925 when the new Seaboard line was extended to Miami, the Orange Blossom Specials were later dieselized and, on a daily basis in the winter season, competed with the Atlantic Coast Line–Florida East Coast Railway Florida Special, with both trains operating as all Pullman sleeping car trains with fine dining and elegant lounge car service. This is a c. 1939 Orange Blossom Special promotional postcard with linen finish.

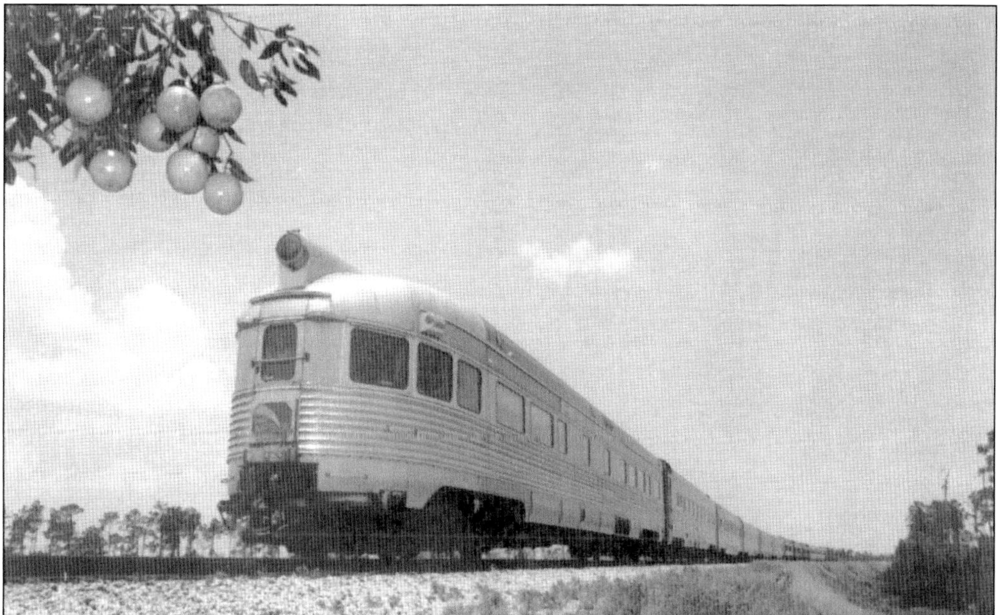

Although the Seaboard discontinued the Orange Blossom Special following the 1953–1954 winter season, it continued to operate at least four trains per day through Broward County for many years thereafter. Its premier streamliner, the Silver Meteor, is shown here.

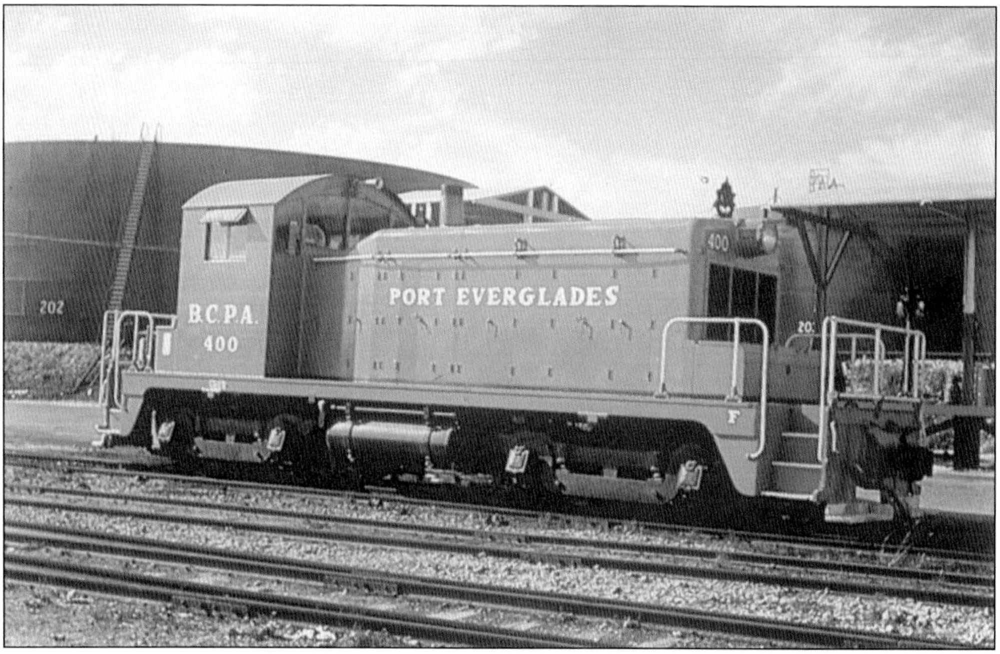

Service between Port Everglades, the Florida East Coast Railway, and the Seaboard was provided by the Broward County Port Authority's (BCPA) own railroad for many years with steam locomotives and later with diesel engines. Diesel engine No. 400 is shown here.

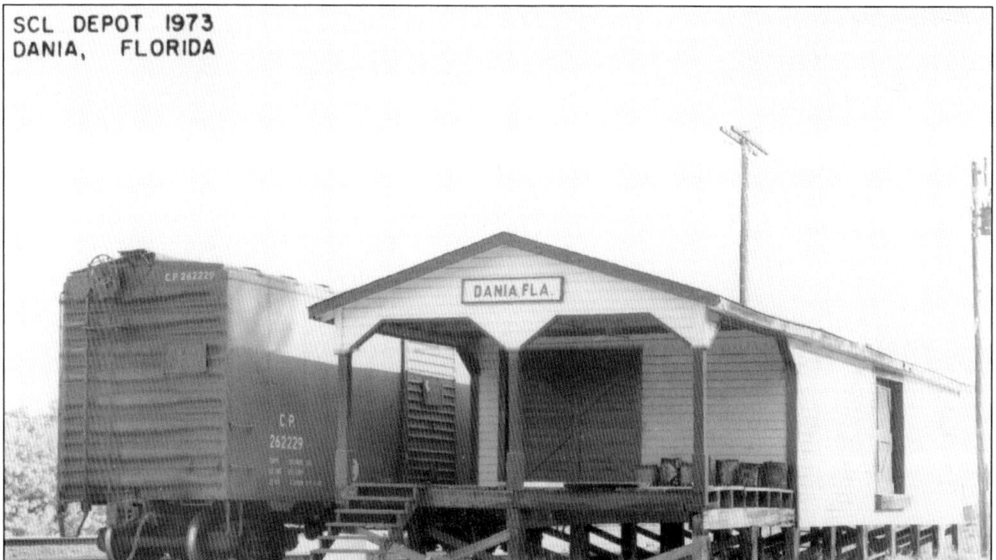

Broward County had a large number of passenger and/or freight stations on both the Florida East Coast Railway and the Seaboard, which was later the Seaboard Coast Line (SCL). All of the SCL stations in Broward County, including Dania, which is shown here, were originally Seaboard depots.

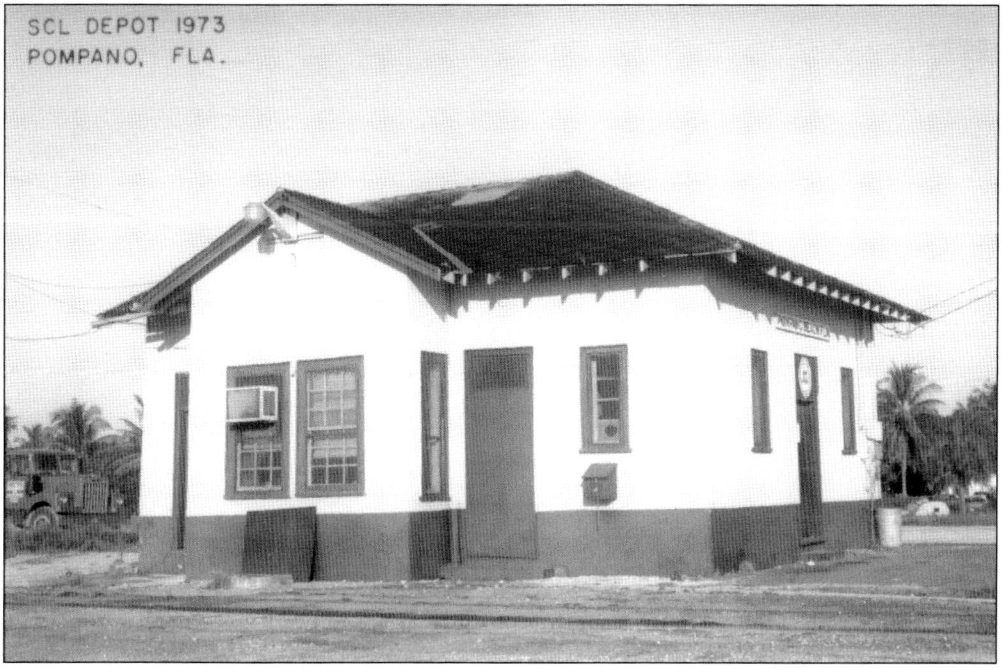

While Pompano Beach was an active and major stop for Florida East Coast Railway trains, only the local or mail trains on the Seaboard/SCL stopped at that railroad's Pompano station, seen here.

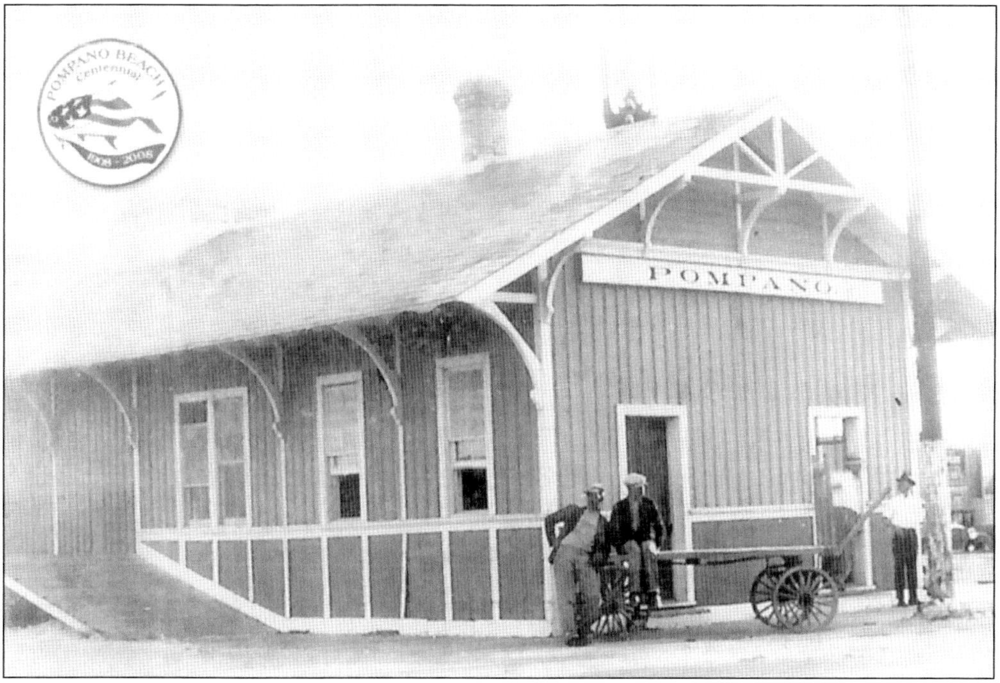

The FEC's Pompano Beach station was commemorated by the Pompano Beach Centennial Committee in 2008 through the publication of this postcard showing the station, which was replaced with a concrete building in the late 1930s or mid-1940s.

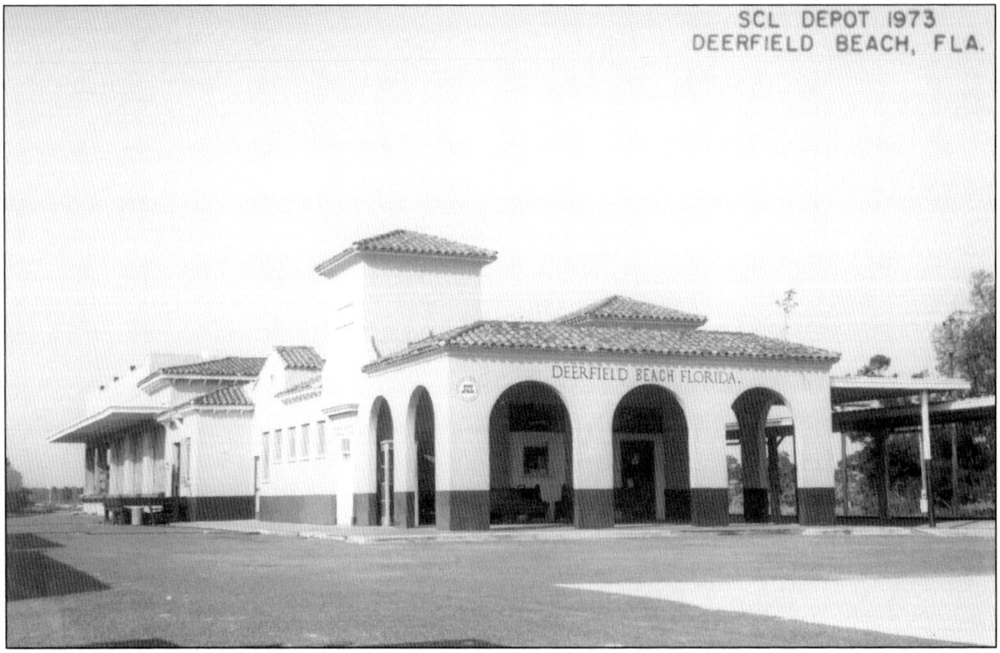

The former Seaboard/SCL station at Deerfield Beach, shown in this southward view, is now used daily by both Tri-Rail and Amtrak passenger trains. It remains the same in appearance.

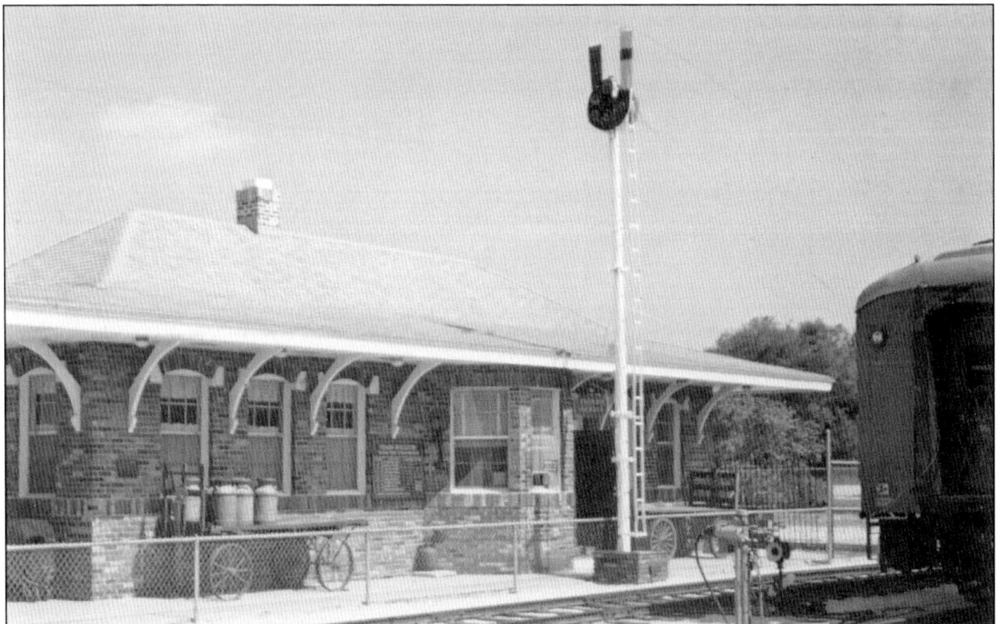

When the Gold Coast Railroad moved to the north side of Fort Lauderdale–Hollywood International Airport, along the BCPA's tracks, it built a brick station named Loisville, in honor of Lois Beekman, one of the major supporters of that all-volunteer railroad, along with car storage space and a locomotive shop to service its steam engines.

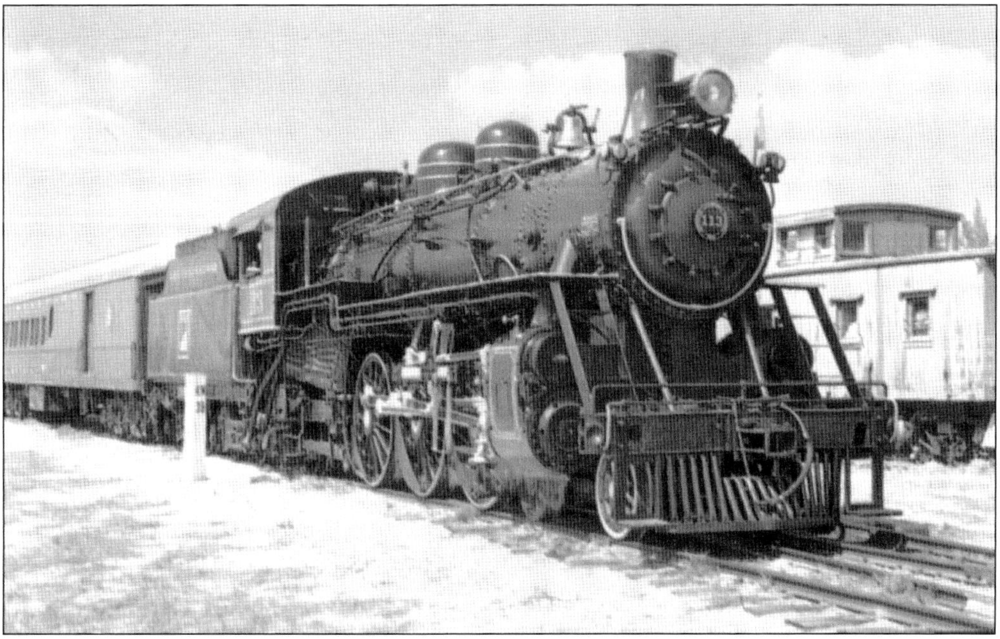

One of the two steam locomotives used by the Gold Coast Railroad between the Florida East Coast Railway and the Seaboard was Florida East Coast Railway 4-6-2 No. 113, shown here with an Apalachicola Northern Railroad caboose in the background and a milepost marker from Key West Extension days to the left of the engine.

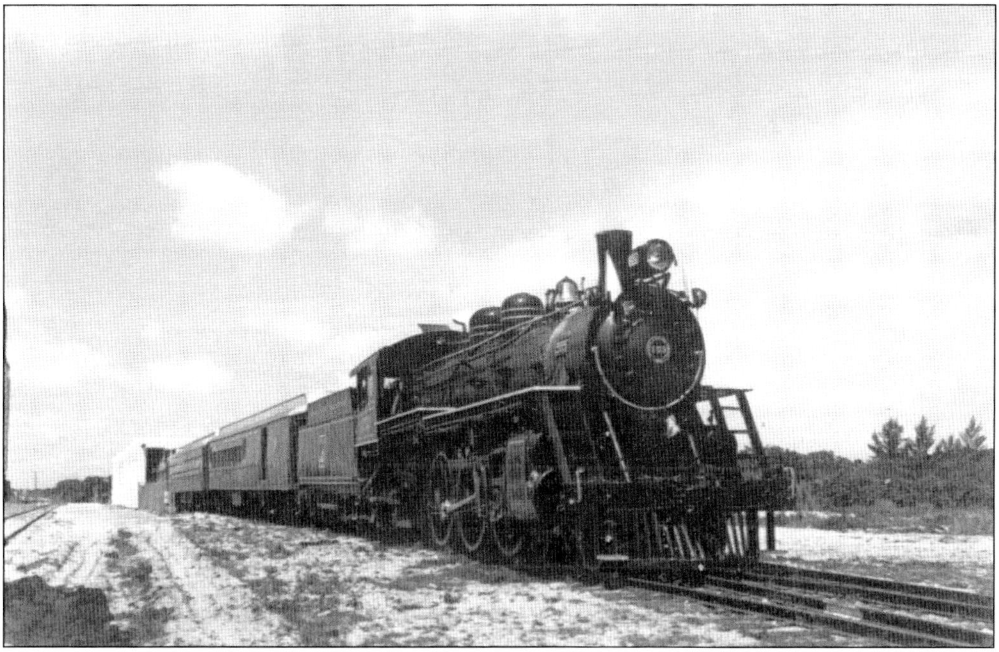

The 4-6-2 engine No. 153 was sold to United States Sugar Company in Clewiston, and along with the No. 113, was eventually donated to the Gold Coast Railroad. In 1984, with Miami Playboy Club bunnies on board, the Gold Coast left Fort Lauderdale to return to its original site at the former University of Miami South Campus, now ZooMiami.

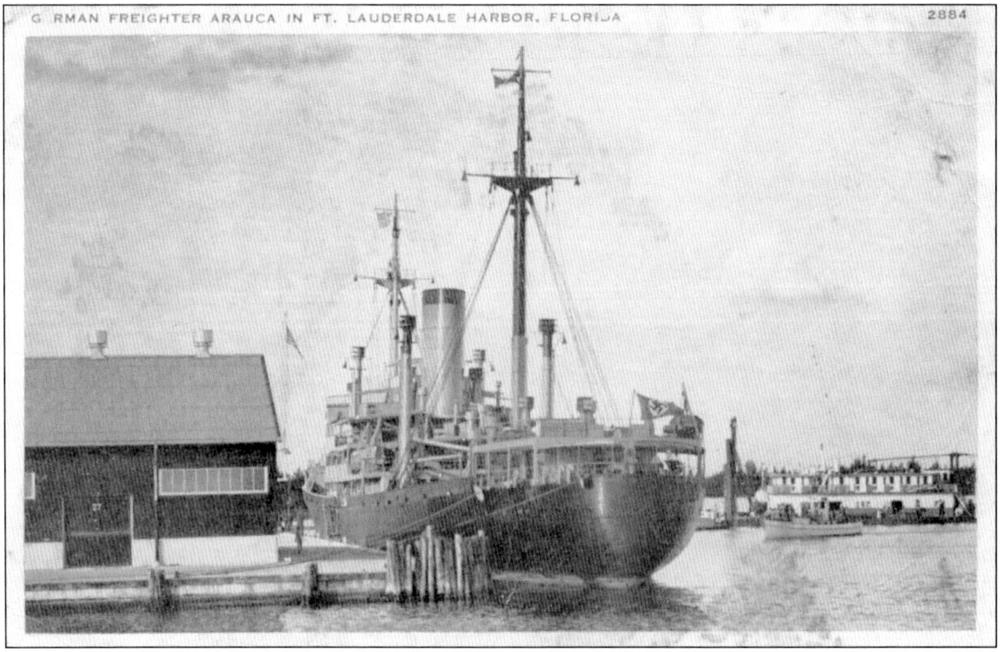

Pearl Harbor had not yet occurred, but England and Germany were already at war. The German freighter *Arauca* is shown here tied up at Port Everglades after outrunning a British cruiser that was sitting just outside the three-mile limit in case the *Arauca* were to make a run for it.

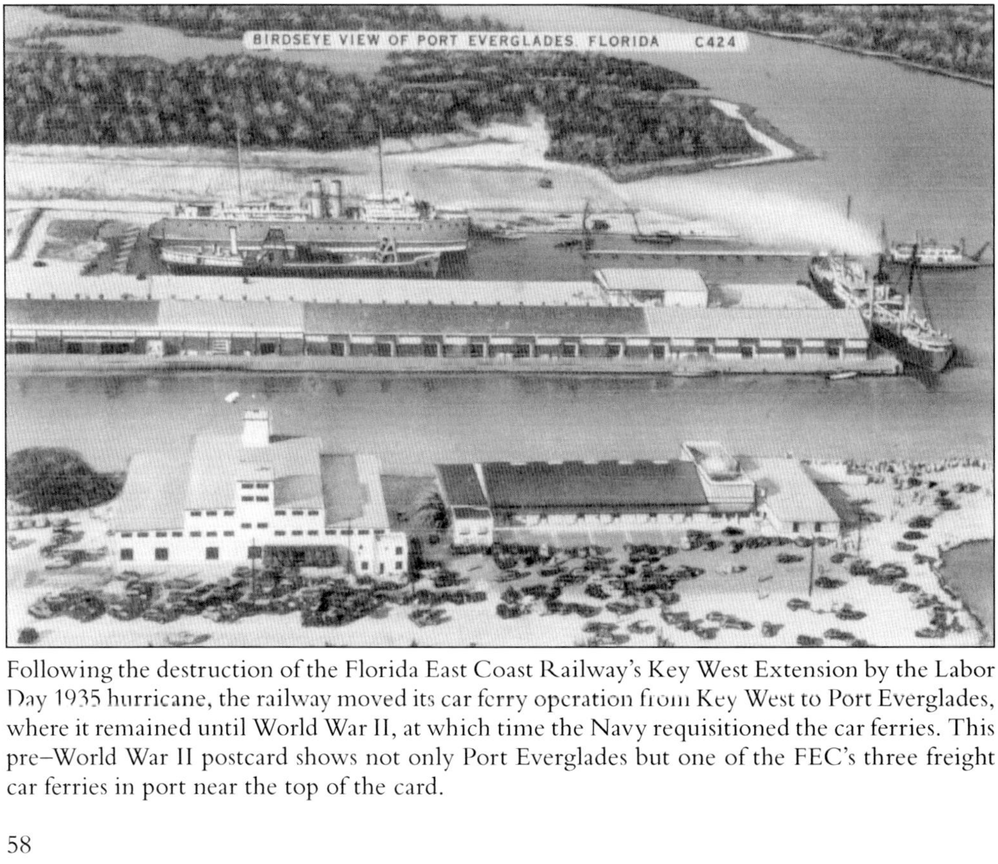

Following the destruction of the Florida East Coast Railway's Key West Extension by the Labor Day 1935 hurricane, the railway moved its car ferry operation from Key West to Port Everglades, where it remained until World War II, at which time the Navy requisitioned the car ferries. This pre–World War II postcard shows not only Port Everglades but one of the FEC's three freight car ferries in port near the top of the card.

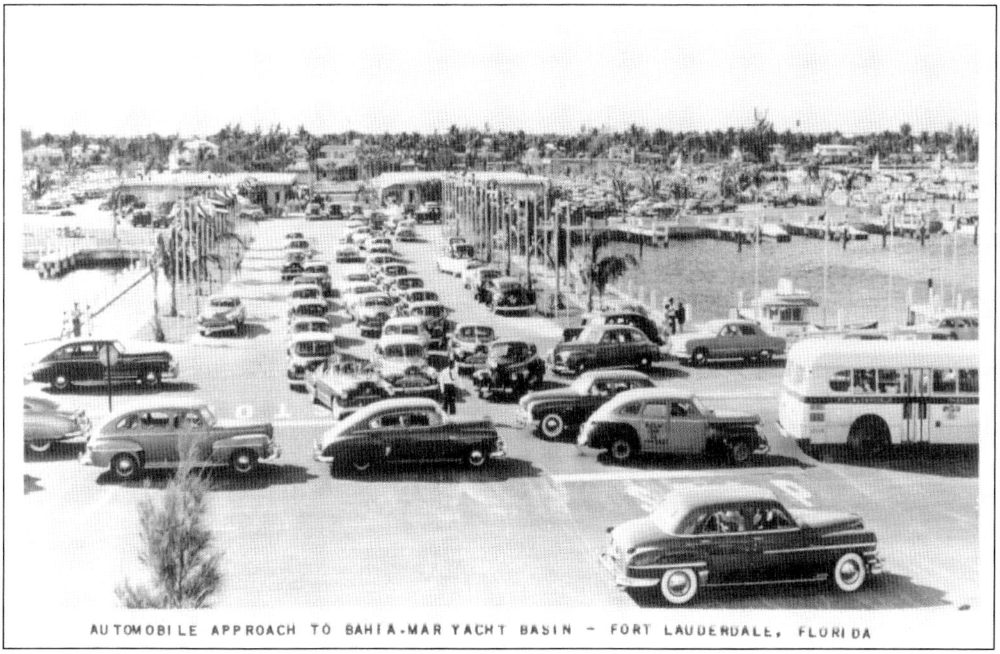

There are incredibly few images of Fort Lauderdale Transit Company buses, so even this partial view of the bus at right, on the "automobile approach to Bahia-Mar Yacht Basin," rates as a true Broward County gem.

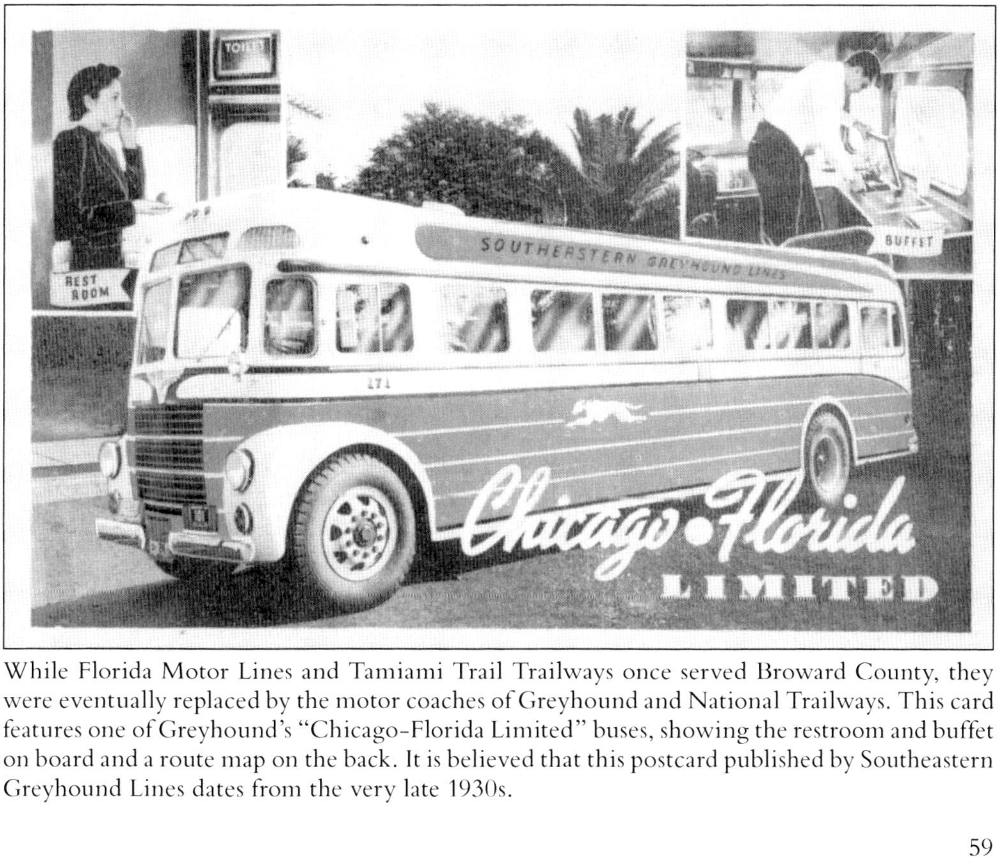

While Florida Motor Lines and Tamiami Trail Trailways once served Broward County, they were eventually replaced by the motor coaches of Greyhound and National Trailways. This card features one of Greyhound's "Chicago-Florida Limited" buses, showing the restroom and buffet on board and a route map on the back. It is believed that this postcard published by Southeastern Greyhound Lines dates from the very late 1930s.

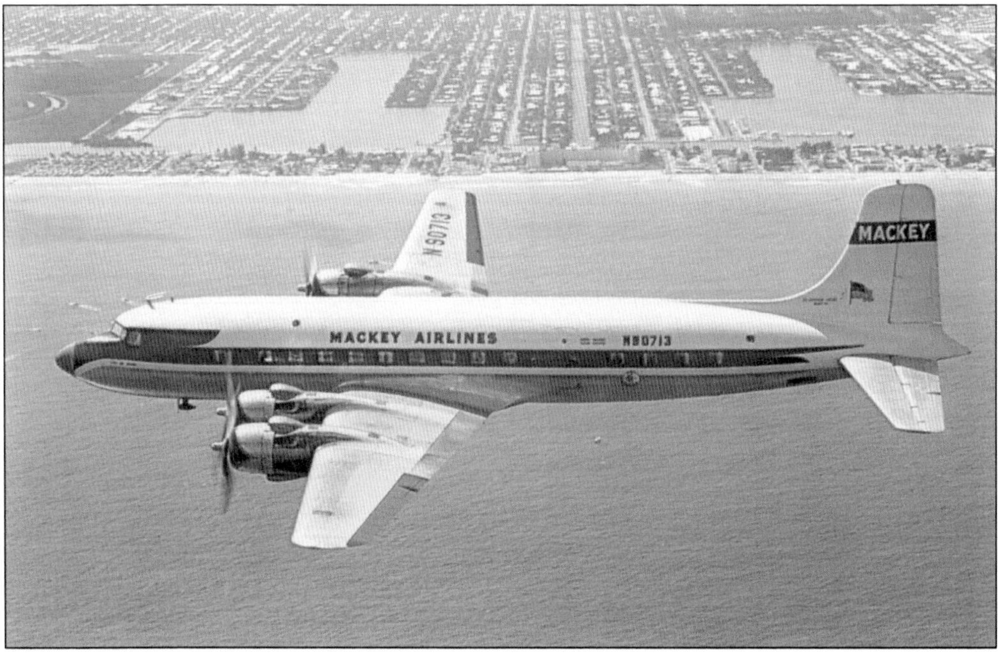

Mackey Airlines, later subsumed by Eastern Air Lines, initiated commercial air service from what was originally called Broward County Airport in 1956. Eventually flying between several Florida cities, Mackey later offered service to Nassau and Havana. Two of its planes are shown here flying over Fort Lauderdale.

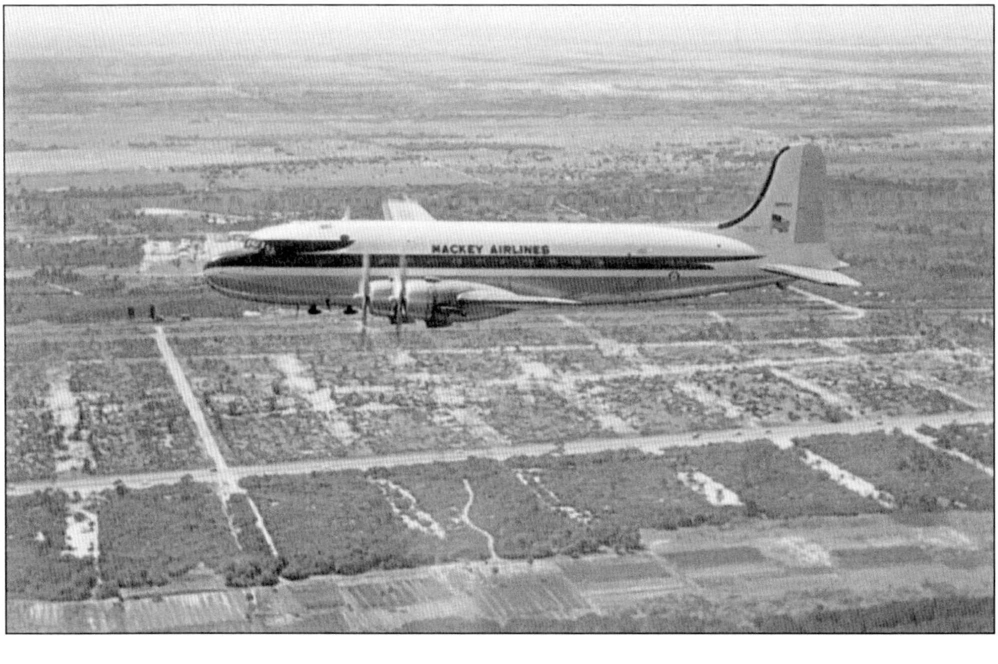

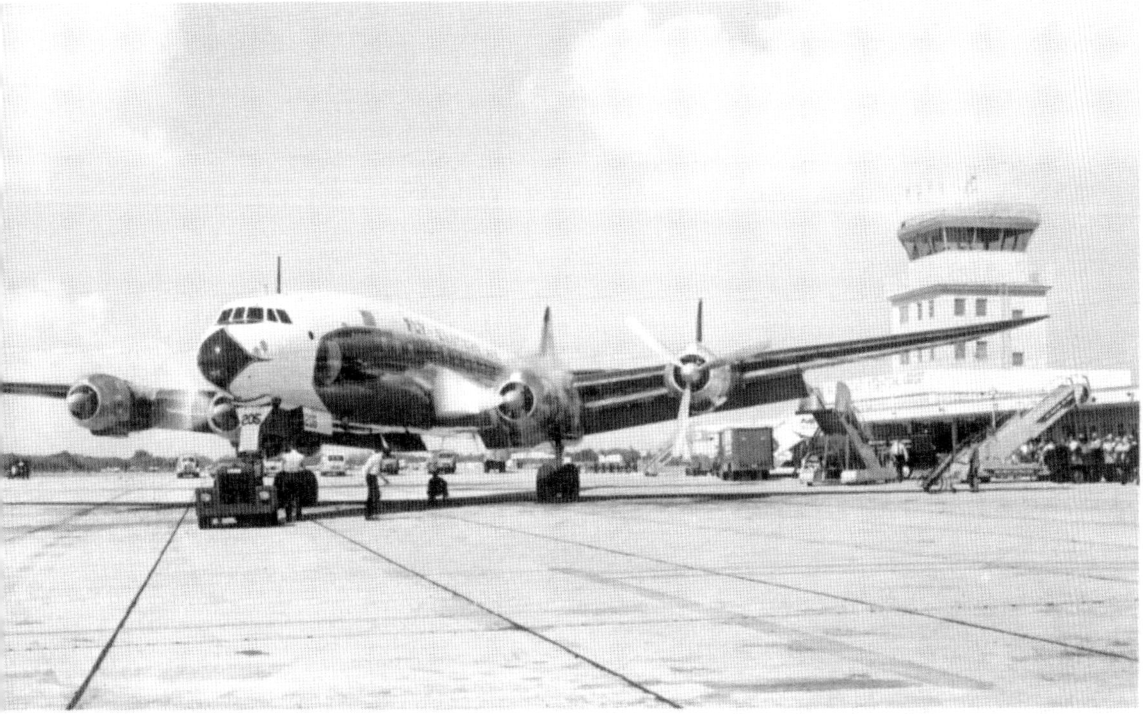

Broward County International Airport, Ft. Lauderdale, Florida

For many years, Eastern Air Lines was a major carrier to and from Broward County International Airport, as it was then known. One of the carrier's Constellations, or "Connies," is shown here shortly before takeoff.

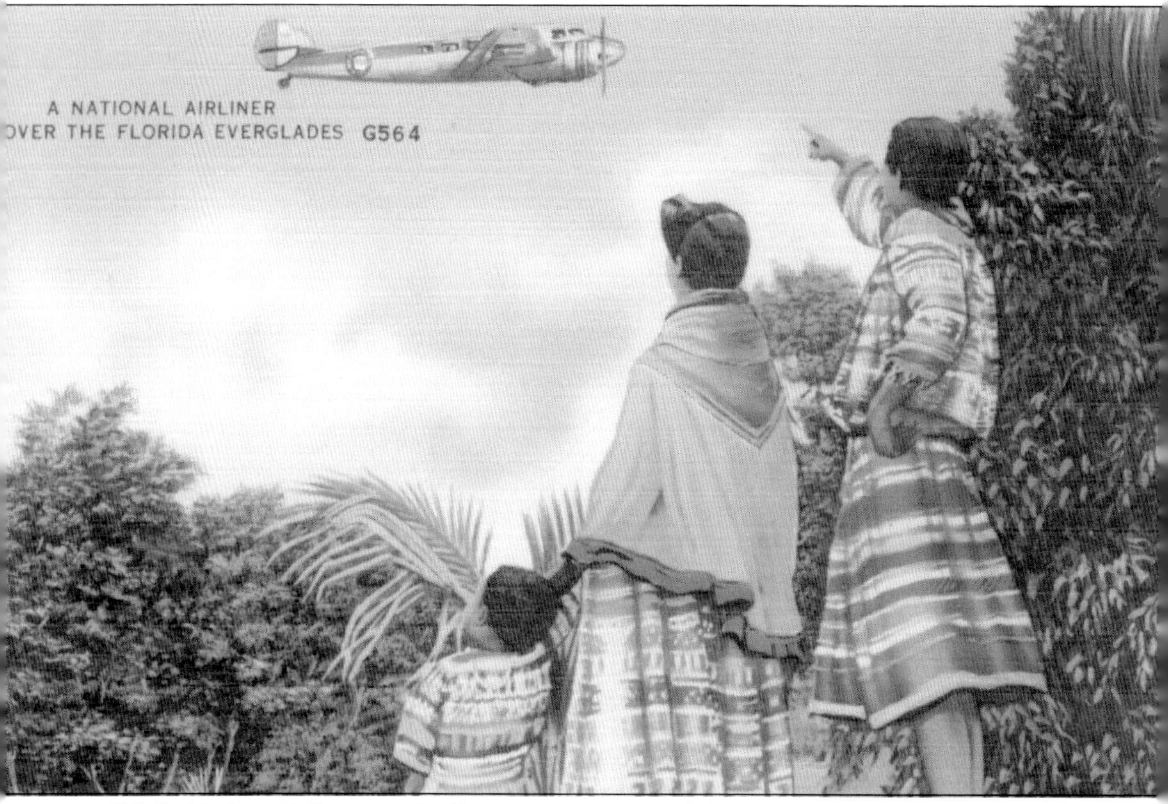

While Mackey Airlines was the first carrier at Broward County Airport, it was later joined by other airlines, including National. In this view, a National plane on what was then known as the "Buccaneer Route" is shown flying out of Broward County Airport, most likely passing over the Seminole reservation on US Route 441.

Five

Bay Mabel and Port Everglades

Although today's Port Everglades is a major shipping origination and destination point for bulk goods and fuel (the port is home to South Florida's fuel tank farms, with millions of gallons stored there for use in gas stations, businesses, and homes) as well as for cruise ships heading for and returning from destinations worldwide, it actually began as an idea for a deep-water port.

The official website of the Broward County Port Authority provides an authoritative history of what would become a world-famous port. That site states that the body of water that would become Port Everglades was known as Lake Mabel or Bay Mabel and became Bay Mabel Harbor in 1911. In 1924, the developer of Hollywood, Joseph Young, purchased 1,440 acres of land and water and called it the Hollywood Harbor Development Company. In 1927, the state legislature established the Broward County Port Authority, and in 1928, the rock barrier separating the harbor from the ocean was removed.

In 1929, the SS *Vogtland* became the first cargo ship and first foreign-flagged vessel to enter the new port. A year later, in 1930, United Fruit Company and its "Great White Fleet" became the port's first official passenger-carrying steamship operation.

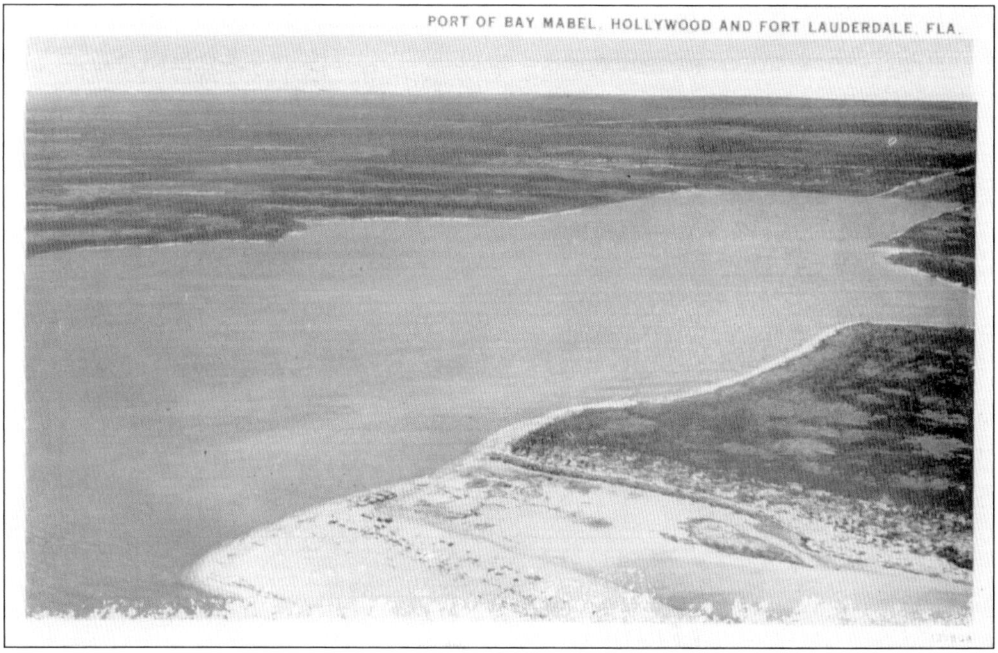

Although the author's Florida postcard collection is immense, this utterly amazing white-border view of "Port of Bay Mabel, Hollywood and Fort Lauderdale, Fla." is one of the rarest cards in the collection, due to the rarity of the c. 1920 card itself and the view of a totally different Port Everglades.

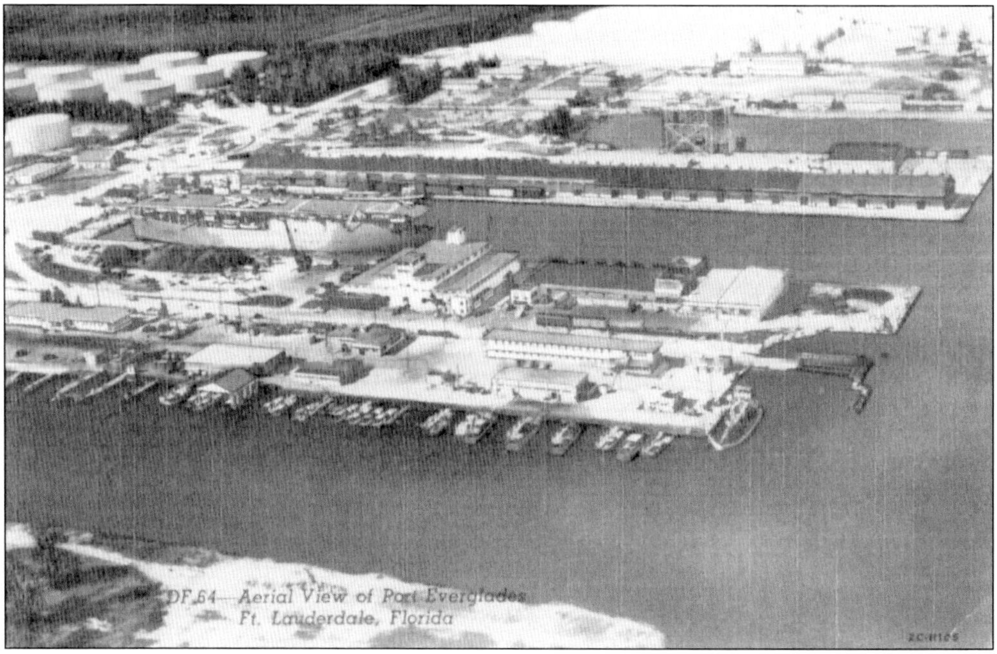

This linen postcard postmarked 1955 is believed to have been made sometime in the late 1940s, shortly after World War II. Though there are numerous items of interest, perhaps the most important is the US Navy aircraft carrier docked at center left. Although Navy ships frequently berthed at Port Everglades, it was rare to have a carrier in port, and this postcard image was taken during one of the very few visits ever made to the port by this type of naval vessel.

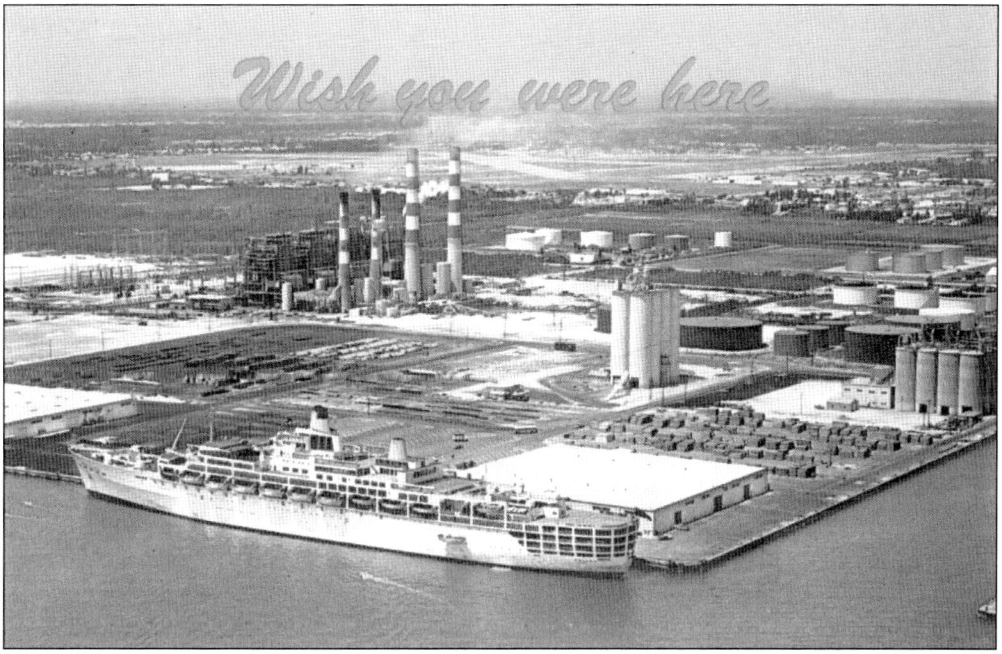

On the back of this late 1950s chrome postcard with a view of Port Everglades that is completely different from what is there today is the statement: "Port Everglades is one of the deepest natural harbors along the Eastern seaboard." While the name of the ship in port is difficult to read, it might possibly be the *Alborg*, a Norwegian cruise vessel.

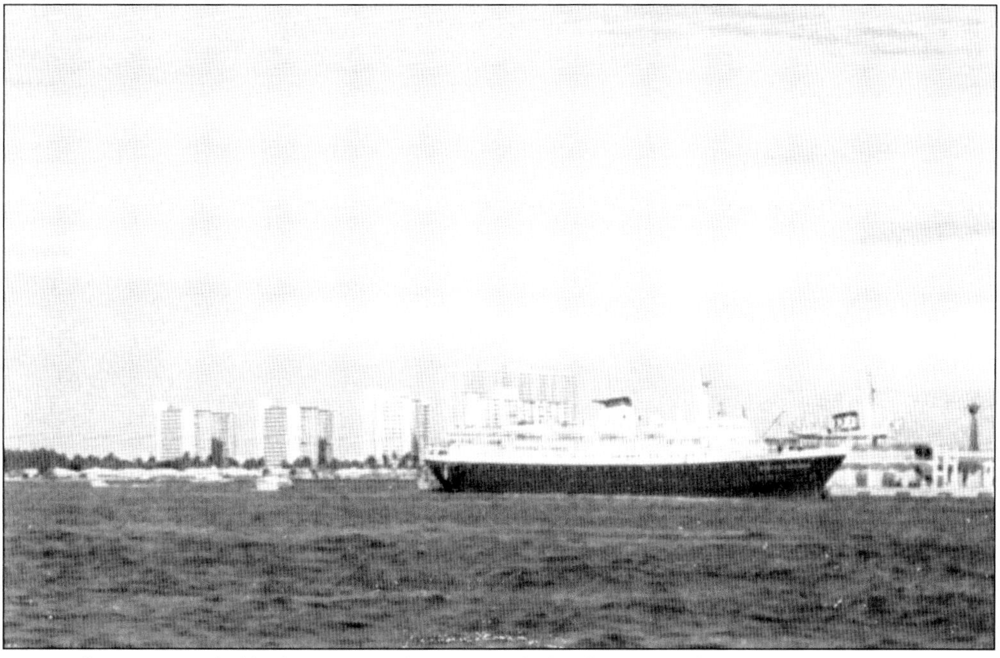

A view from Bay Mabel looking toward Port Everglades shows new high-rise apartment buildings in the background. The scene at the port today, approximately 35 years after this postcard was made, is so totally different as to be almost unrecognizable.

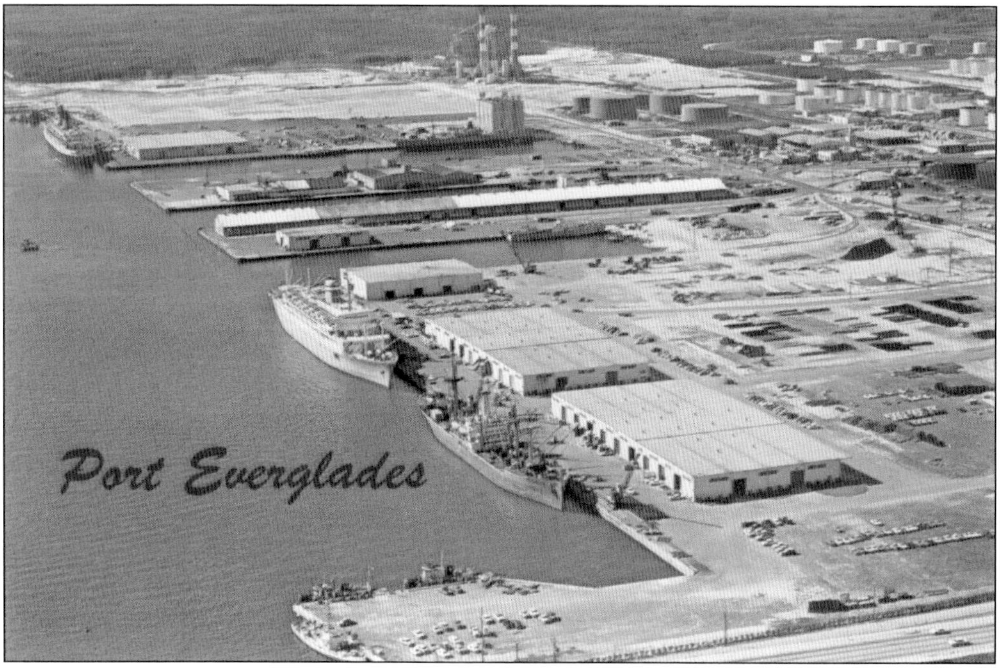

This view from the air shows both a docked passenger liner and a freighter in port. Part of the tank farm is visible in the background at right, while the power plant is visible in the distant background at center.

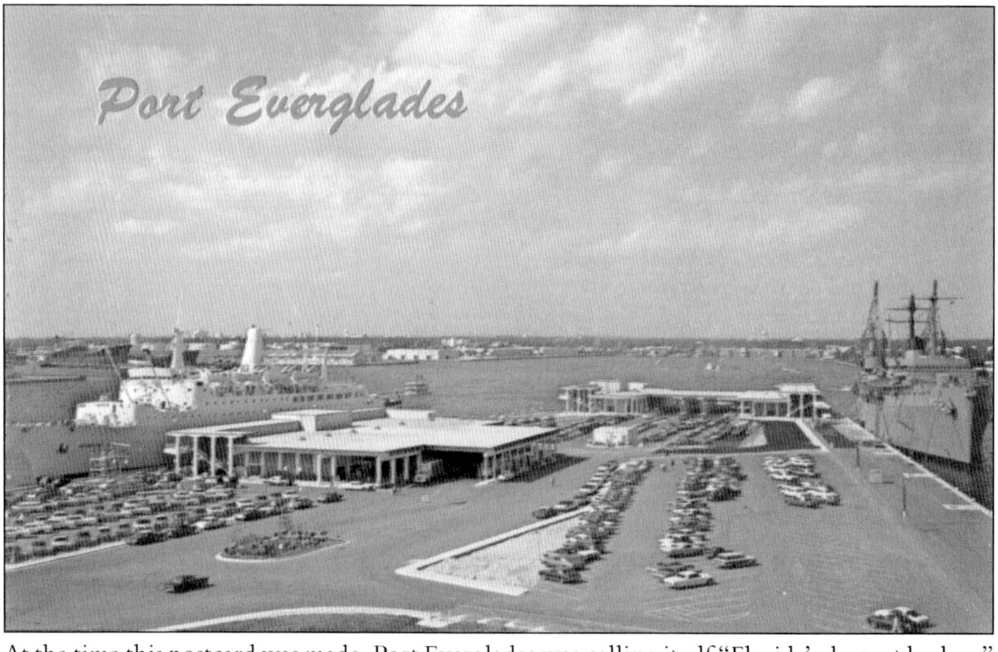

At the time this postcard was made, Port Everglades was calling itself "Florida's deepest harbor," with the depth then at 37 feet. The new cruise port is shown here, with a US Navy vessel on the right and a passenger liner docked at left.

Six

Fort Lauderdale and Wilton Manors

Fort Lauderdale is one of the most famous cities in America. Made even more famous than it had been by the 1960 Connie Francis movie *Where the Boys Are*, Fort Lauderdale, which celebrated its centennial in 2015, is not only a major Florida metropolis but the largest city in and county seat of Broward County.

The original US Army stockade named Fort Lauderdale was built in 1838 during the first Seminole War. It was later the site of fighting during the Second Seminole War. The fort, which had been named for Maj. William Lauderdale (1782–1838), the younger brother of Lt. Col. James Lauderdale, was abandoned in 1842 after the end of the war, and the area remained virtually unpopulated until the 1890s.

Fort Lauderdale's first major development began during the Florida land boom of the 1920s. Although growth was seriously stunted following the 1926 hurricane and the Great Depression, World War II brought new life to the area. The city became a major US Navy base, with a Naval Air Station (NAS) to train pilots, radar and fire control operator training schools, and a Coast Guard base at Port Everglades. In 1948, as noted in chapter four, the NAS was turned over to Broward County and eventually became Fort Lauderdale–Hollywood International Airport.

After World War II ended, service members returned to the area, spurring an enormous population explosion that dwarfed the 1920s boom. Today, Fort Lauderdale is a major yachting center, one of the nation's most important tourist destinations, and the seat of a county with a population closing in on two million people.

The slogan of Wilton Manors, which refers to itself as "Island City," is "Life's Just Better Here." Indeed, for a great many in that city, which was founded as a community known as Colahatchee, it is. The name Wilton Manors was conceived by a transplant from Georgia, Ned Willingham, in 1925, although his reason for deciding to call it that is unknown. In 1947, the city was formally incorporated.

The city not only boasts a sizeable LGBTQ population, but attracts a large contingent of winter visitors who frequent the stores, shops, nightclubs, and gay-owned businesses along Wilton Drive, the city's main commercial street. A city web page notes that the police department, which has gay and lesbian officers in its ranks, conducts sensitivity training sessions geared toward the gay community. All of the city commission's members, with the exception of Vice Mayor Scott Newton, are gay.

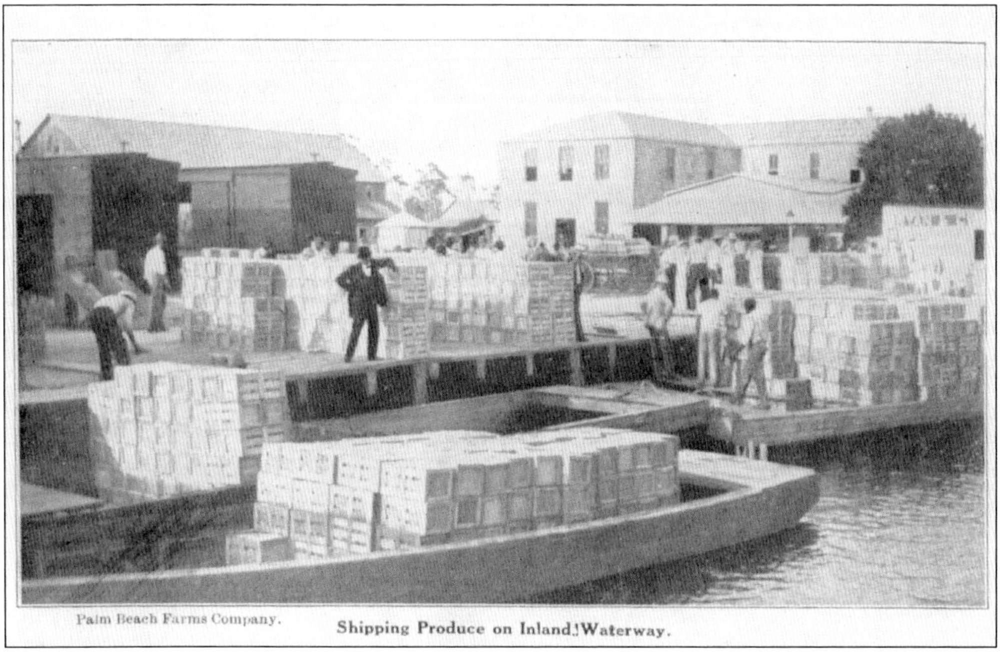

Fort Lauderdale's early commerce began at the junction of the New River and the Florida East Coast Railway's shipping dock. In this c. 1912 Palm Beach Farms Company postcard, barges laden with produce and citrus fruit are awaiting unloading, with the produce to be transferred to the refrigerator cars visible at left.

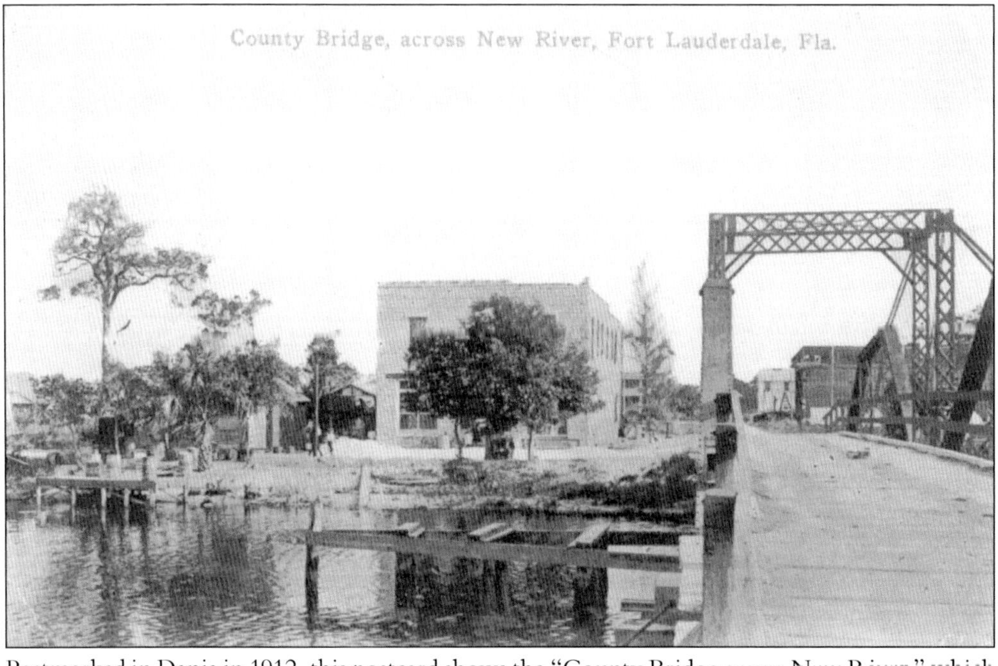

Postmarked in Dania in 1912, this postcard shows the "County Bridge across New River," which the author believes was the original Andrews Avenue bridge. Replaced at least four times, it now has four lanes and supplements the US Route 1 tunnel under the New River, which also has four lanes and is one of only two vehicular tunnels in Florida (the other one is at PortMiami).

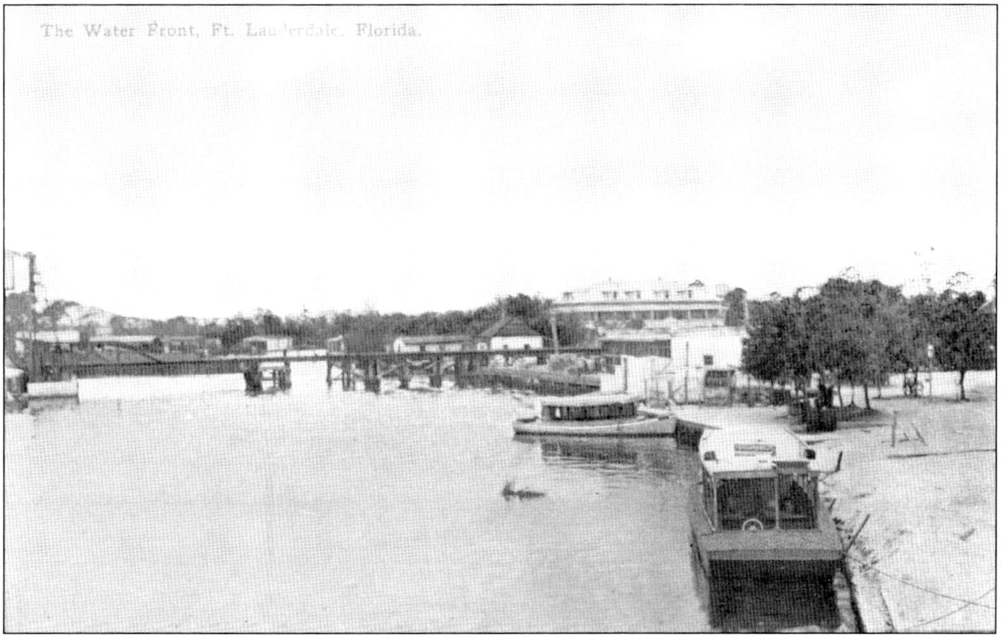

With the New River Inn in the background, this view is now vastly different than the one shown on this postcard. The Florida East Coast Railway's drawbridge is at center.

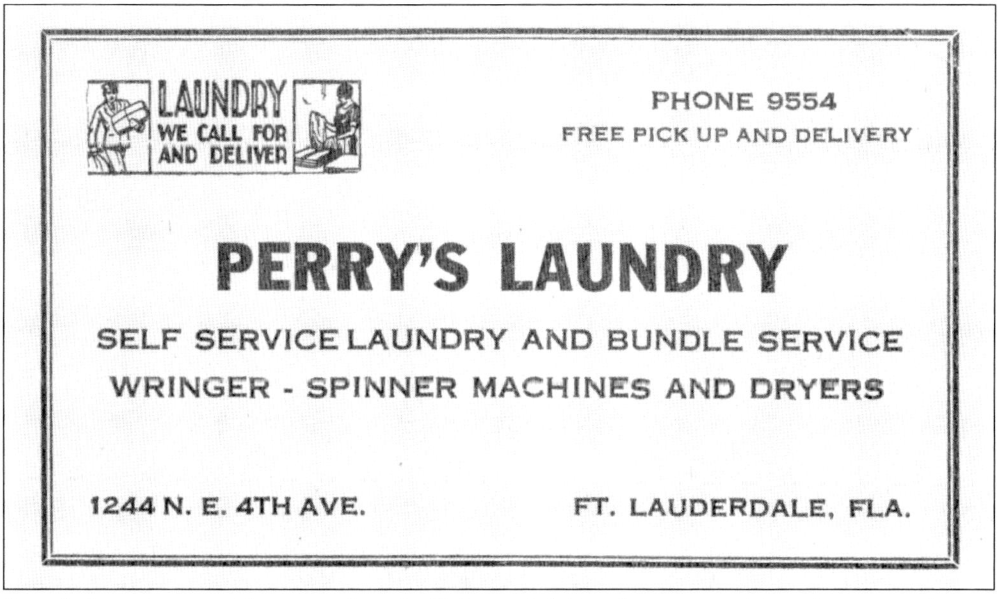

Perry's Laundry would at one time "call for and deliver" customers' laundry at no charge. Although it was apparently located at 1244 Northeast Fourth Avenue, other than this card, there appears to be no other record of the existence of this business.

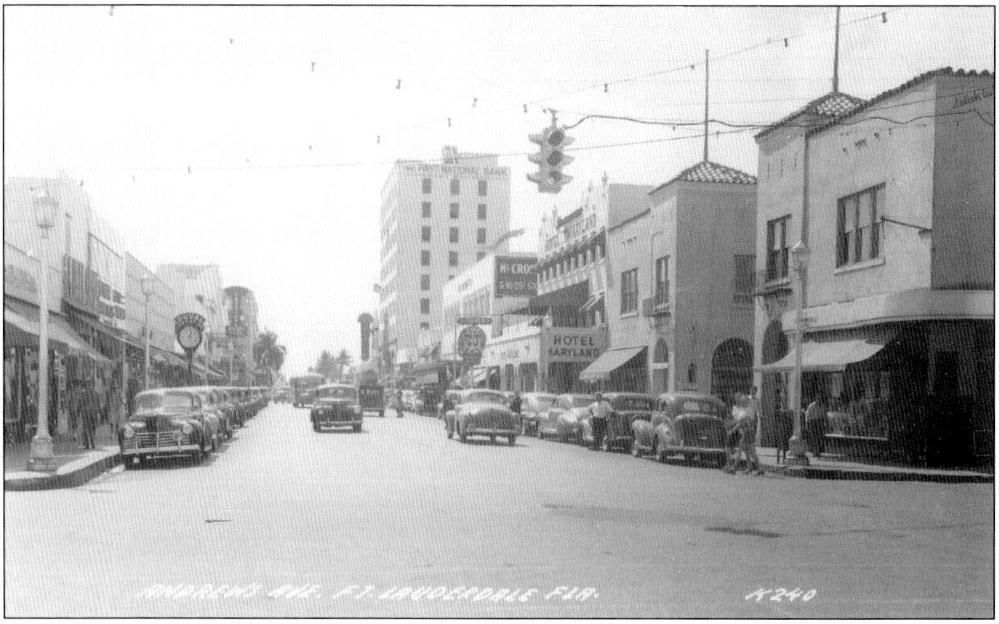

Until the great growth of Fort Lauderdale and Broward County to the west, Andrews Avenue was, for many years, the city's (and the county's) most important business and commerce location, replete with clothing stores, banks, at least one movie theater, professional offices, and a variety of eateries. This late 1930s postcard shows Andrews Avenue with the Hotel Maryland, McCrory's 5 and 10 Cent store, and the Sunset Theater in the First National Bank building at right.

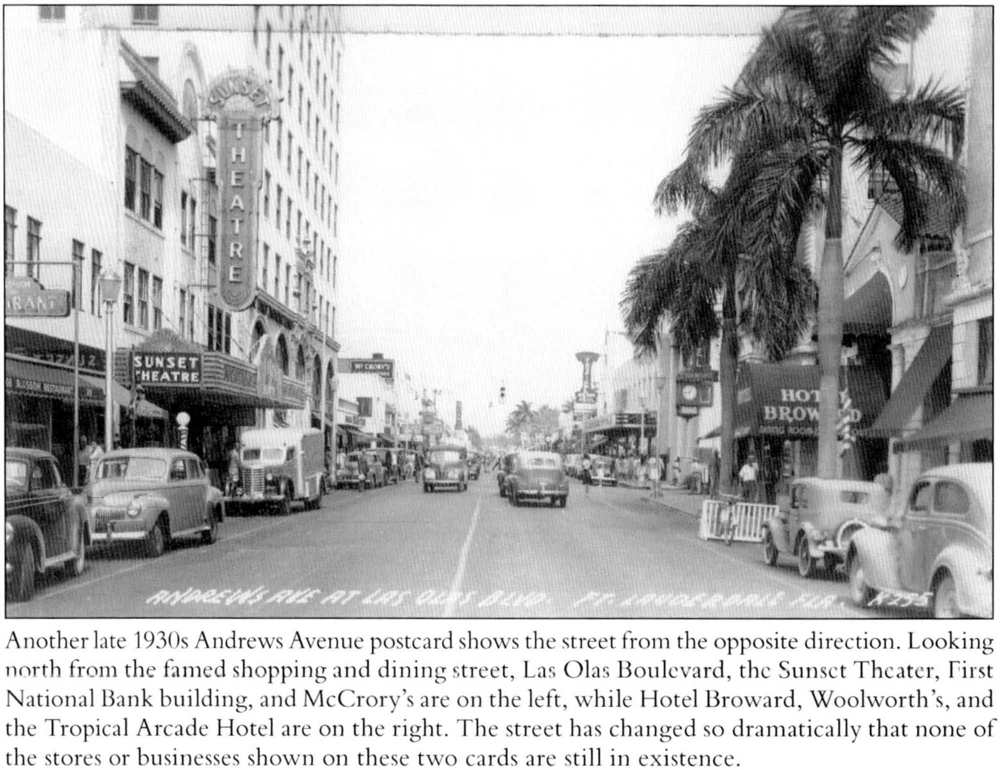

Another late 1930s Andrews Avenue postcard shows the street from the opposite direction. Looking north from the famed shopping and dining street, Las Olas Boulevard, the Sunset Theater, First National Bank building, and McCrory's are on the left, while Hotel Broward, Woolworth's, and the Tropical Arcade Hotel are on the right. The street has changed so dramatically that none of the stores or businesses shown on these two cards are still in existence.

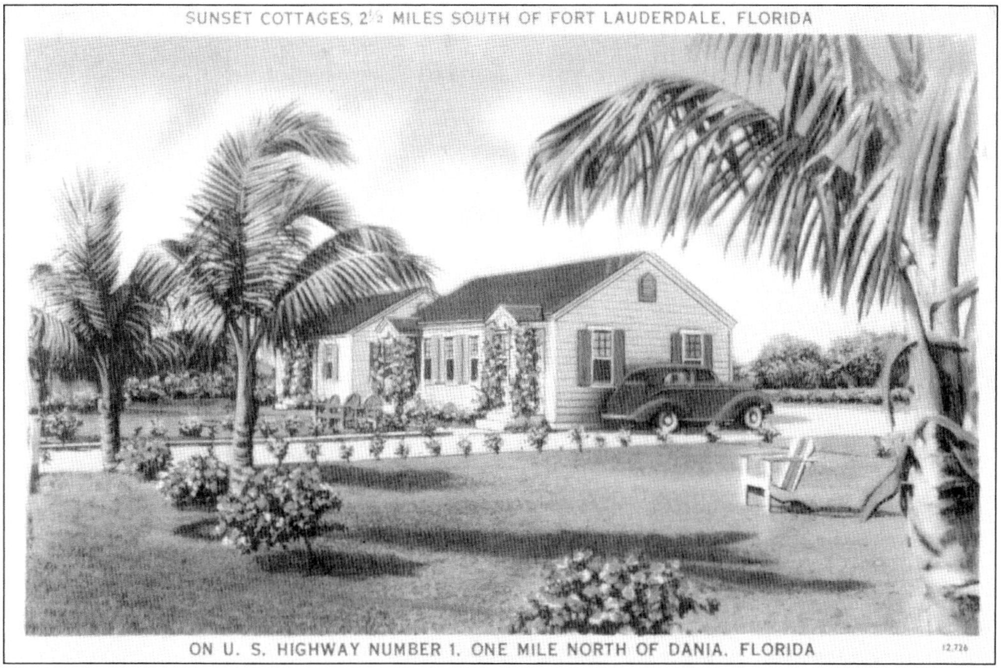

Sunset Cottages was shown as being "2 1/2 miles South of Fort Lauderdale" and "One Mile North of Dania, Florida," which would have been in the area taken over by the state for the widening of US Route 1 and the federal government for the enlargement of the Fort Lauderdale–Hollywood International Airport. With "21 modern, heated cottages and electrically equipped kitchenettes," it was one of the last of the cottage/tourist court hostelries along Route 1 in South Florida.

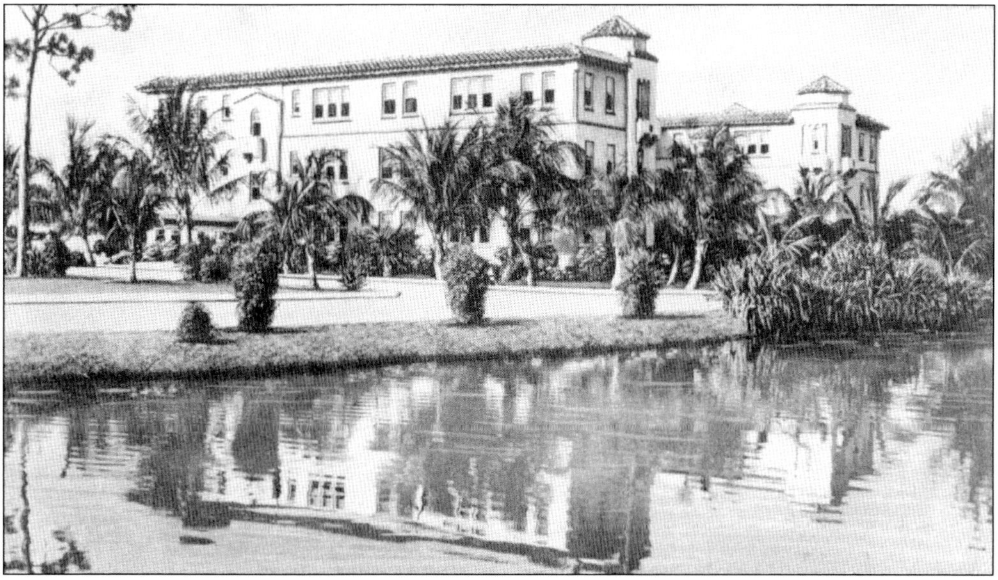

The Towers Apartments faced Himmarshee Waterway and were at the corner of Southeast Second Street and Ninth Avenue. Advertising itself as "semi-fireproof" (whatever that means), the 34-unit apartment building claimed to be the "largest and finest in Fort Lauderdale and Broward County." While maid service was listed as an amenity, the card also states that the apartments were restricted to "selected clientele," meaning Jewish guests were not welcome.

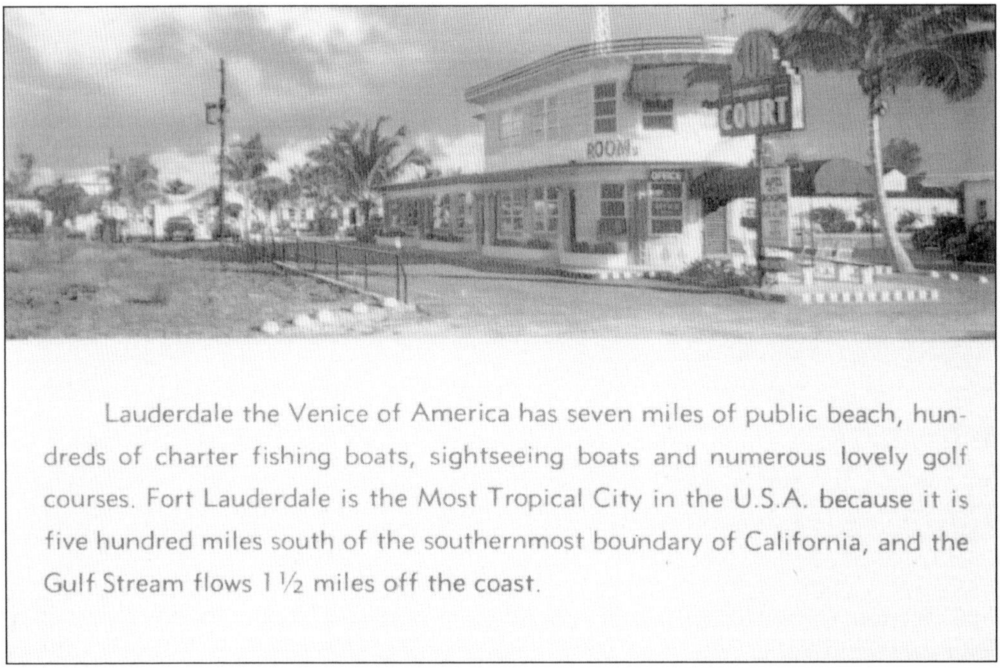

The front of this postcard featuring the Jones Sun Court Apartments and Hotel claims that Fort Lauderdale was "the Most Tropical City in the USA." The back left side of the postcard, which is usually left blank for messages, is filled with a list of the advantages and amenities of the Sun Court. Located at 614 Northeast Sixth Avenue (and now gone for many years), the Jones Court, like the Towers Apartments, catered only to "selected clientele."

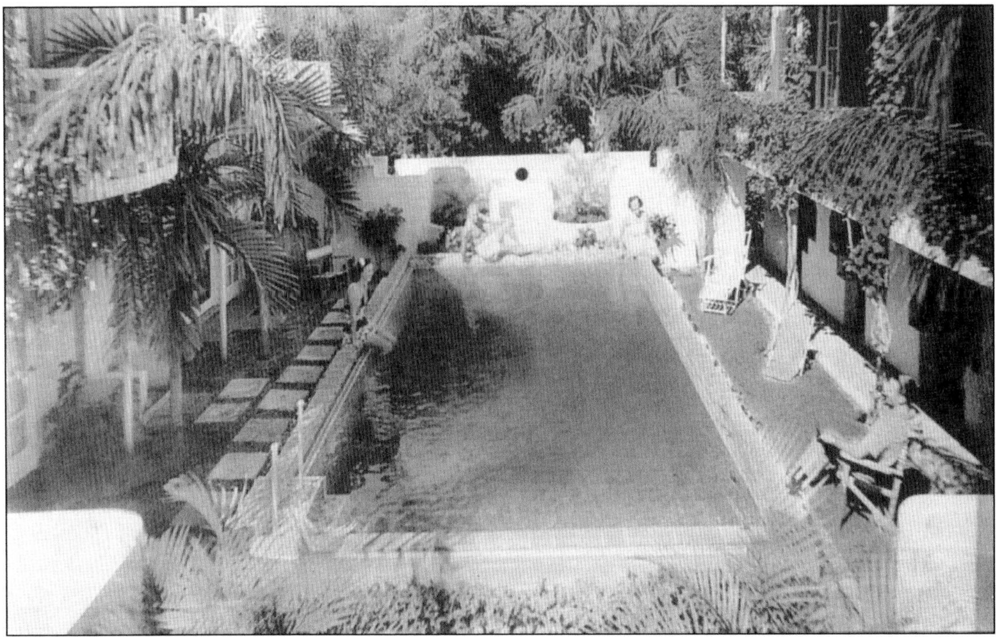

This absolutely beautiful, hand-colored postcard shows the pool and sun deck at Castillo Apartments, "On the Beach [with no address] Fort Lauderdale, Fla." The last line in the blurb states "restricted clientele."

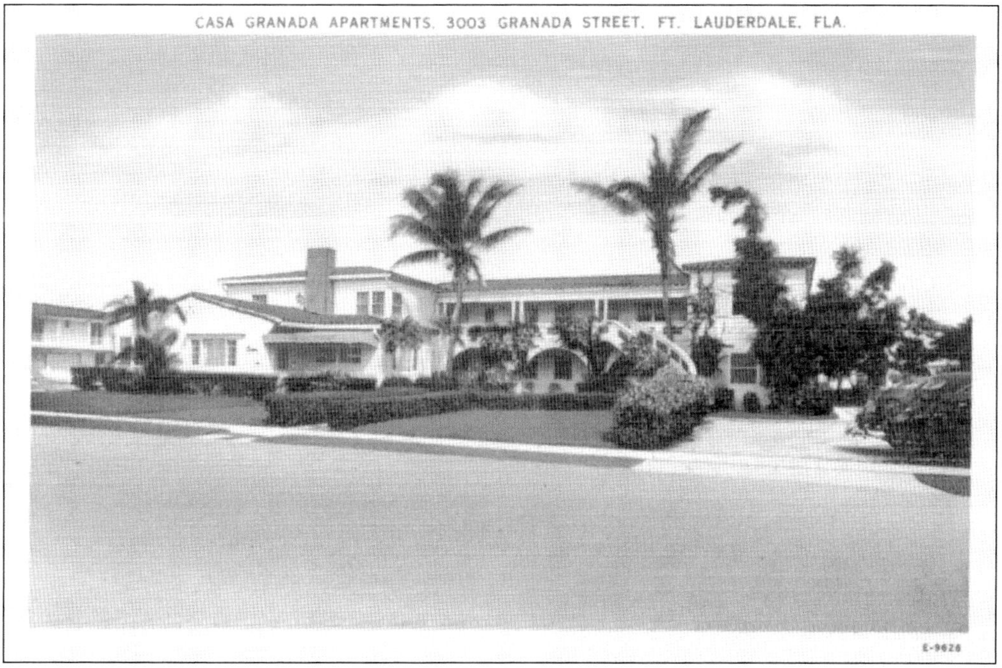

Casa Granada was located at 3003 Granada Street. Offering "Furnished Apartments and Hotel Rooms Ideally Located One Block from the Ocean," the apartments discriminated against Jewish guests. The card highlights the building's "select clientele."

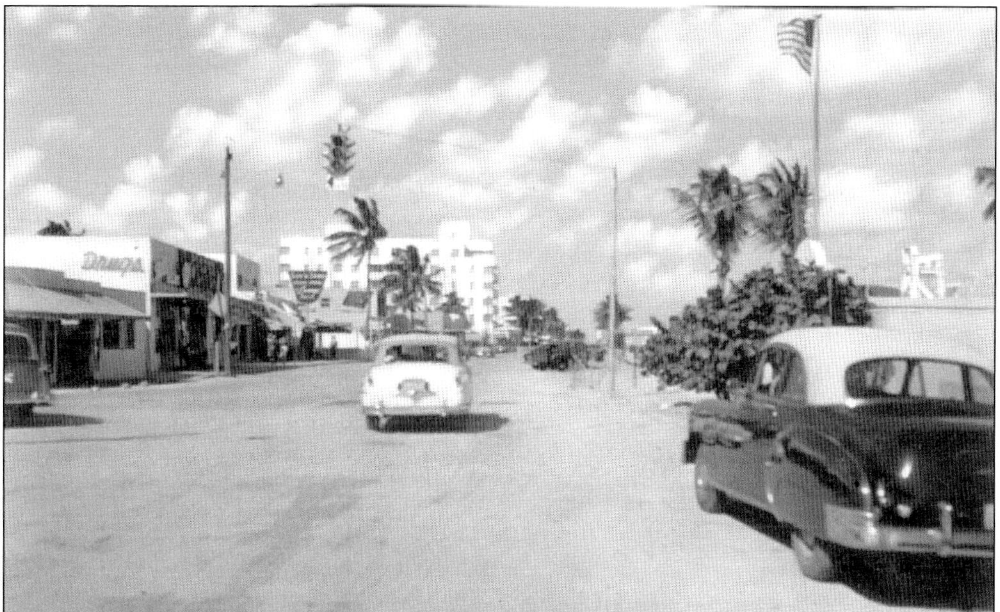

This wonderful c. 1952 chrome postcard looks north on Atlantic Boulevard from Las Olas Boulevard. Now a major intersection with a completely different vista, this corner is protected by several traffic lights.

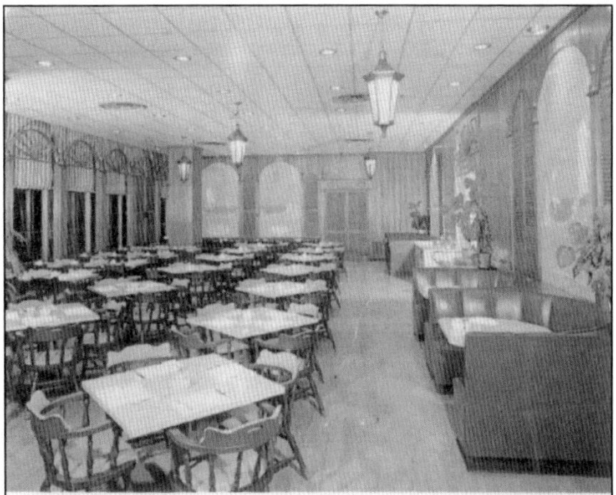

For many years, the Forum Restaurant on the corner of Las Olas and Atlantic Boulevards was a favorite dining spot for nearby residents. It had two separate serving areas, the dining room (top) and the Sportsman's Room (for more casual dining).

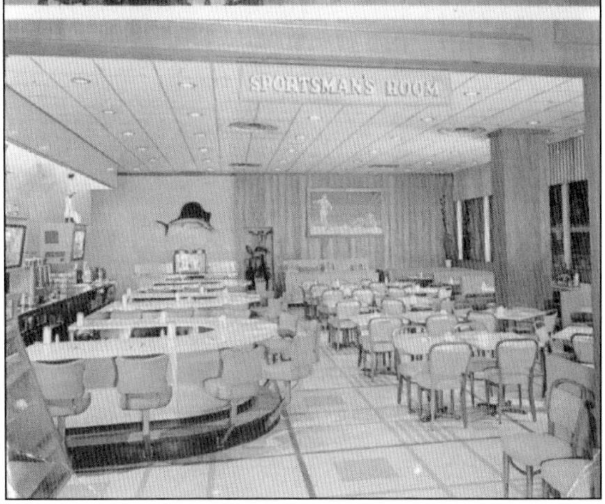

Owners Henry Vogt and Fred Wenner were not shy about using superlatives on the back of this postcard for the Seahorse, which was located at 904 East Las Olas Boulevard. Not only does the card state that it was "Florida's most beautiful restaurant and lounge," it also claims that it was "nationally known for good food."

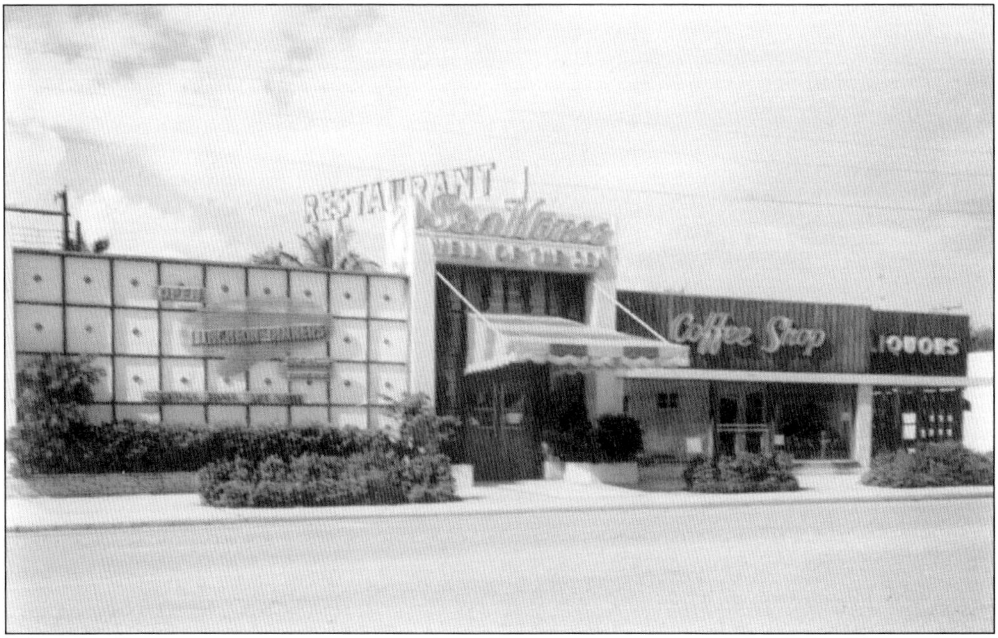

The Caves Restaurant and Lounge, located at 2205 North Federal Highway, was owned by Jacquie and Saul Hochman, pictured in the center of the card. The Caves was a unique dining emporium, advertising that guests would "journey to pre-historic days via the stone age décor and hearty feasting."

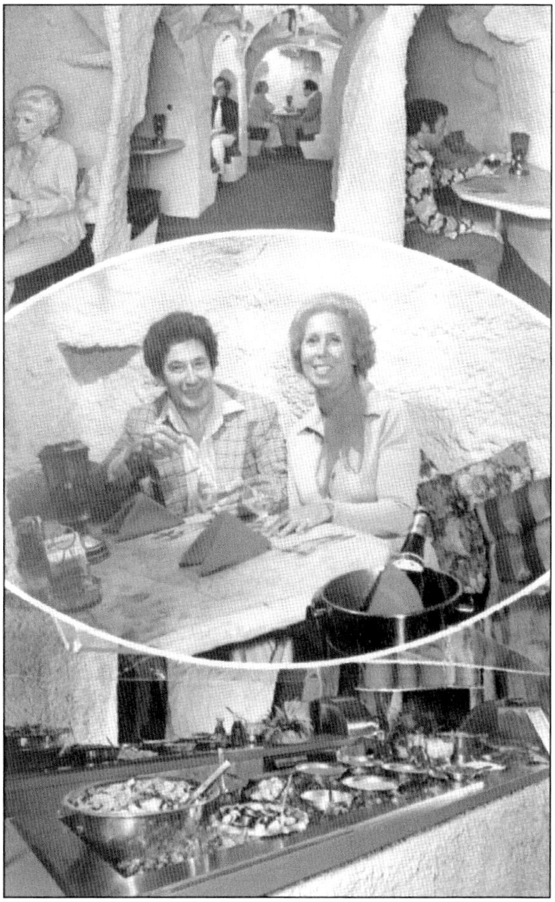

Just as the Dodgers held their spring training in Vero Beach for many years, the New York Yankees held theirs in Fort Lauderdale from 1962 until 1995. Located at 1401 Northwest Fifty-Fifth Street, the stadium is on land owned by the Fort Lauderdale Executive Airport. The Yankees left after the 1995 season.

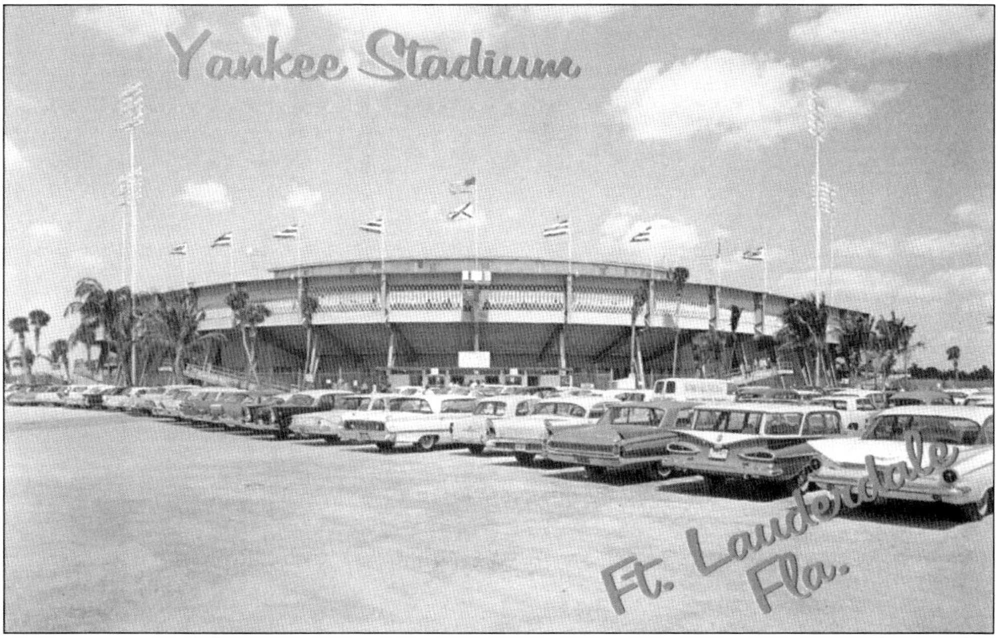

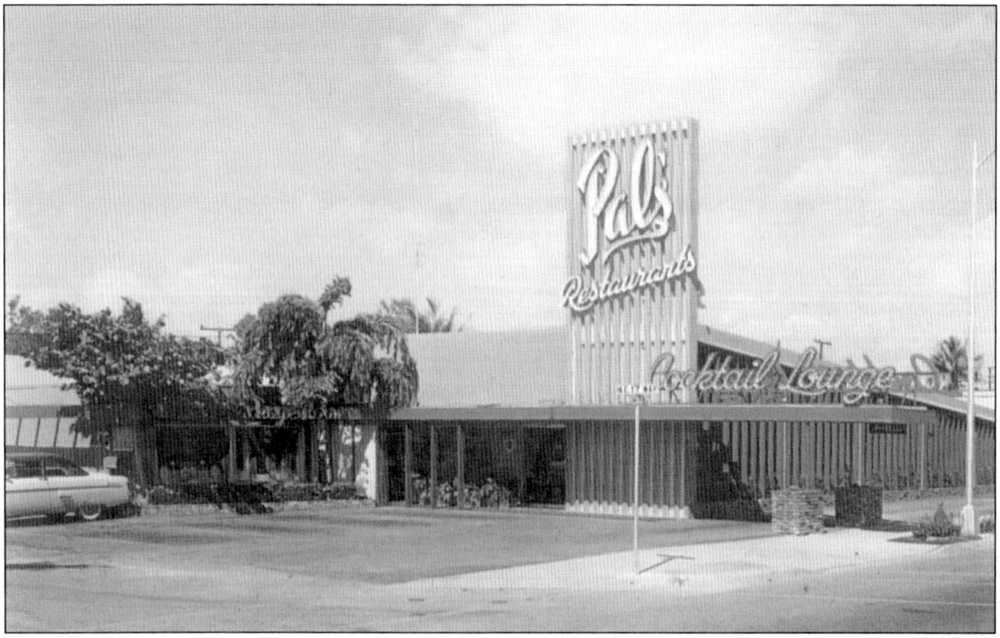

When it was owned by Hank Hagmann, Pal's Restaurant operated under that name and had fine-dining operations in both Fort Lauderdale and Pompano Beach. After the business was sold, the names were changed to Pal's Captain's Table, but this pre-sale card shows the restaurant on US Route 1 (Federal Highway) and Northeast Seventeenth Way in Fort Lauderdale.

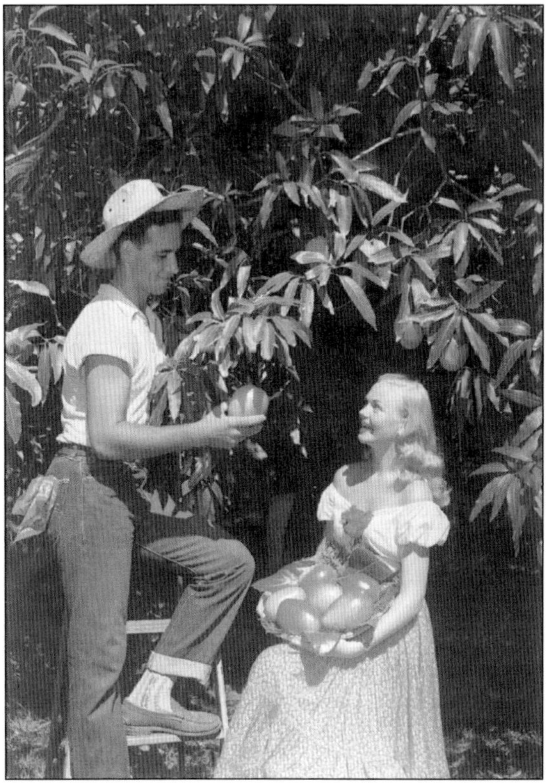

One of the most famous Florida fruit-growers was the late Al Roth. Roth left Miami Beach in the late 1950s and opened his grove west of Fort Lauderdale, becoming a major producer of citrus, mangos, and papaya. When he was old enough, Al's son Robert (Bob) took over the operation, which is still in the same place, flourishing on the south side of Interstate 595 and still producing great fruit! Although the people shown are unidentified, this super-sized postcard, made by the well-known South Florida photographer H.W. Hannau, shows mangos at their peak of perfection and is a perfect example of the fruit that the Roth family still produces.

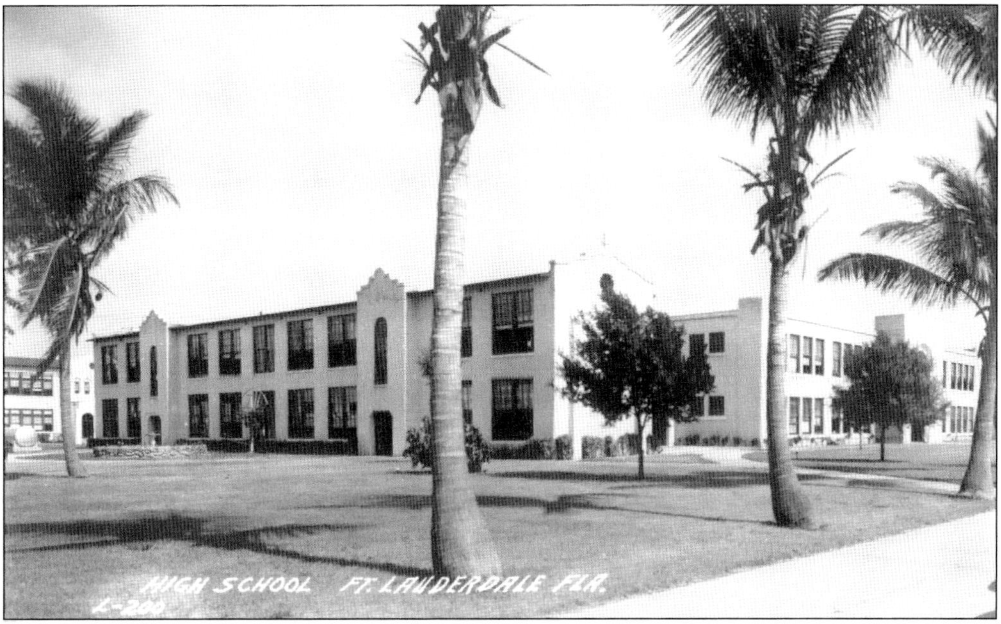

Fort Lauderdale High School, "Home of the Flying L's," was originally on North Federal Highway. In 1962, the property was sold by the school board, and a new Fort Lauderdale High School was built on Northeast Fourth Avenue, retaining both the name and the nickname of Broward County's oldest public school.

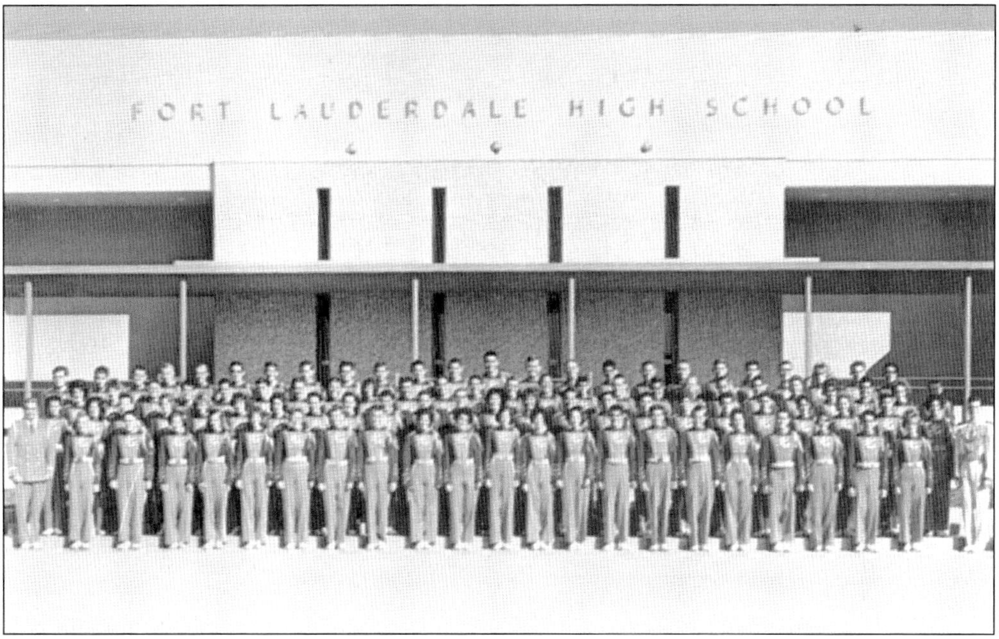

The Flying L's concert band is shown here in full regalia. In the late 1980s, for its 25th annual Winter Concert Series, band director William H. Bennett commissioned a series of color photographs to be published as postcards to commemorate a quarter-century of great music for the people of Broward County. Bennett is at far left in the first row.

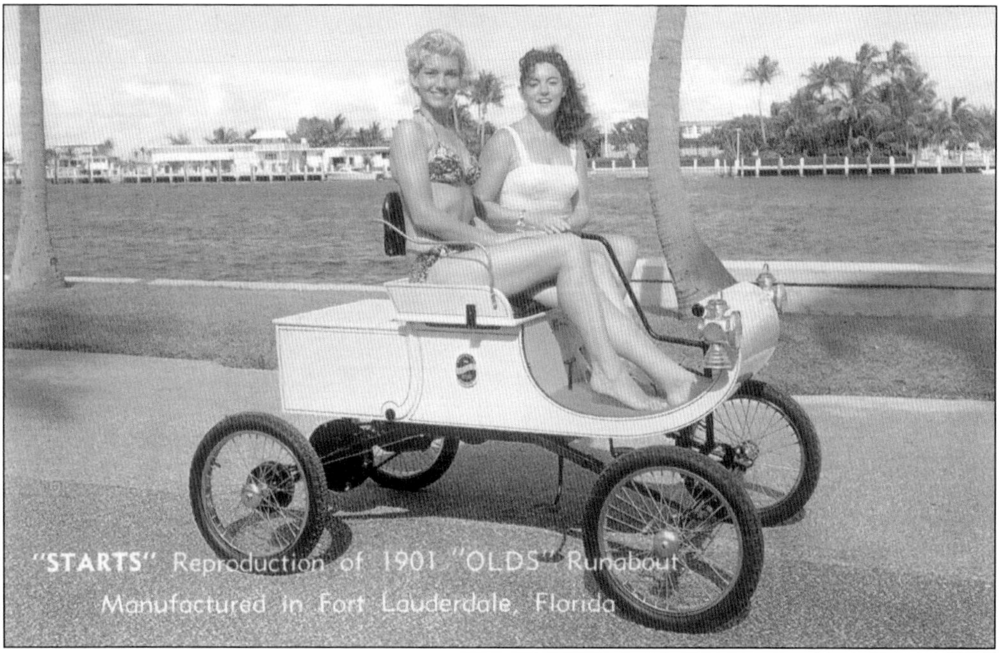

Although no longer in business, Starts Manufacturing Company, located at 230 Southwest Twenty-Ninth Street, produced a series of reproductions of early automobiles, including this 1901 Oldsmobile, in the 1980s and early 1990s. The reproductions actually ran, and this postcard, one of several utilizing beautiful young women as models, ballyhooed the fact that the cars, utilizing a Continental gasoline engine with an electric starter, got 100 miles to the gallon and could operate at 35 mph.

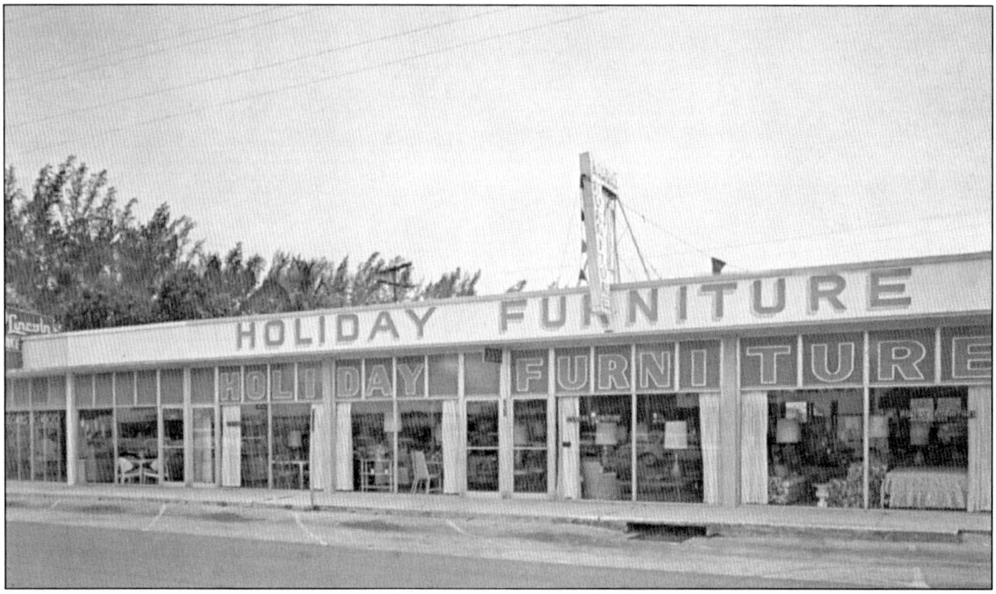

While there appears to be a dearth of Wilton Manors postcards, this one, showing Holiday Furniture at 2031 Wilton Drive (Northeast Fourth Avenue), shows a building that is extant. Owned and operated at the time by Burt Kurlander, the building is still in place, although it is now under different ownership and has different tenants.

Seven

Pompano Beach and Lighthouse Point

According to Pompano Beach Historical Society, the city celebrated the 100th anniversary of its incorporation on July 3, 2008. It is the second oldest city in Broward County and the fifth oldest in all of South Florida; only Key West, West Palm Beach, Miami, and Dania Beach are older.

The first train arrived in the small Pompano settlement on February 22, 1896, and Frank Sheen supposedly named the community after jotting down the name of the fish he had for dinner on his survey of the area! The arrival of the railroad led to development farther west from the coast.

On July 3, 1908, a new municipality was incorporated in what was then Dade County: the Town of Pompano. John R. Mizell was elected the first mayor. In 1915, Broward County was established, with a northern boundary at the Hillsboro Canal. Thus, within eight years, Pompano had been part of Dade County, then Palm Beach County, and then Broward County.

In 1947, following the population boom after World War II, the City of Pompano merged with the newly formed municipality on the beach and became the City of Pompano Beach. By 1950, the population of the city had reached 5,682, and as of the writing of this book, it has passed 105,000, making it one of Broward County's major economic engines.

Although often thought of as part of Pompano Beach, Lighthouse Point is a separate and distinct municipality, and the city graciously provided this historical material:

> In 1951, the first acreage was acquired for development by R.E. Batemen and the first home in a new subdivision called Hillsboro Isles was completed that same year, with a civic association being formed in October, 1953.
>
> On June 13, 1956, the Town of Lighthouse Point came into being when 107 of about 600 people living here voted to incorporate. City Hall operated from a store front at 1811 NE 24th Street with fire protection being provided by Pompano Beach Highlands volunteers.
>
> In June 1957, Lighthouse Point received its state charter and officially became a City. A City Hall building was completed at 22nd Avenue and 38th Street in 1959 and by 1963, the City was able to employ a fire chief and ten reserve firefighters. In 1965 a police building was constructed across from City Hall to accommodate both police and fire departments. The two shared space until a new fire station was built later on.
>
> The city's land area, after several annexations, is now 2.36 sq. miles with a population of nearly 9,500. In 1996 the city celebrated its 40th birthday with a City-wide party at which many of its pioneers and benefactors were honored.

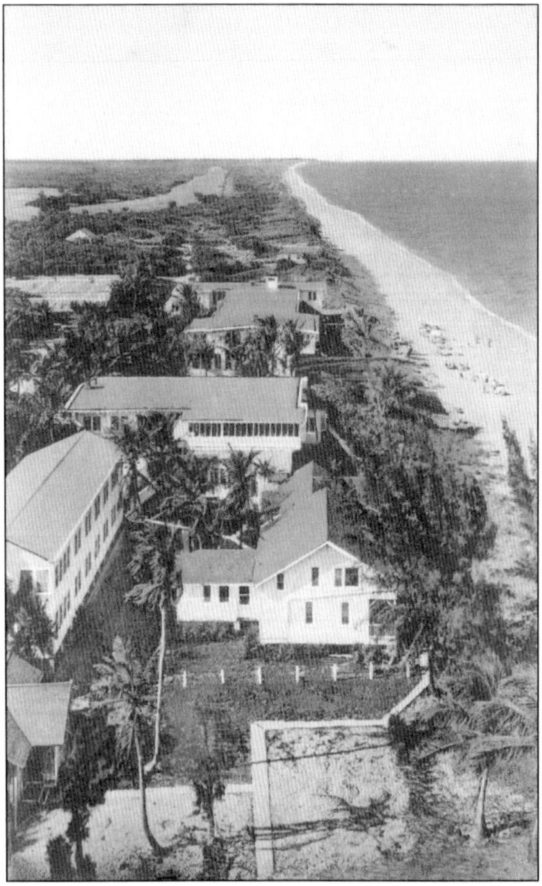

This 1940 view of the Hillsboro Club, then owned by H.L. Malcolm, shows an idyllic Florida beach scene far different from today. With 1,000 feet of "private" beach, the club was a delightful pre–World War II vacation resort. It began in 1923 as the winter campus of the Adirondack School and is now privately owned by its members and still very much in operation.

Kester Brothers Ocean Homes was getting ready to reopen for the 1941 season when this postcard was mailed on November 17, 1941. Blissfully unaware that Pearl Harbor was right around the corner, the Kester brothers were predicting, on the back of the card, "a larger season than ever before." The *Fort Lauderdale Sun-Sentinel* has reported that although the Kester brothers are long gone, a number of the solidly built houses are still in place and in use.

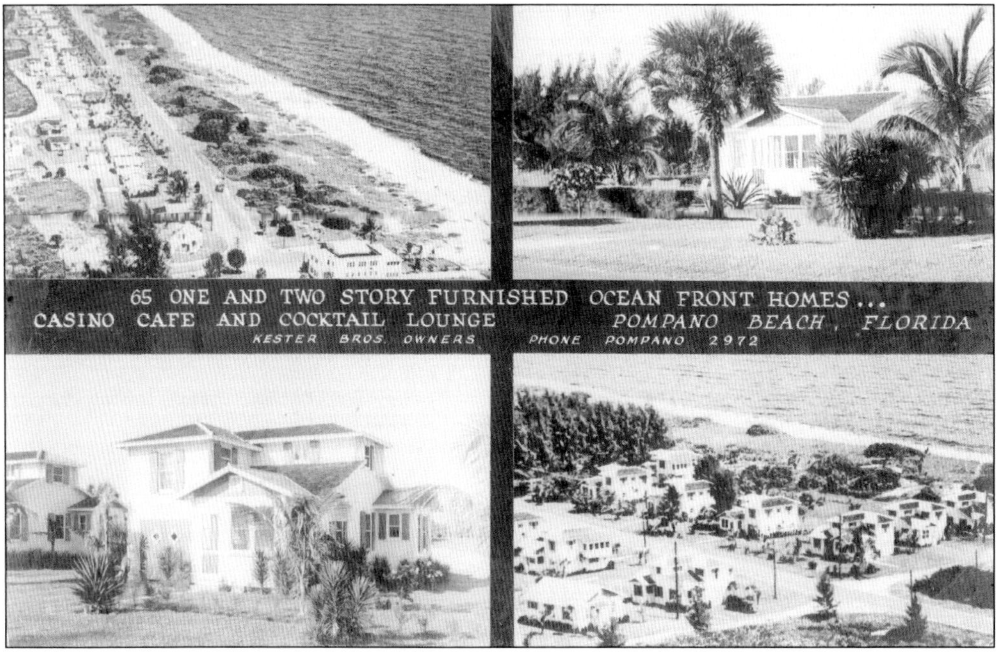

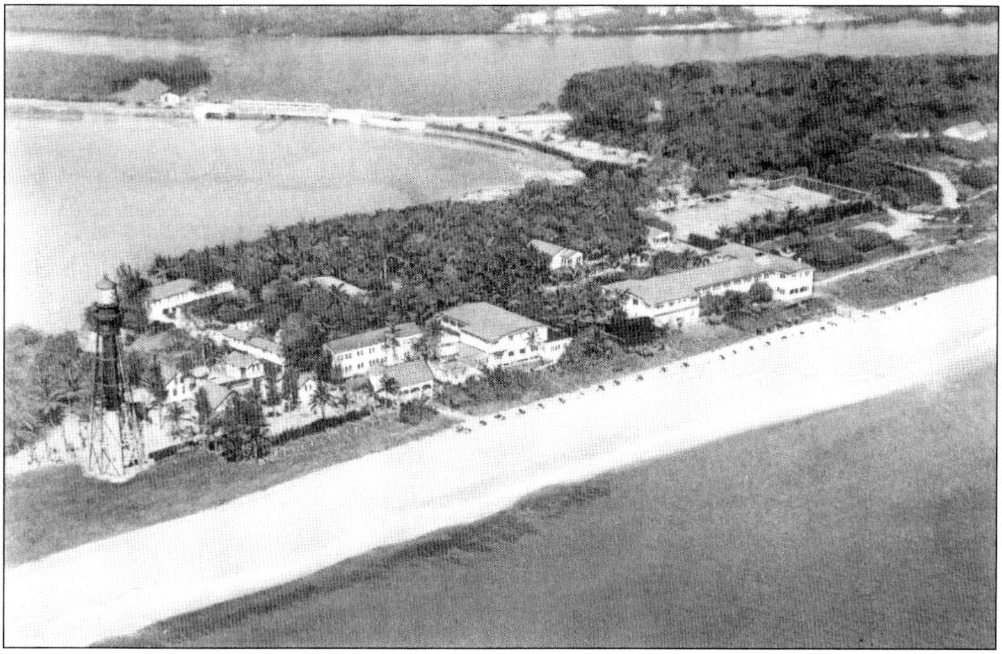

Hillsboro Club founder H.L. Malcolm used this October 15, 1941, aerial view of the Hillsboro Club as an advertising piece on this color postcard. Looking east from the Atlantic Ocean, this view gives a definitive look at the property.

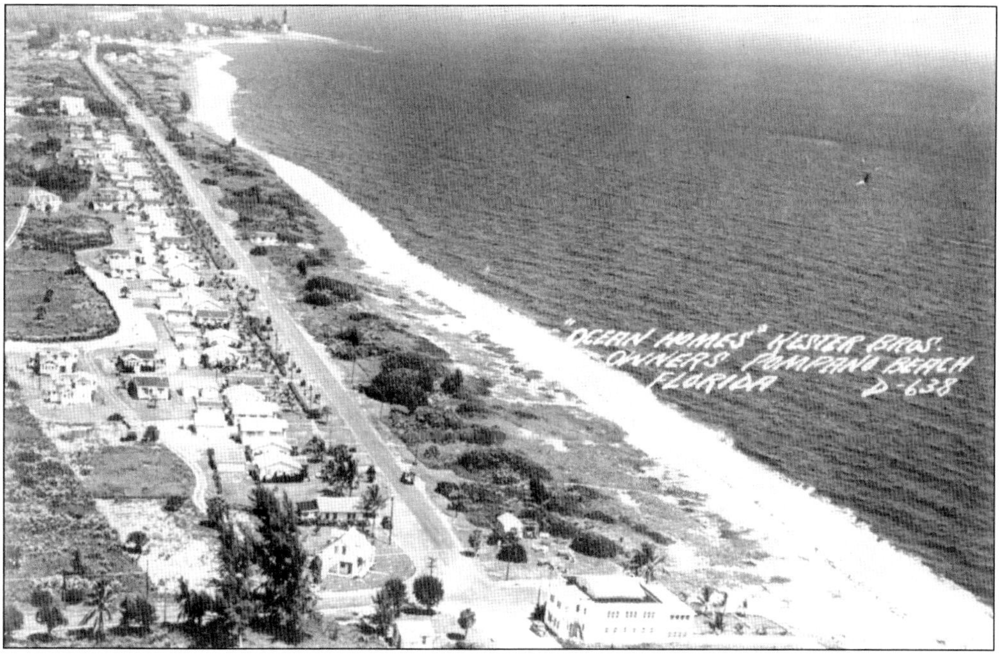

This general view from the air shows the Kester Brothers Ocean Homes in late 1941. The advertisement on the back of this card advises to renters that "we have added a separate dining room to all two-story houses as well as gas heating in all homes."

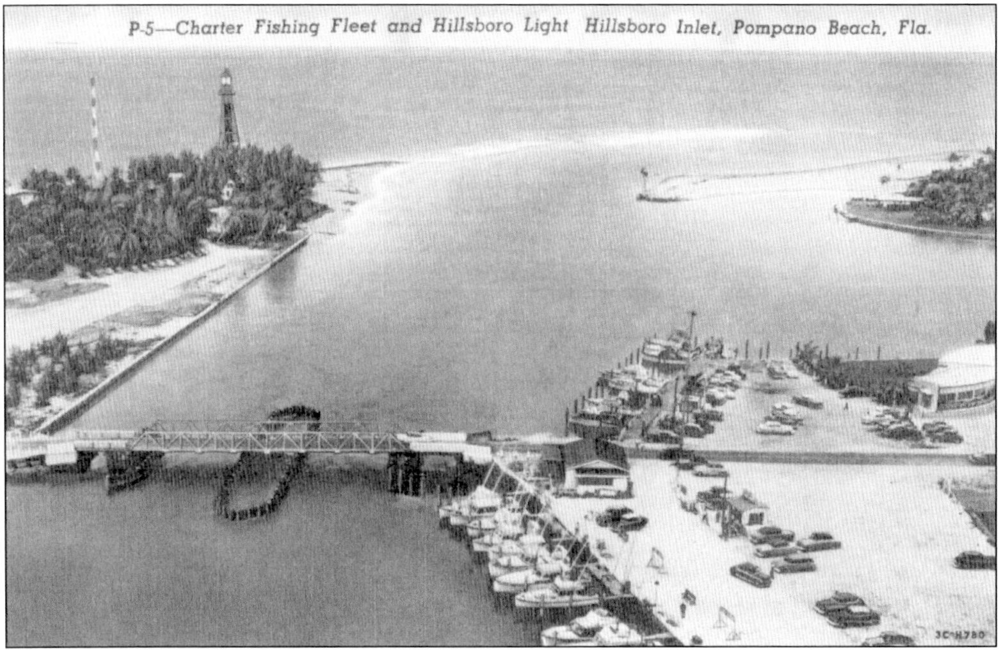

This 1940s linen card features the charter fishing fleet and, at left, the Hillsboro Inlet lighthouse. One of the anecdotal stories regarding "the barefoot mailman," who delivered mail on foot from Lake Worth to Arch Creek before the coming of the railroad, claims that the disappearance of that brave and hardy soul occurred here.

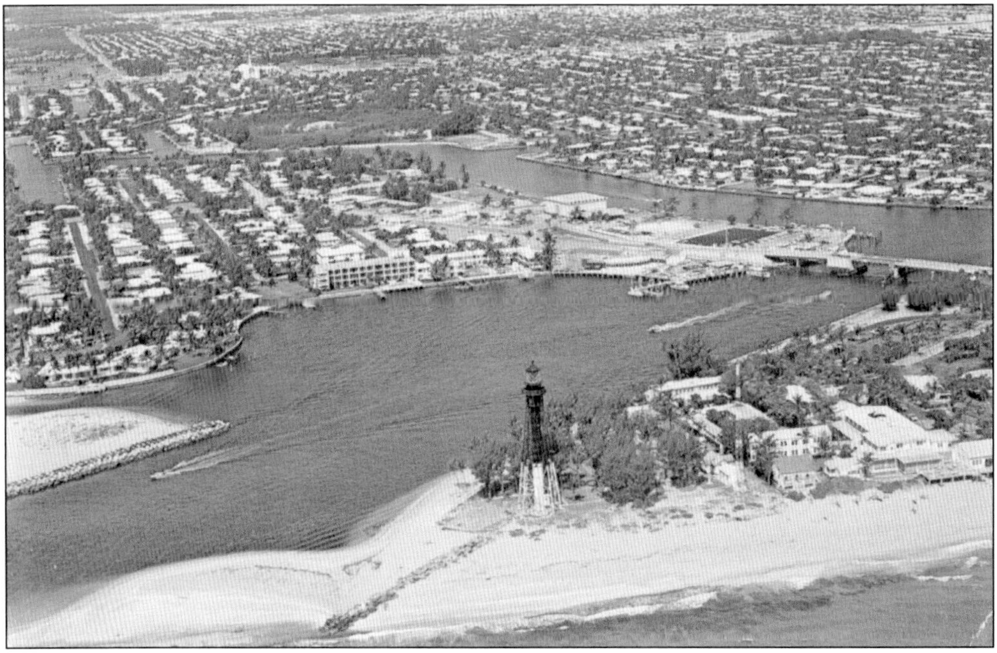

This 1967 aerial view looks west from above the Hillsboro Inlet Lighthouse toward the burgeoning city of Pompano Beach. The Intracoastal Waterway is directly behind the lighthouse. This is the approximate location of the northern limit of the underwater Florida coral reef.

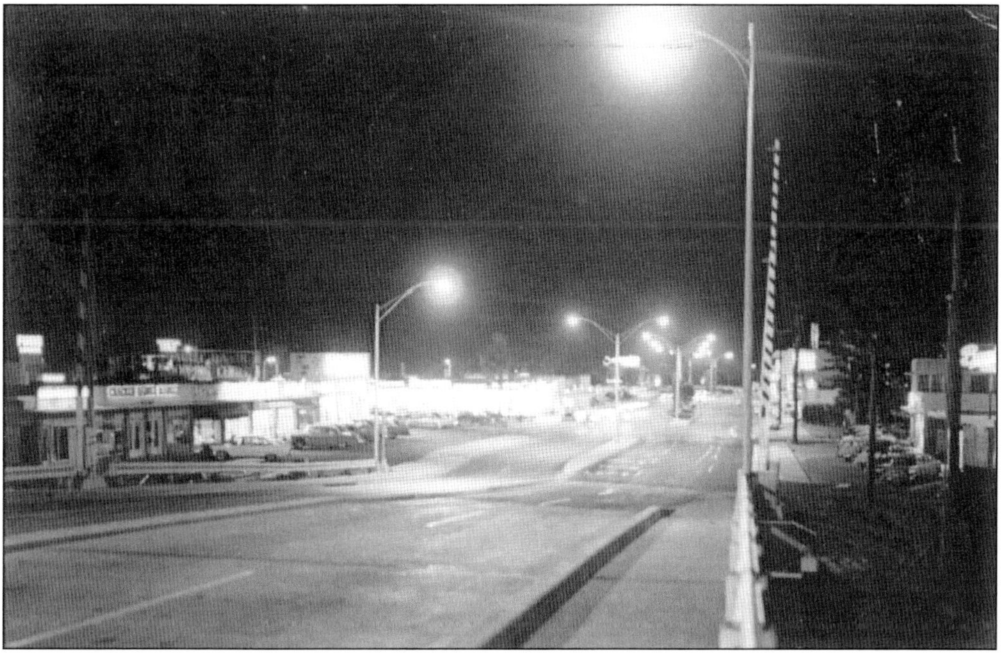

Atlantic Boulevard is Pompano's main east-west street and runs from the Atlantic Ocean into western Broward County. This unusual 1960 nighttime view looks west from the Intracoastal Waterway bridge and shows the boulevard devoid of traffic.

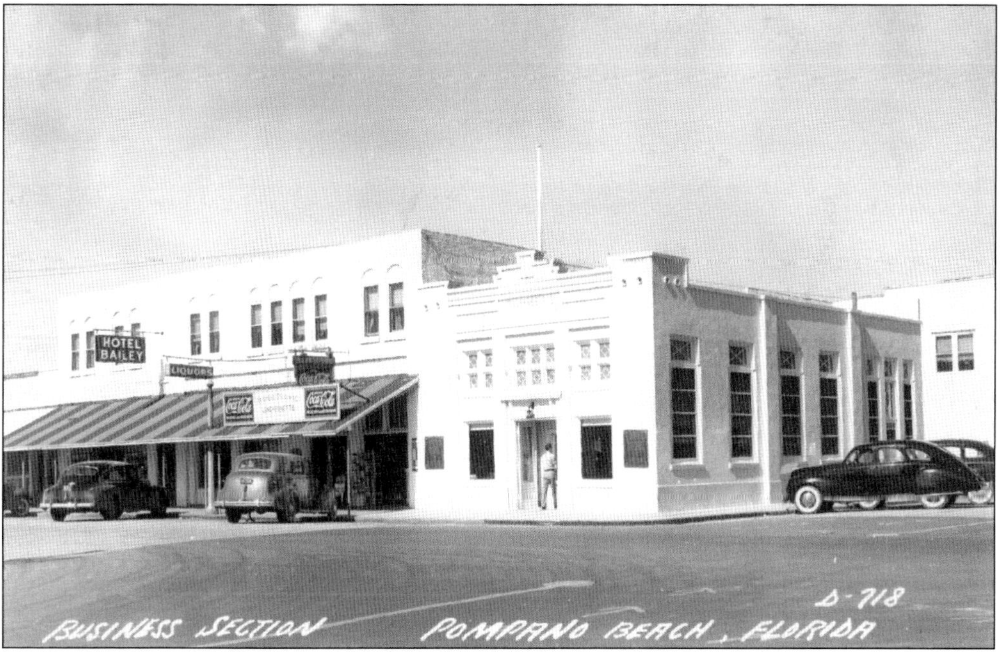

Stating that this is the "Business Section" of Pompano Beach, this postcard understates the size of that section, even though this postcard was published shortly after World War II. The Hotel Bailey is the two-story building at center left; Pompano Pharmacy and Luncheonette were the main tenants. (Note the Coca-Cola sign on the canopy.) The Farmers Bank of Pompano Beach is on the corner.

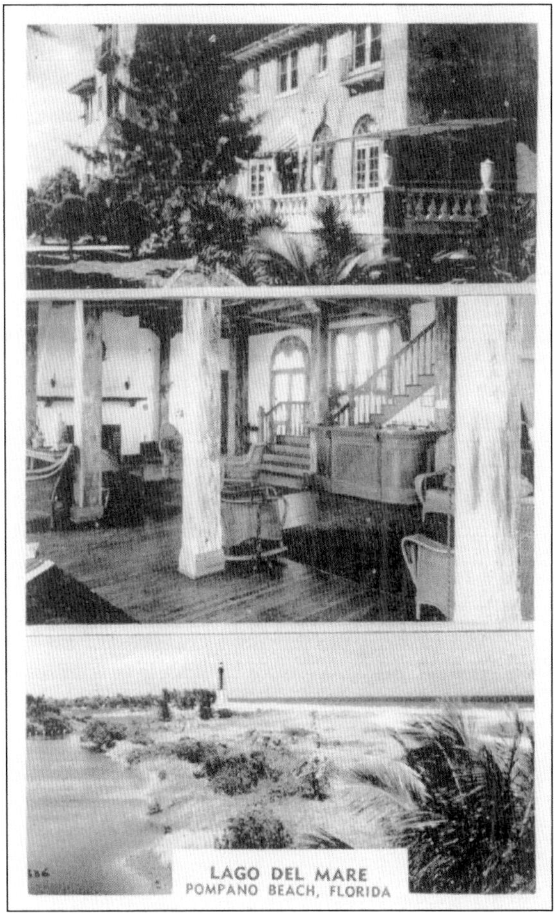

This three-section black and white postcard features Lago Del Mare, "On the Atlantic Ocean, Pompano Beach." Lago Del Mare was the home of Dr. Carlson's School of Corrective Motor Education, which boasted a summer session in East Hampton on Long Island in New York. It is unknown whether the school dealt with automobiles or human motor functions.

Although it now has a different name and a somewhat altered configuration, the Beacon Light Shopping Center is still located on Federal Highway (US Route 1) in Pompano Beach. Other than the 1950s automobiles, this postcard features a Dairy Queen at left, next to the drugstore.

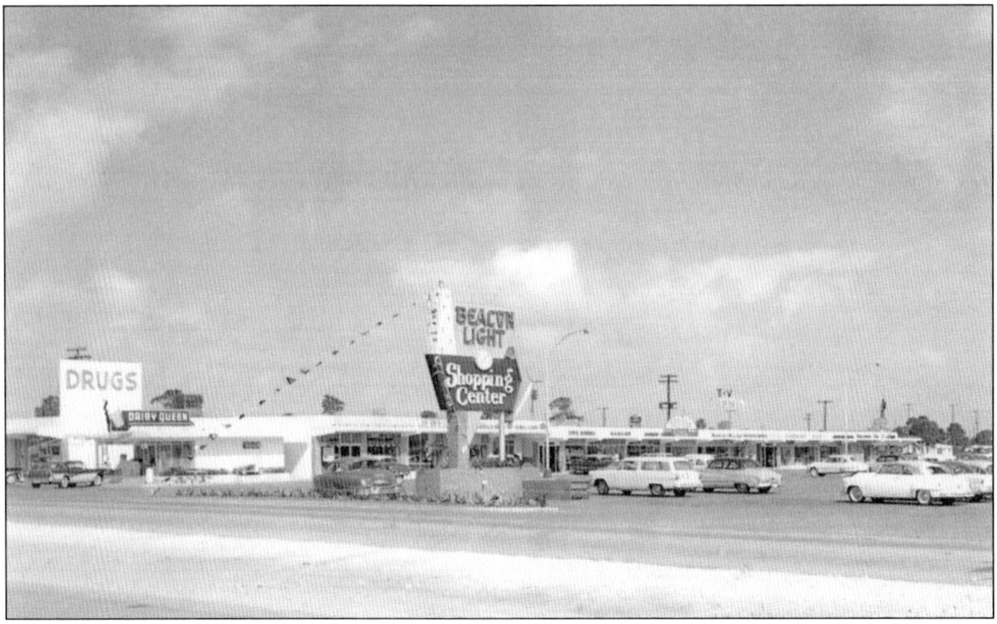

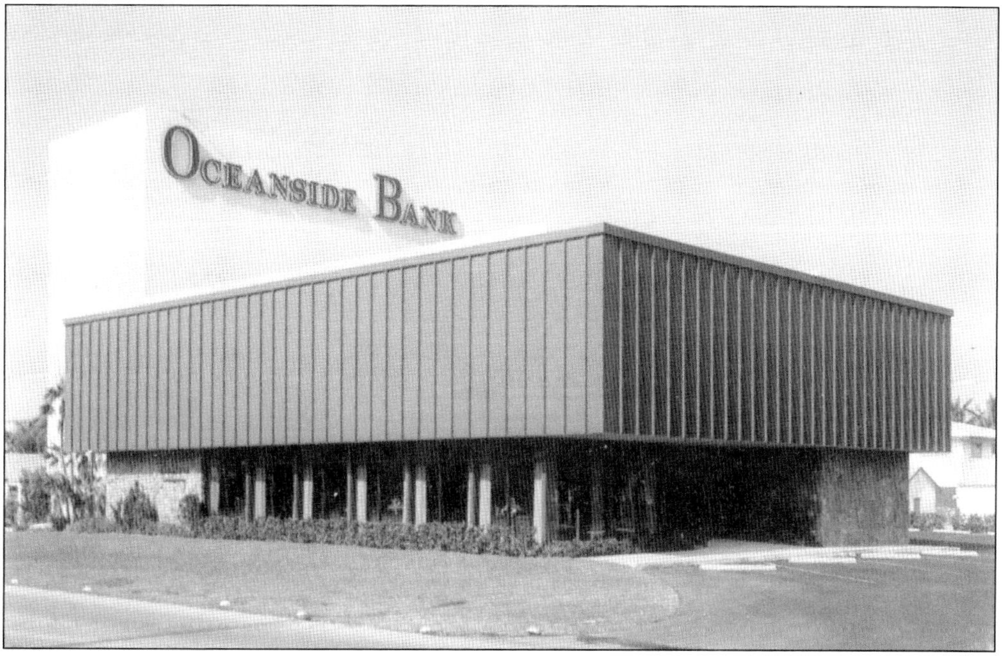

Oceanside Bank, at 101 South Ocean Boulevard on the beach side, was a local, community-owned bank. Taken over by Bank of America in the late 1980s, it remains a branch of that behemoth.

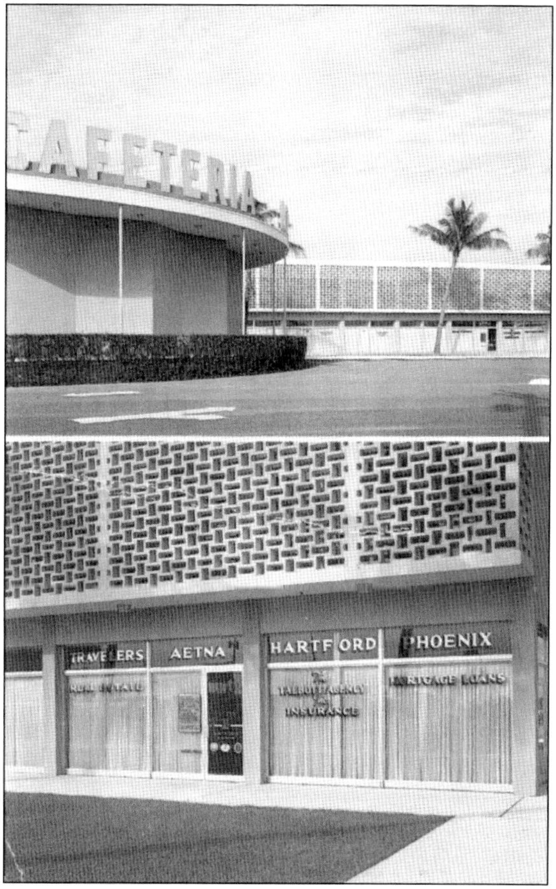

While it appears at first glance that this might be a promotional card for a cafeteria, it is not—the card was published by Talbot Insurance in the early 1960s. The lower half features the offices of that company, which are shown in the background on the upper half of the card.

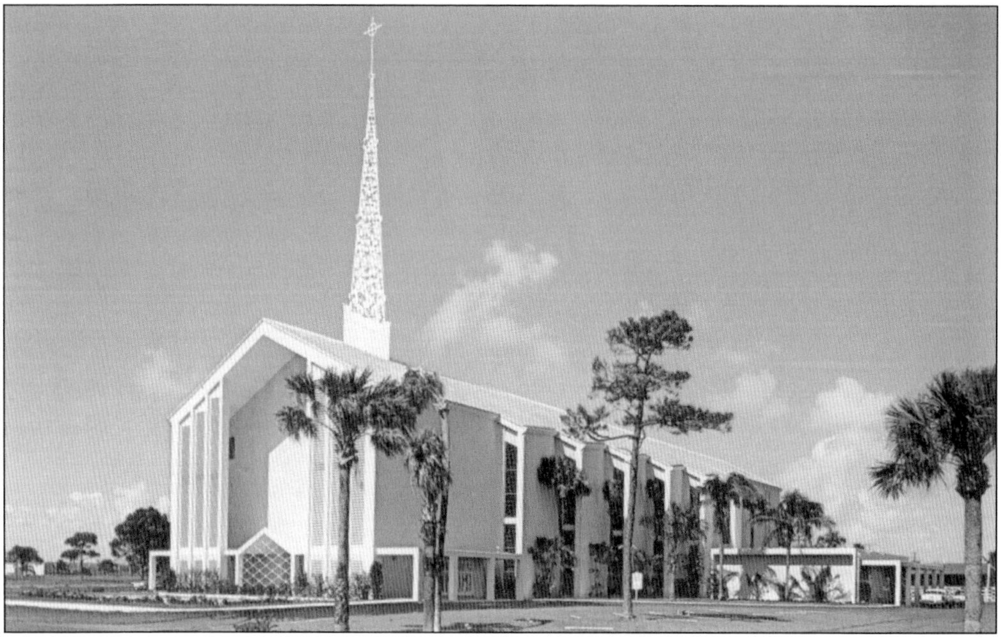

This is the First Presbyterian Church of Pompano Beach. This card, published in 1961, was mailed in March 1962 and features the church's then-new house of worship.

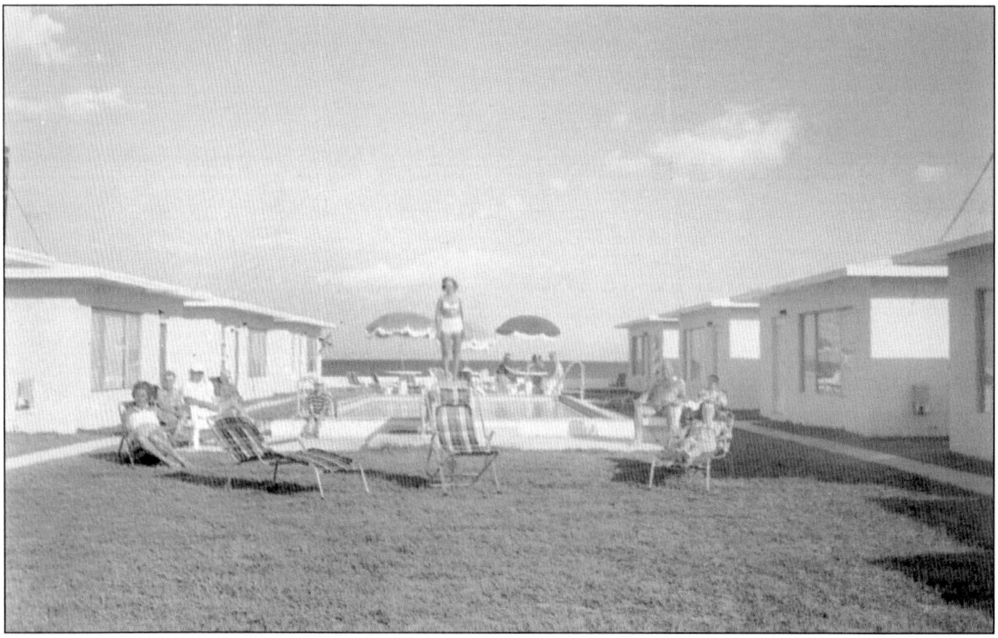

Caribe Villas was directly on the ocean and provided maid service and utilities. While it advertised a selection of villas, efficiencies, and hotel rooms, this postcard also notes that it discriminated against Jewish guests, serving only a "restricted clientele."

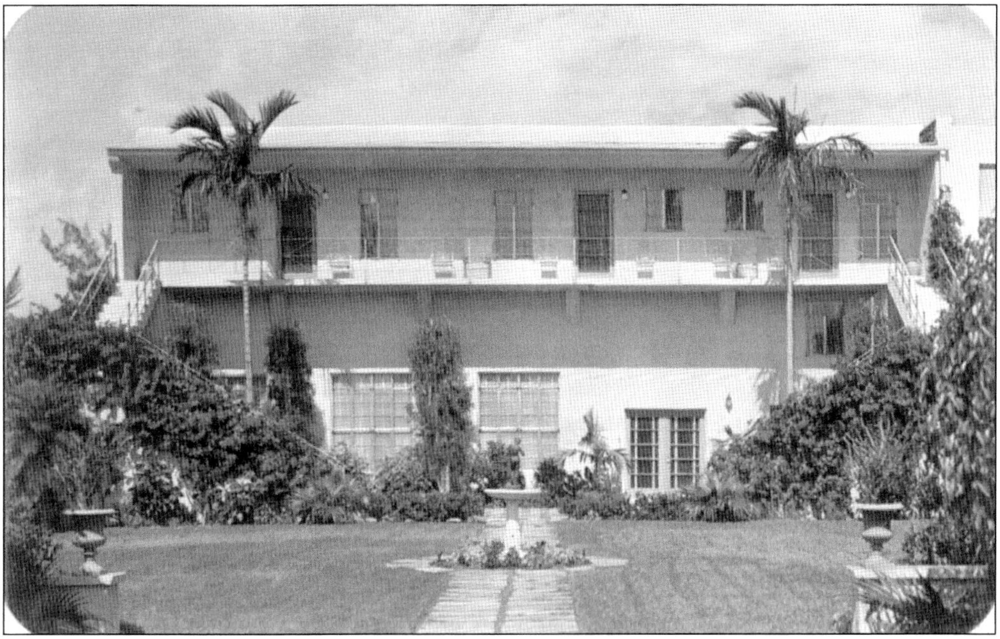

Floranada, on US Route 1 (Federal Highway), was operated by Earle B. Smith & Co. The advertising blurb on the back of the card begins with some unique phrasing: "Renting apartments to a select clientele, and showing the finer." After 59 years of collecting Florida postcards, the author still cannot figure out what the second phrase in that sentence means.

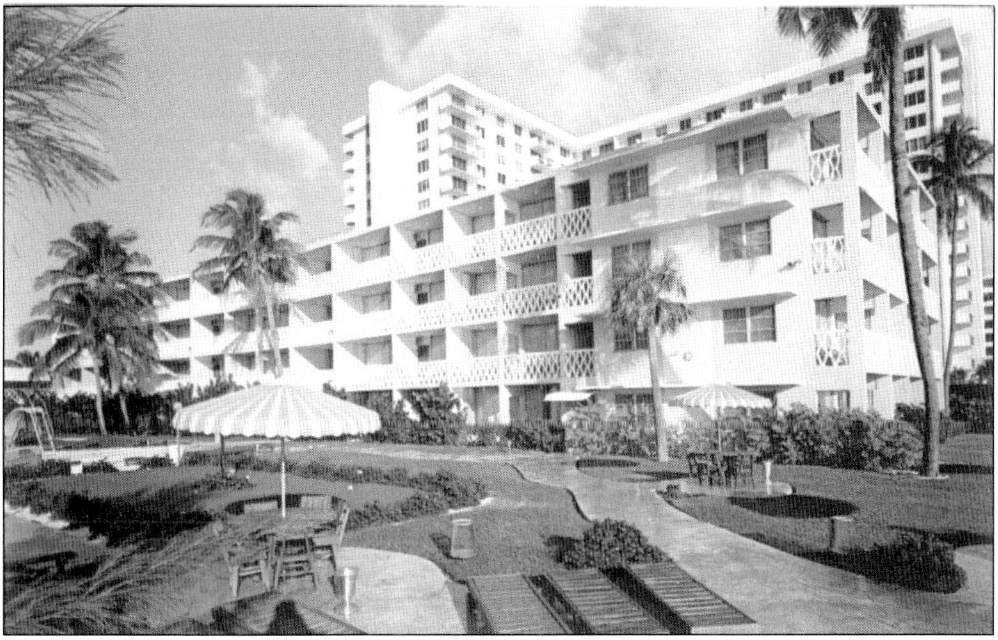

The Native Sun (a unique name for a hostelry!) was at 1950 South Ocean Boulevard. Offering efficiencies and hotel rooms, this property, at least as shown on the back of this postcard, offered every service to its guests and renters except food and beverages.

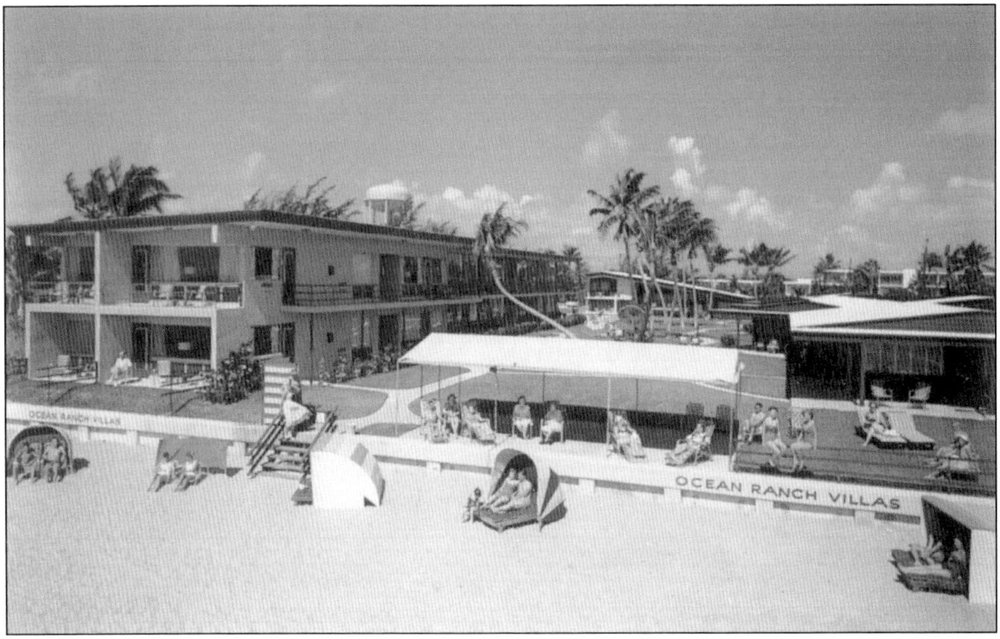

Ocean Beach Villas, on Ocean Highway (same as Ocean Boulevard; both Florida state road A1A), offered a telephone in every room and a large putting green. It too catered to "selected clientele."

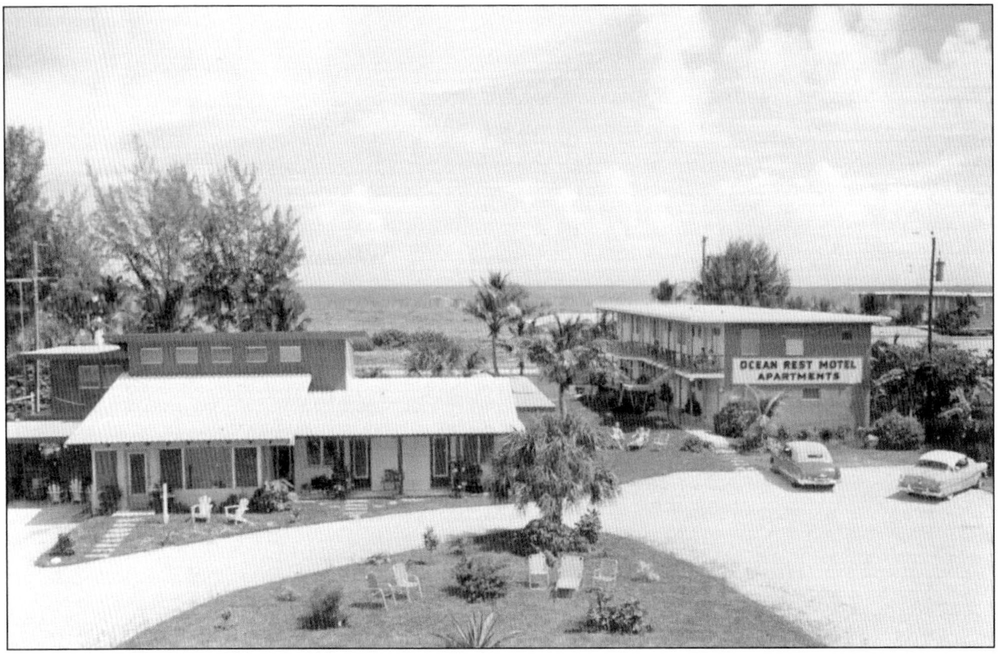

Olah's Ocean Best Motel & Apartments was at 212 South Ocean Boulevard. The phone number at the time this postcard was published was "Pompano 9190," indicating that it was produced sometime in the mid- to late 1950s.

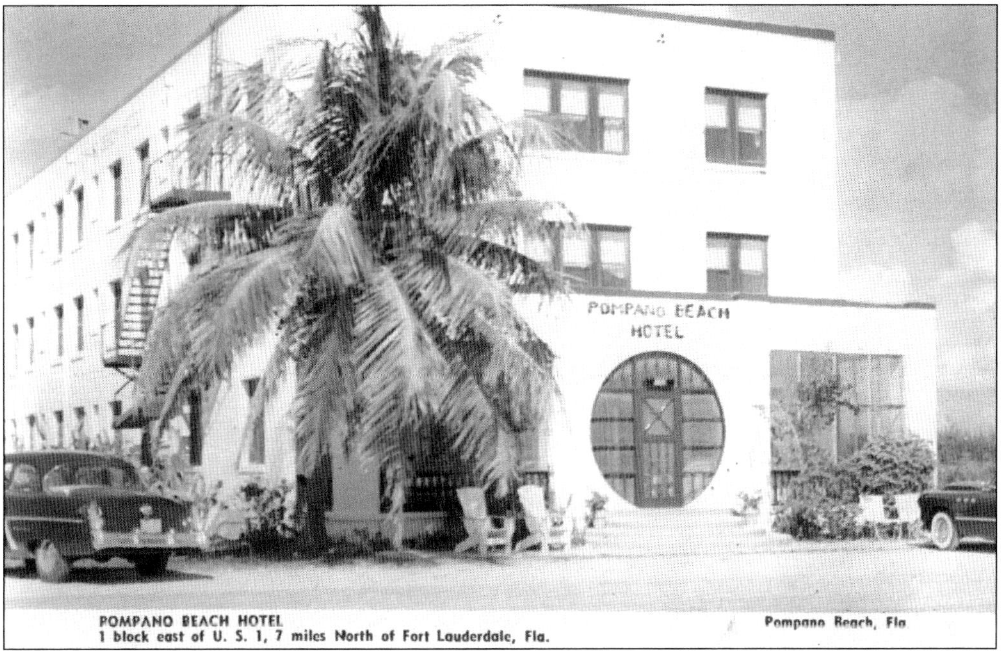

Interestingly, there is no exact address on this Pompano Beach Hotel postcard. The card notes only that the property is "Halfway between W. Palm Beach and Miami." With "moderate rates and a homelike atmosphere," the hotel featured an "excellent dining room."

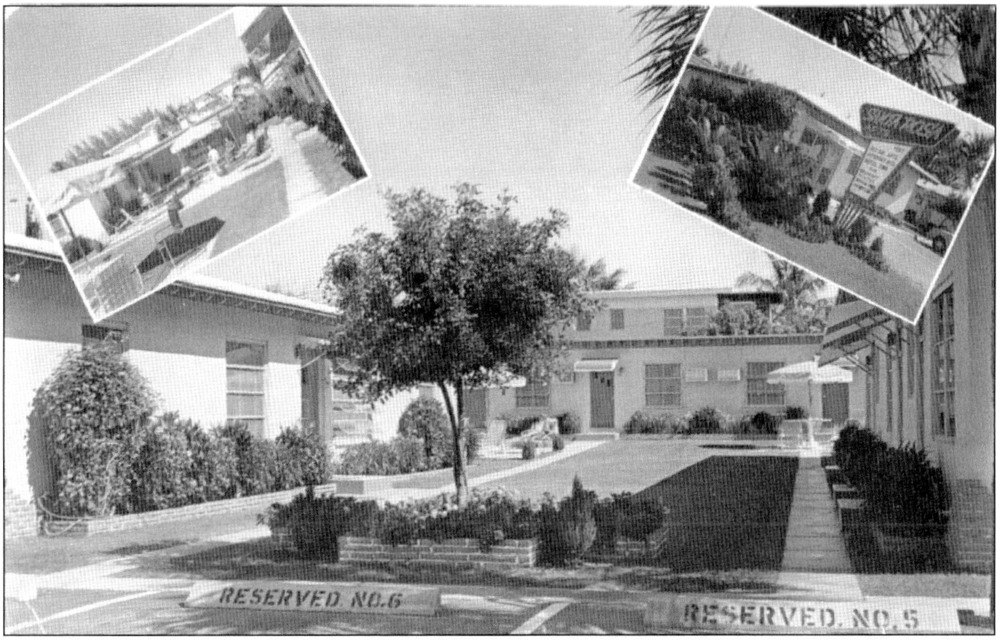

Santa Rosa Apartments, at 308 South Ocean Boulevard, was "300 feet from beach, two blocks from shopping center." The card also states that it is "a homey spot catering only to refined, select clientele."

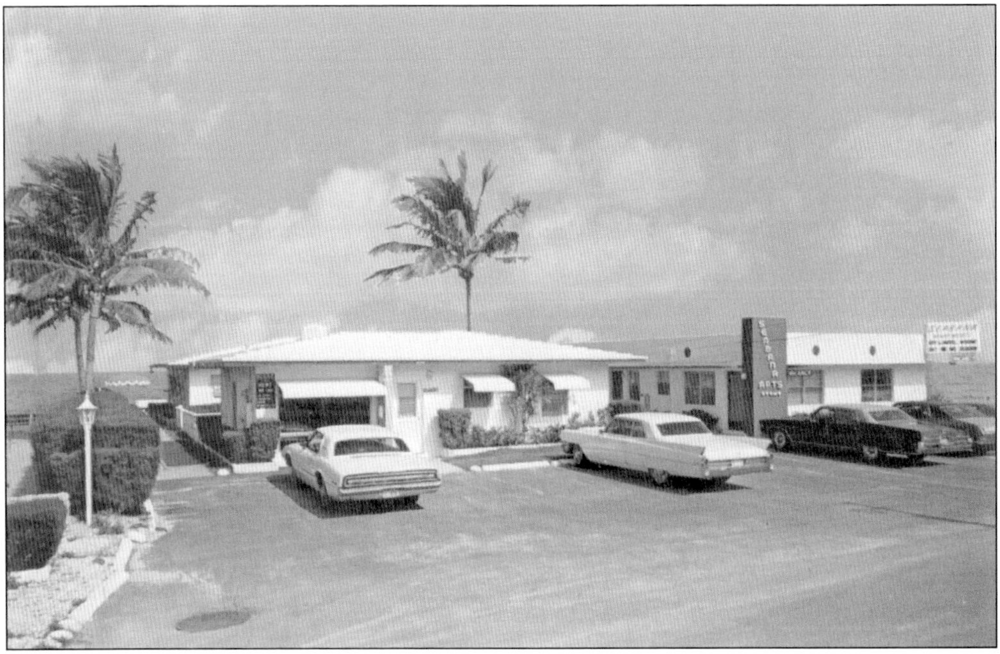

Seabana Apartments was on the beach side at 800–802 Briny Avenue. It was open to adults but did not allow pets. The phone number is complete with the "305" area code, which was changed to "954" in the late 1980s.

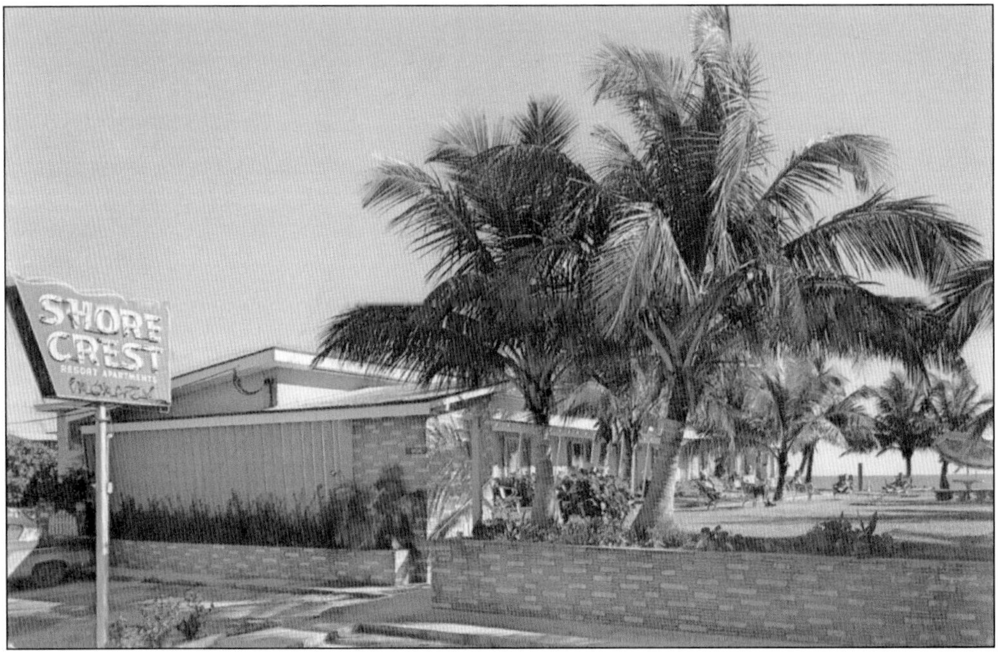

Advertising itself as being "Thirty-five Miles North of Miami," Shore Crest Apartments was located at 700 North Ocean Boulevard. Unlike many—if not most—of its competitors, it offered beachfront cabanas for daily, weekly, monthly, or seasonal rentals.

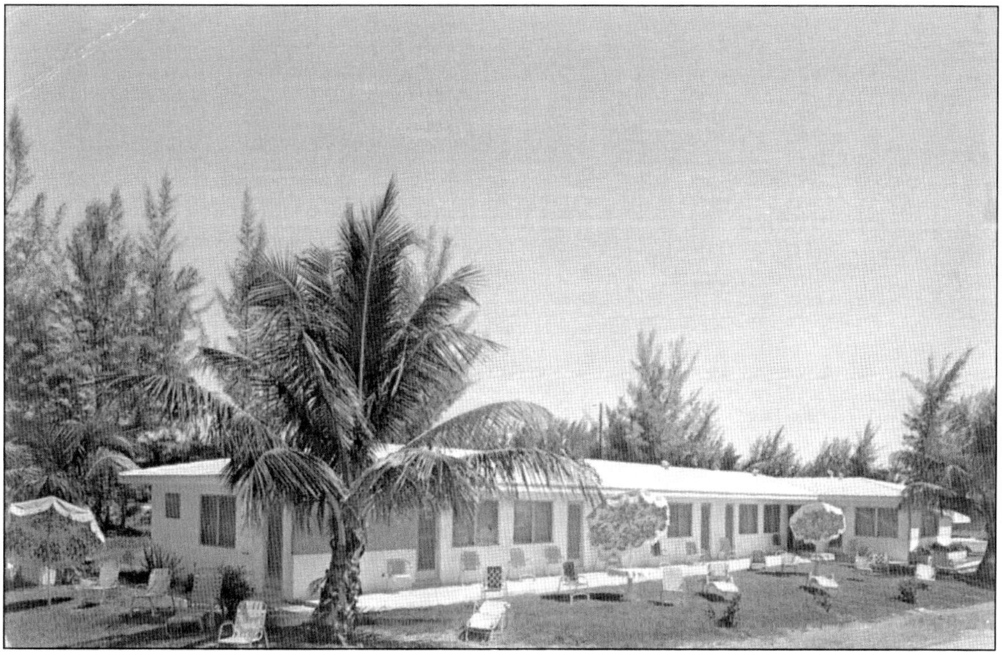

The Sun Ranch Apartments were two blocks from the ocean at 1500 Riverside Drive. As with so many of the local seasonal properties of the 1950s, the Sun Ranch's postcard noted that it was "Open November 1st to May 1st."

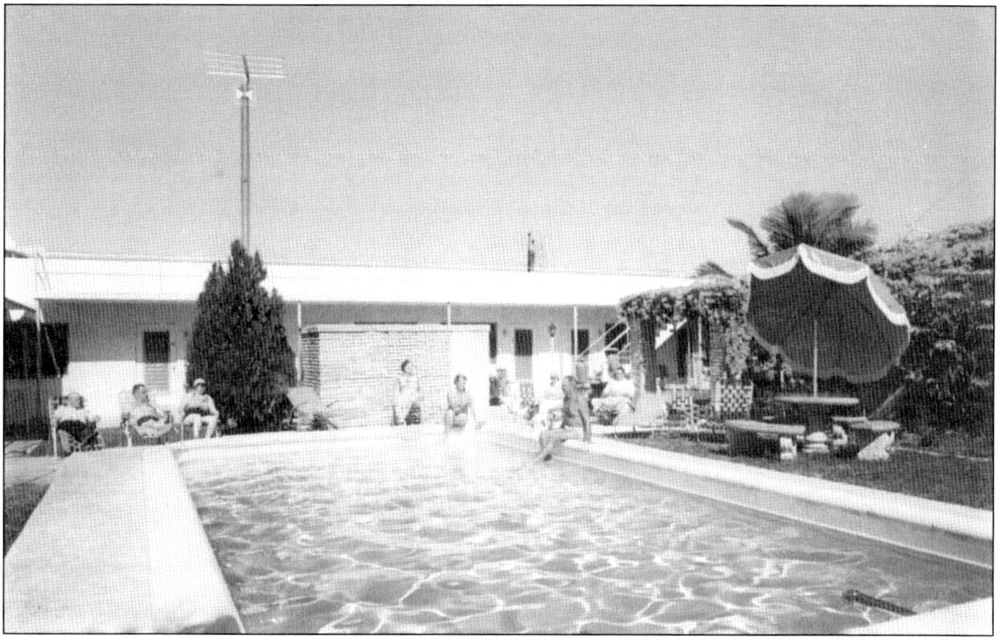

Offering efficiency apartments and hotel rooms, Villa Nova Apartments featured shuffleboard courts, a swimming pool, and a television room. It was located at 812 South Ocean Boulevard.

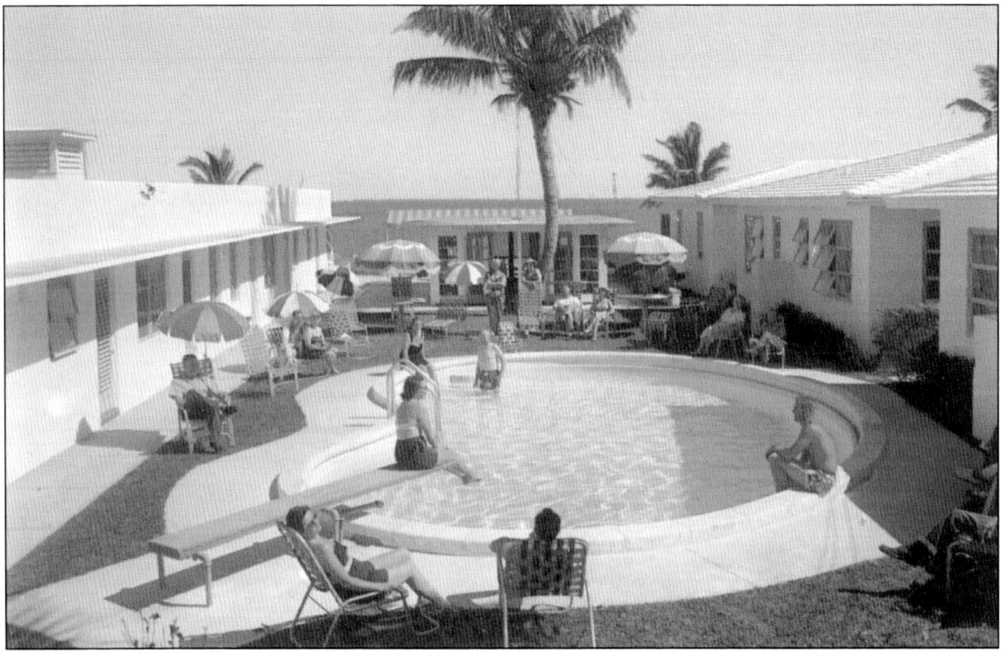

Like the Pompano Beach Hotel, Vista Del Mar (View of the Sea) offered no address for prospective guests, noting only that it was "located on the Seashore of the Atlantic Ocean," meaning Ocean Boulevard. This is another 1950s postcard, and the phone number on the back of the card is listed as "4401."

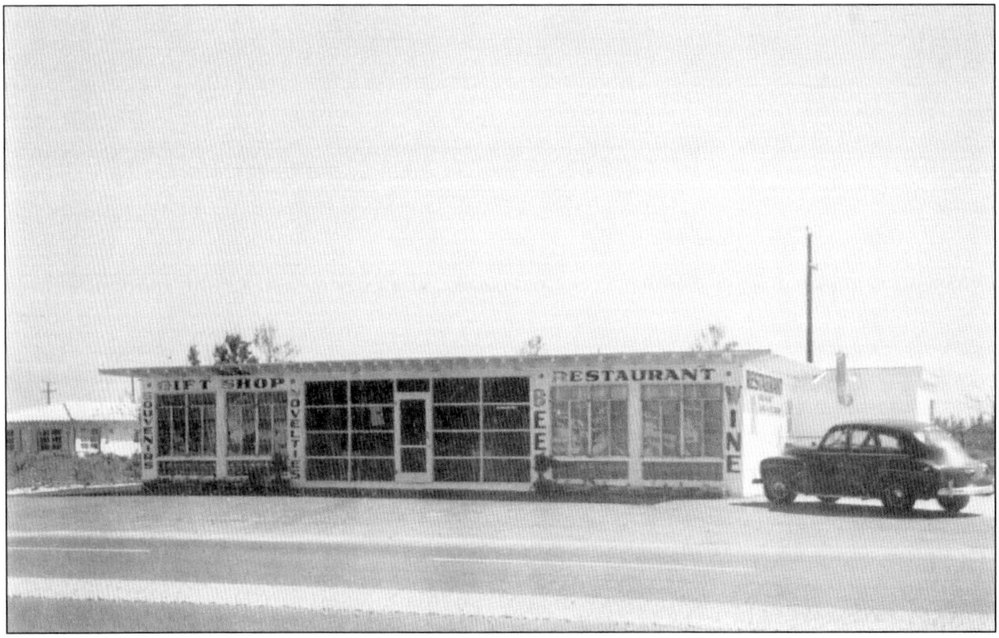

While this postcard explains that Martin's Restaurant–Gift Shop was on US Route 1, was open for "Breakfast—Lunch—Dinner," and had a post office box (shown on the back), it did not include an address. This card was made in the early 1950s by Raymond Studios in Miami.

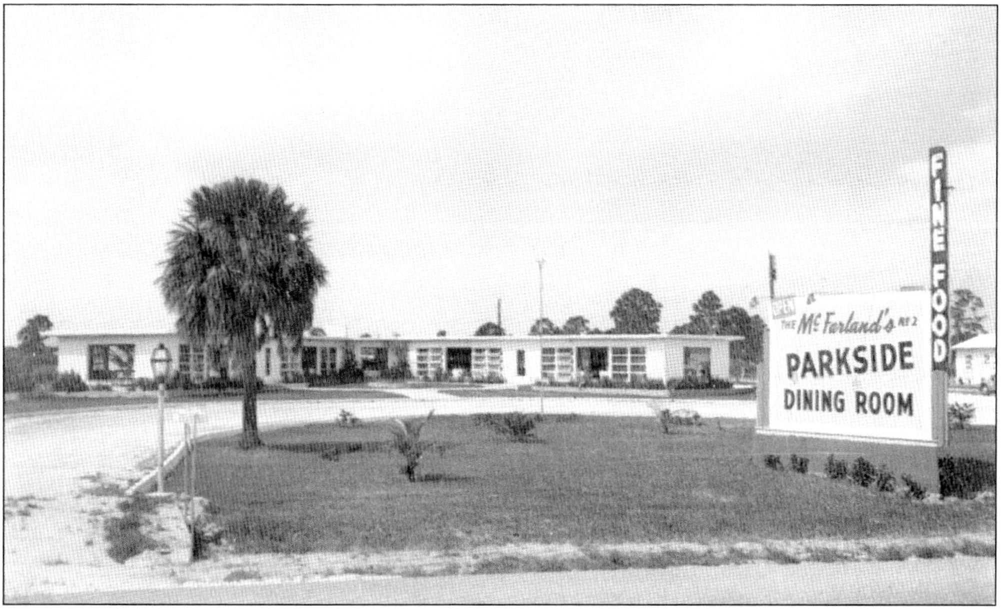

McFarland's Parkside Dining Room offered French cuisine in "Florida's most beautiful and newest dining room." Although this postcard does not include a street address, one could figure out where it was, as the location was shown as being on US Route 1, "located 2 miles North of traffic light."

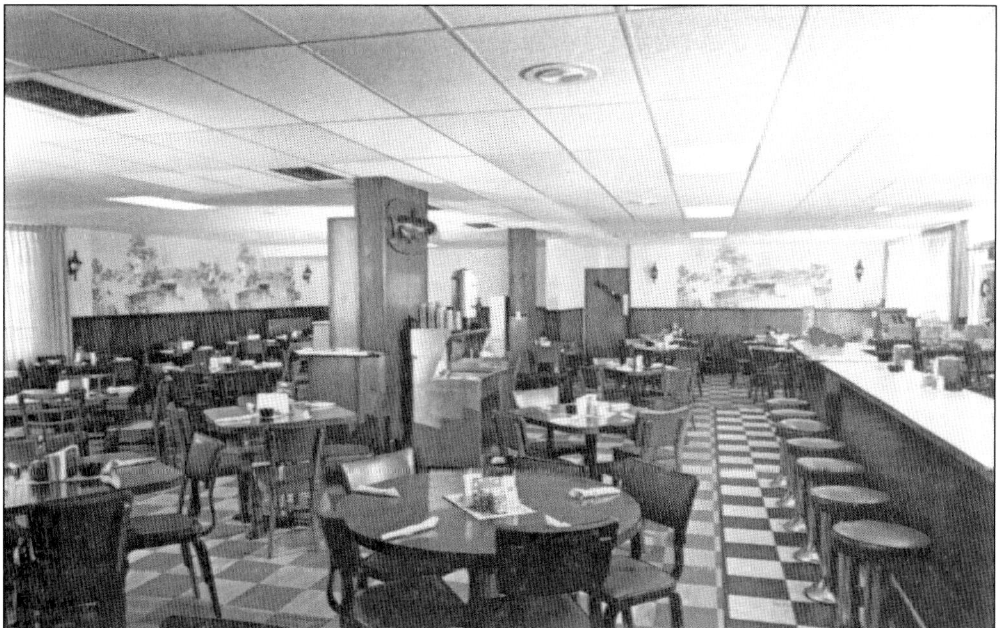

C.L. Norris owned and operated the Norris Catfish Restaurant at 4701 Atlantic Boulevard Extension, "two miles west of town at Sunshine Turnpike Exit P, No. 24—or one block east of State Road 7 (Hwy 441)." The restaurant, which served the Florida specialty noted in its name along with hushpuppies (a variety of fried dough), included Trotter's Lounge and Bar.

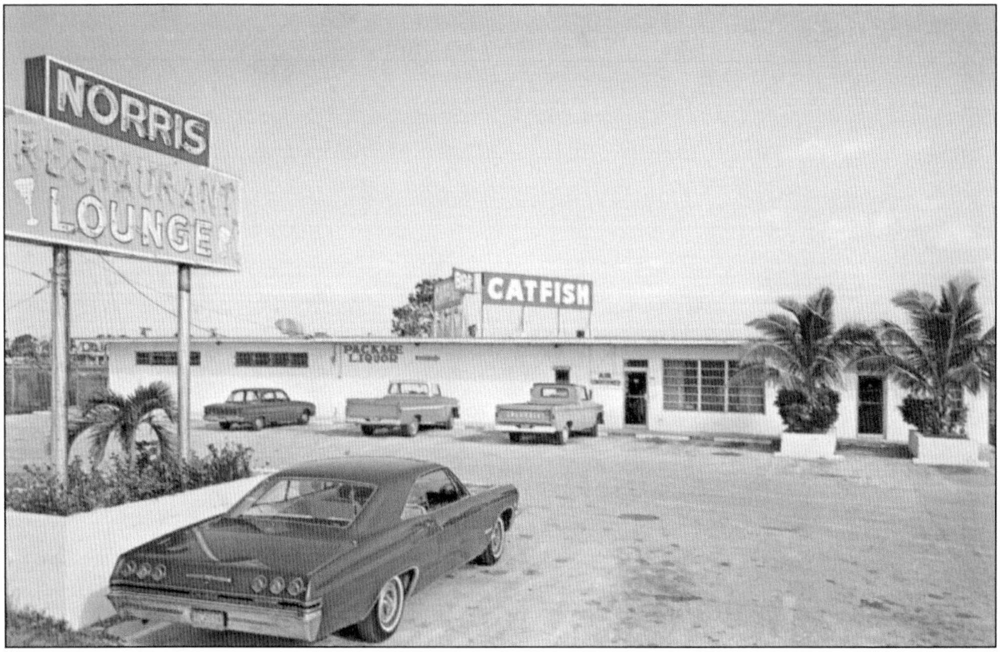

This is an exterior view of the Norris Catfish Restaurant taken in the mid- to late 1960s. The restaurant had closed by the late 1970s.

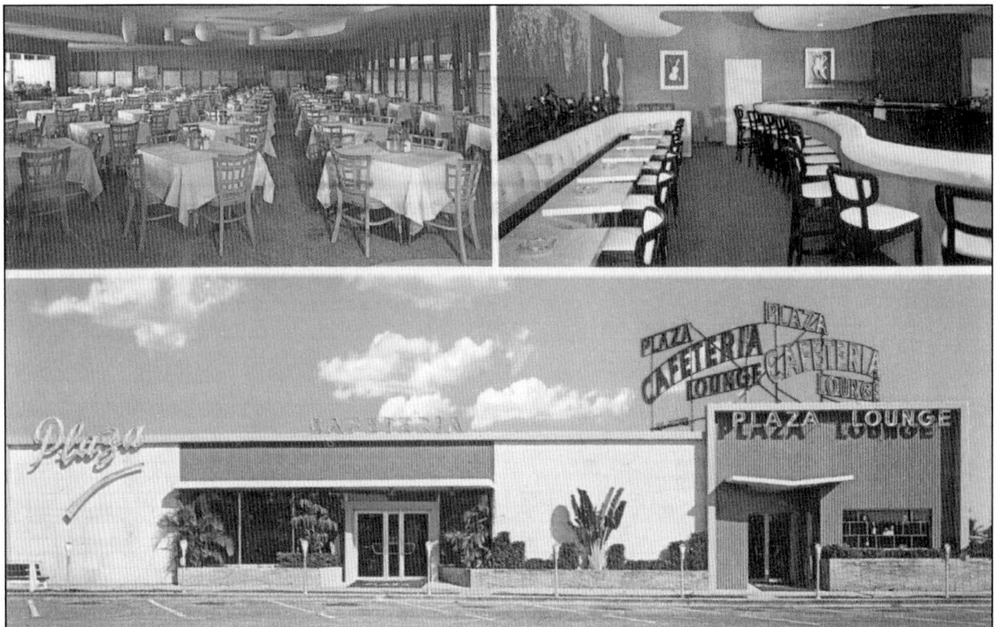

Plaza Cafeteria and Cocktail Lounge was sold to St. Clair's, the cafeteria chain, in either the very late 1950s or in 1960. This food and beverage operation was at 2715 Atlantic Boulevard.

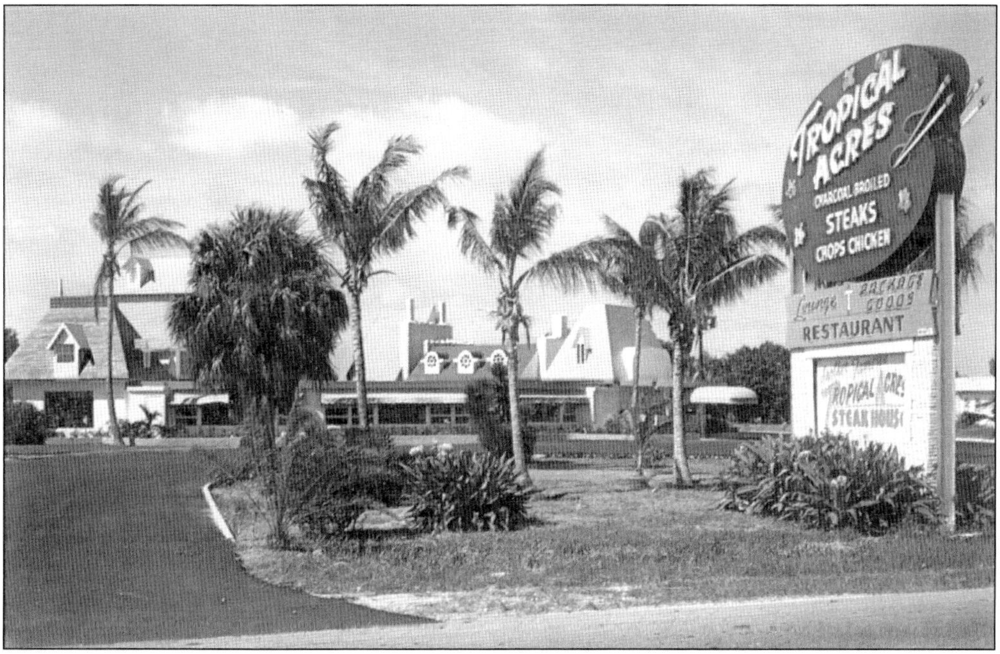

In addition to its flagship location on Griffin Road in Dania, Tropical Acres operated restaurants in Boynton Beach, Florida; Yonkers, New York; and, as shown here, at 2711 North Federal Highway in Pompano Beach. "Famous for Charcoal Broiled Steaks," the Dania store is the only one still in operation.

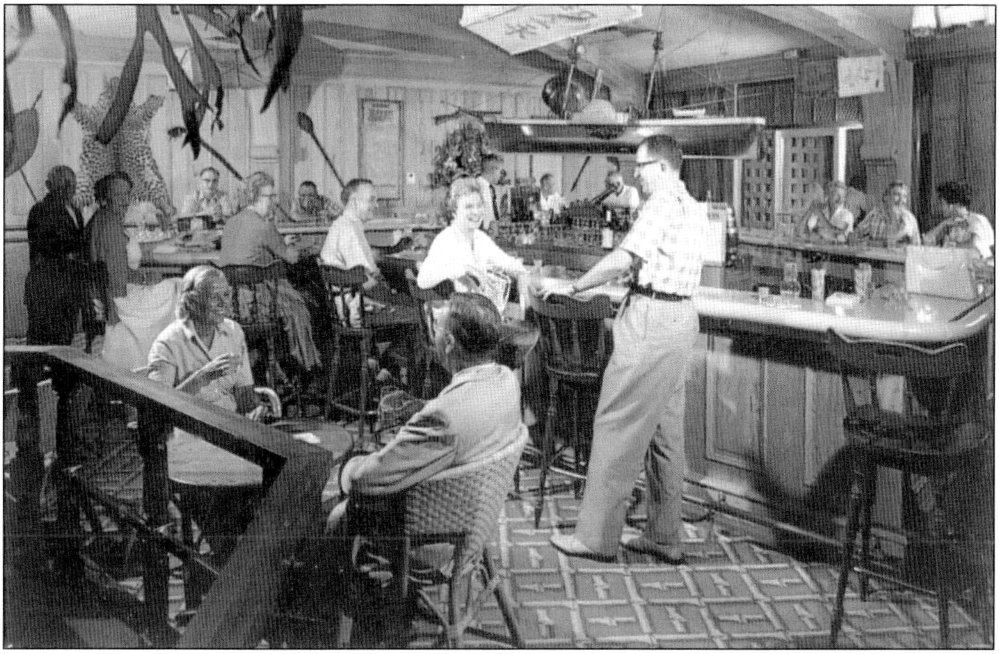

Traders Wharf was in the Traders Resort-O-Tel at 1600 South Ocean Boulevard. The back of this postcard notes that the establishment was a "popular meeting place for the fun and sun lovers."

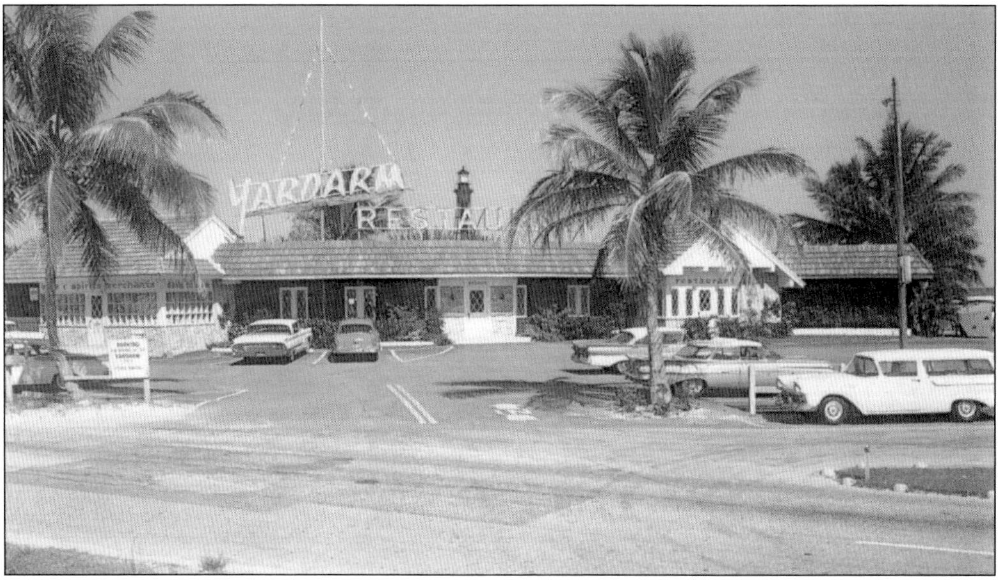

This 1957 postcard shows the Yardarm Restaurant at "Hwy A1A at the Hillsboro Inlet." Offering "a touch of New England," the restaurant was successful for many years, but its owners became mired in years of lawsuits when they wanted to build an 18-story hotel on the site. Numerous accounts of their battles against the City of Pompano Beach are easy to find.

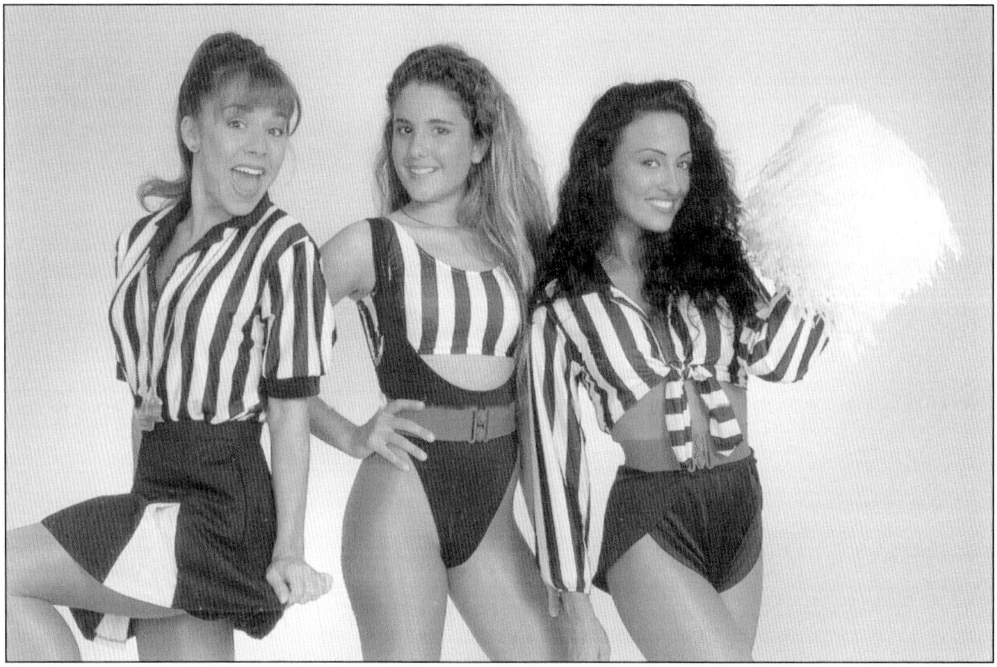

The girls on this postcard represent a Pompano Beach business. Although they are unidentified, they are, on this and several other advertising postcards, representing Class Act Designer Uniforms, which, in this case, was offering "Hot New Looks for Football Season" to restaurants and clubs. While this postcard and others in the author's collection from the company are postmarked from 1991 through 1995, the company is still in business at 290 Southwest Twelfth Avenue in Pompano Beach and is still making a variety of Class Act uniforms.

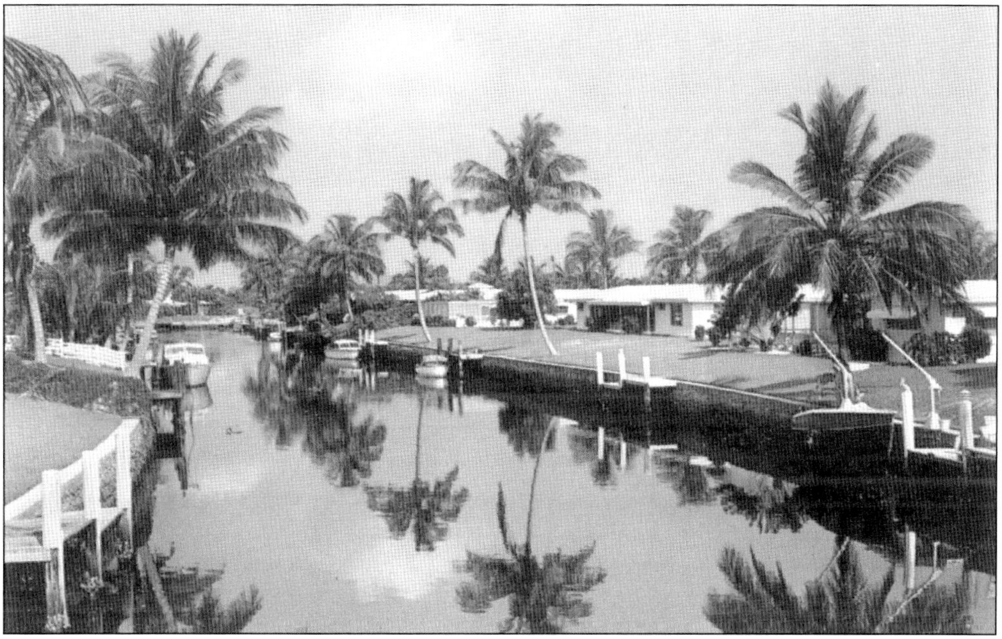

Two views of the beautiful homes and waterways that make up most of Lighthouse Point are shown here. The houses and waterfront property are part of what makes Lighthouse Point a grand place to play and live.

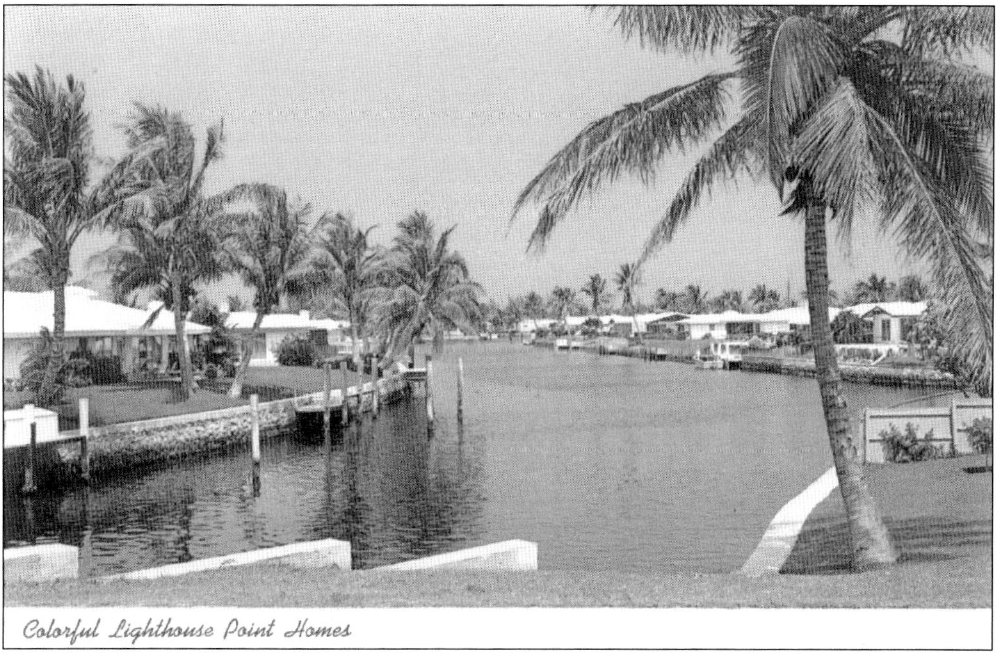

Colorful Lighthouse Point Homes

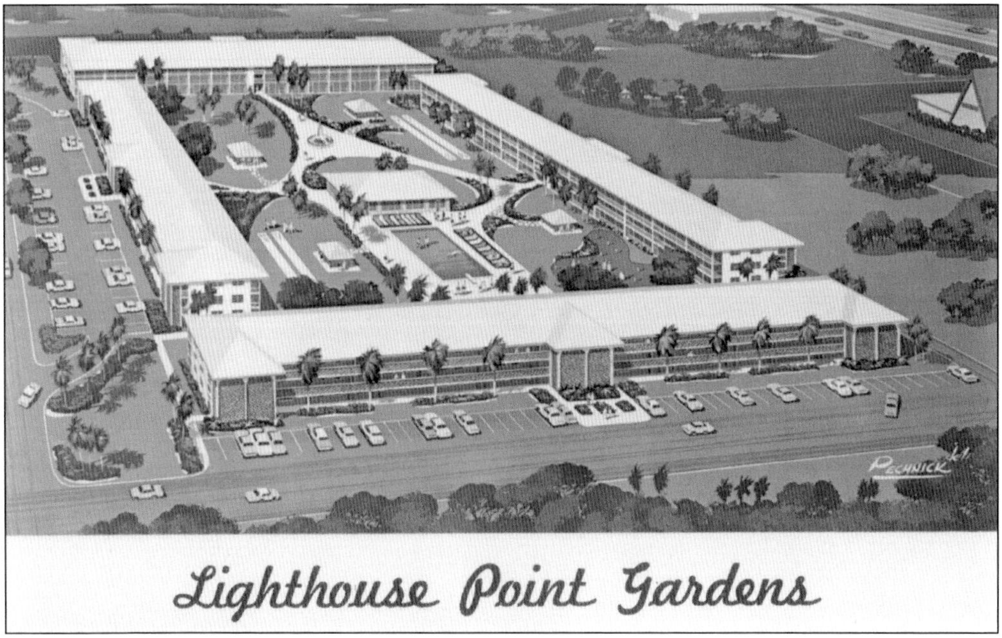

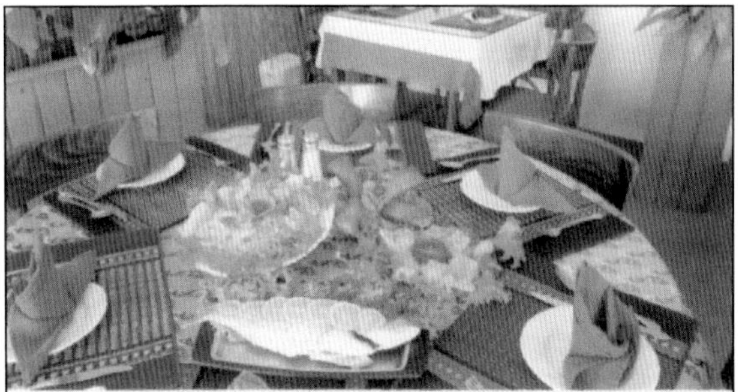

According to the back of this postcard, Lighthouse Gardens was "the newest creation in condominium living by John Bargas," who must have been the builder. With prices ranging from $8,900 for a one-bedroom apartment and $10,500 for two bedrooms and two baths, the card can be dated to the late 1970s or very early 1980s.

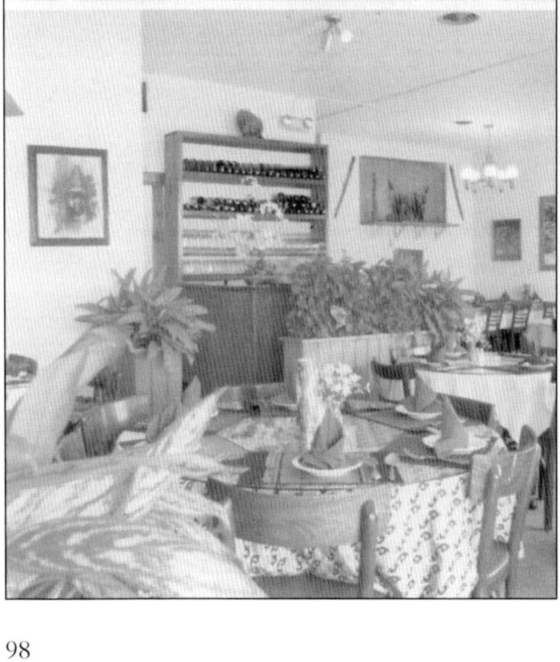

The Taste of Siam was one of the first of the new wave of Thai restaurants that popped up in South Florida beginning in the late 1980s. Taste of Siam is still open just north of Sample Road in Main Street Plaza at 4610 North Federal Highway in Lighthouse Point.

Eight

Deerfield Beach

On June 22, 1898, a post office was established in Deerfield to serve a population of 20 settlers. It is believed that the town's name was chosen because of the numerous deer that grazed along the Hillsboro River, which formed the northern boundary of Deerfield.

The present-day intersection of Hillsboro Boulevard and Dixie Highway was the focus of Deerfield's businesses in 1910, although Dixie Highway was then only a nine-foot-wide dirt trail. The community was home to four or five stores, a lodge, the post office, and the Australian and Pioneer Hotels. The key to the village's economy lay at the produce shed adjacent to the Florida East Coast Railway depot, where farmers brought their vegetables and fruits for shipment north. (At the time, the depot doubled as a site for civic activities.)

In 1911, the Hillsboro River was dredged and became the Hillsboro Canal, linking Deerfield to Lake Okeechobee, 45 miles to the northwest.

The Town of Deerfield incorporated on June 11, 1925. George Emory Butler Jr. was elected as the town's first mayor. The first public library in Deerfield opened in 1925 to serve a population that had climbed to 1,300 residents. In 1939, the name of the town was changed to Deerfield Beach, and the population numbered about 1,800.

One of Deerfield's most influential civic organizations, the Lions Club, formed in 1947. Its first project was establishing Pioneer Park along the banks of the Hillsboro Canal. The Lions cleared the scrub growth and fashioned a picnic area and a baseball diamond complete with stands and barbecue pits. The park has since been expanded to include recreational buildings, boat ramps, and lighted tennis courts. To raise funds, the club held several chicken and ribs barbecues. The fundraiser became so popular that it became an annual celebration now known as Founders' Day.

In 1951, the town's name was changed to City of Deerfield Beach. The economy gradually shifted from agriculture toward tourism. Today, Deerfield Beach's economy is heavily diversified and includes distribution, manufacturing, and office space, in addition to tourism. The sustained year-round population of more than 50,000 people offers evidence of the strength of the local economy.

Today, the city works diligently to provide customer-oriented services to residents and visitors to create a quality of life that encourages both residents and employers to enjoy South Florida and prosper in an ever-growing international economy.

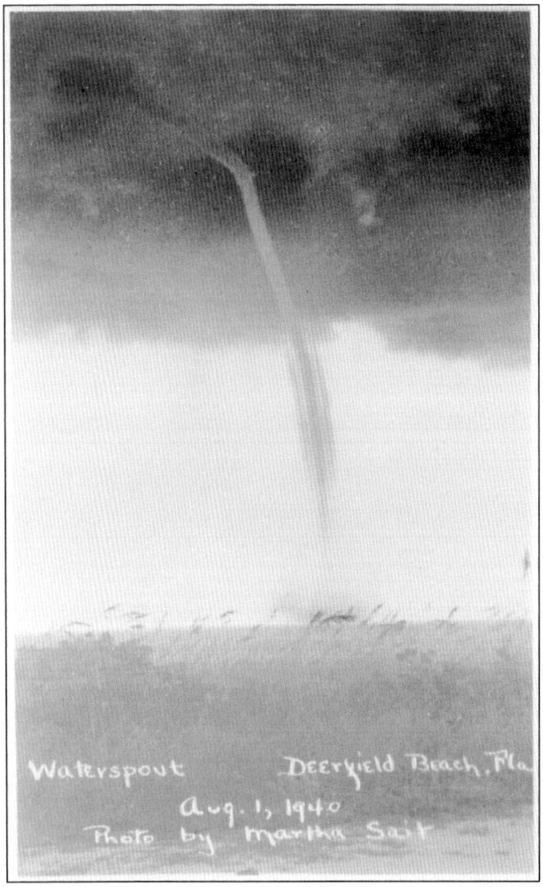

On August 1, 1940, while standing on the dunes overlooking the beach and the Atlantic Ocean, and with great presence of mind, Martha Sait took this photograph of one of the great wonders of nature, a water spout. Similar to tornados but occurring over water (and generally seen in the Atlantic Ocean), these natural phenomena rarely reach the shore. This postcard was mailed from Boca Raton, just north of Deerfield Beach, on February 24, 1941.

Always an important part of any town, city, or regional business community, the chamber of commerce plays a large role in facilitating, increasing, and improving interactions between businesses and the community at large. The Deerfield Beach Chamber of Commerce building was completed in 1960 and is still at the location shown on this postcard, 1601 East Hillsboro Boulevard. The phone number on the card, "8752," is now (954) 427-1050.

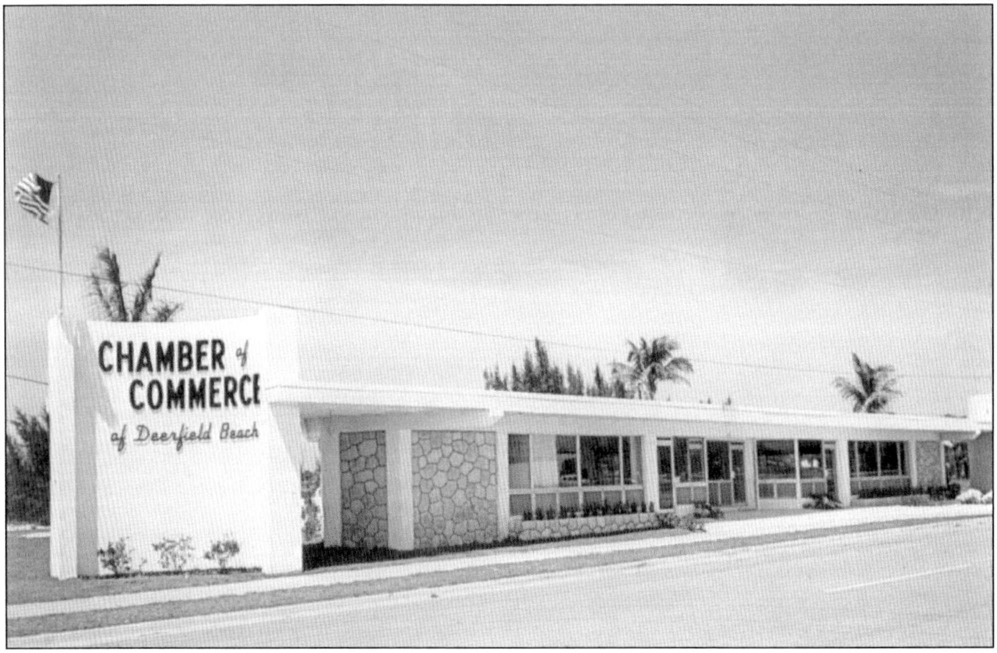

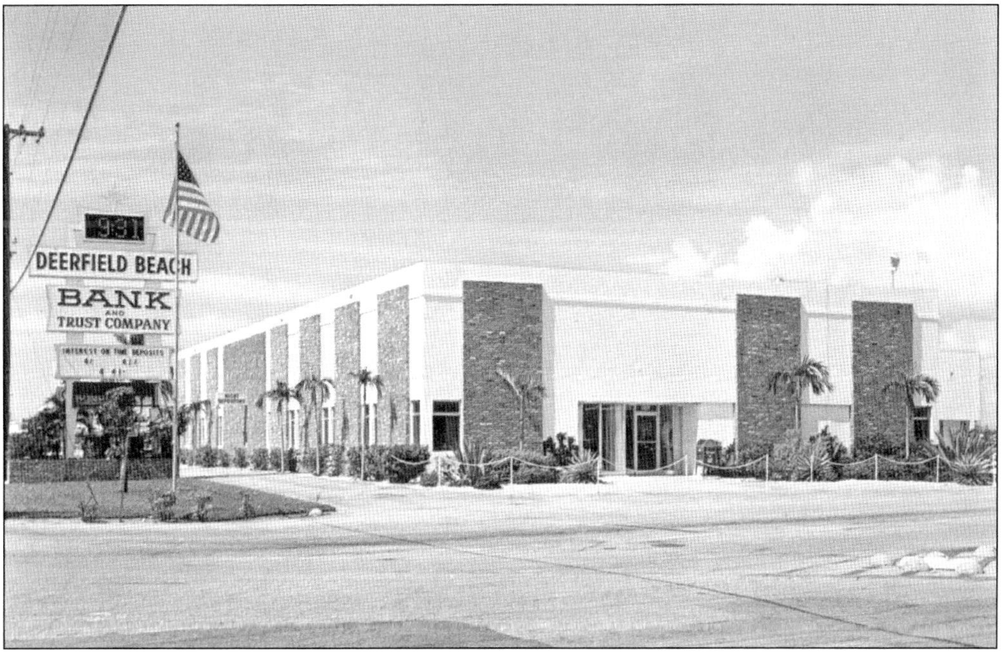

Deerfield Beach Bank and Trust Company was located at 1007 South Federal Highway when this postcard was made around 1960. It appears that Bank of America bought or took over the bank at some point and moved across the street to 1000 South Federal Highway, where that branch is now located.

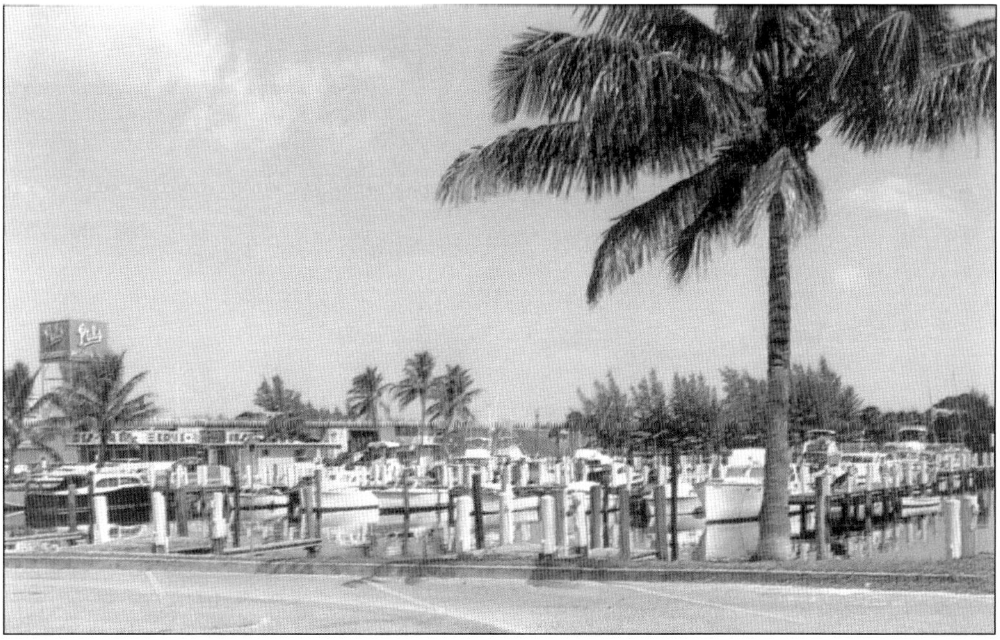

This is the Cove Yacht Basin with the Deerfield Beach Pal's Restaurant in the background at left. Now known as Cove Marina (and greatly enlarged), the business is located at 1755 Southeast Third Court and is a very active major dockage and ships stores operation.

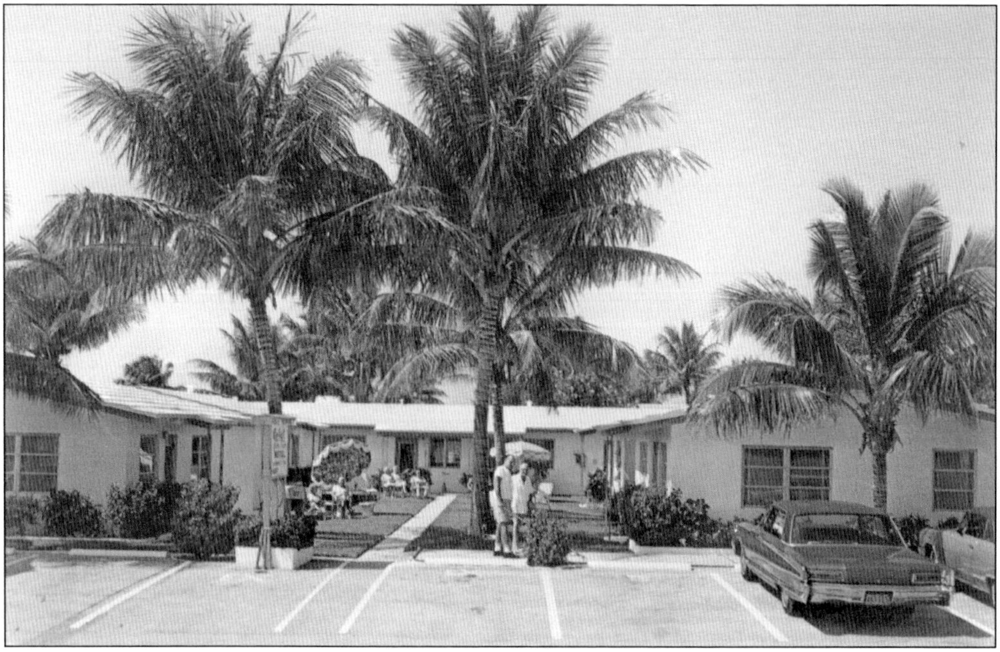

Gobel Apartments was owned by Julia and Thomas Gobel. Located on State Road A1A at 97 Southeast Twentieth Avenue, Gobel Apartments offered the usual amenities for the time, including shuffleboard.

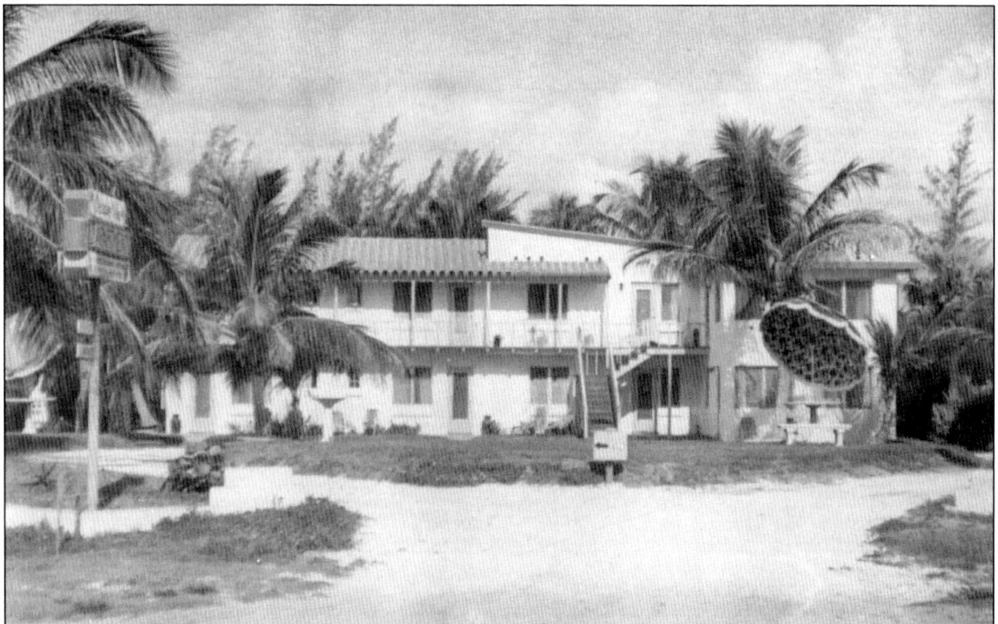

Ocean Vue Apartments, also on State Road A1A, was owned by Mr. and Mrs. Chabot. Handwritten on the back is: "$70 a wk. for efficiency/$125 for bedroom. Those were the days!"

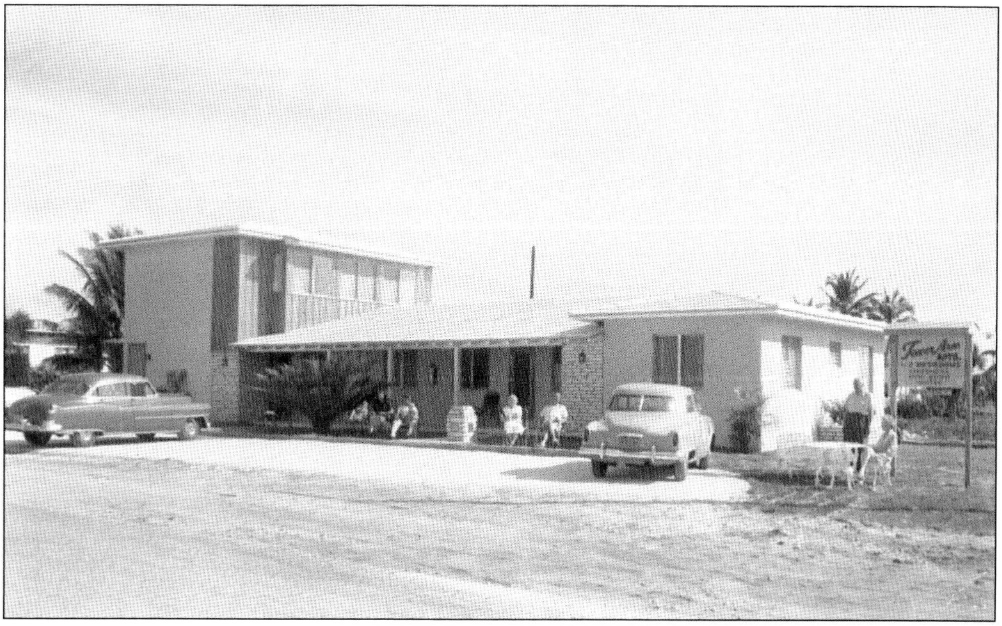

Although Tower Arms Apartments was located on State Road A1A in Deerfield Beach, the mailing address was "Box 1245, Route 2, Pompano Beach." Written in ink at the top left of the card is "Tel. Boca Raton 2551." This c. 1951 postcard was mailed from Pompano Beach on May 15, 1953.

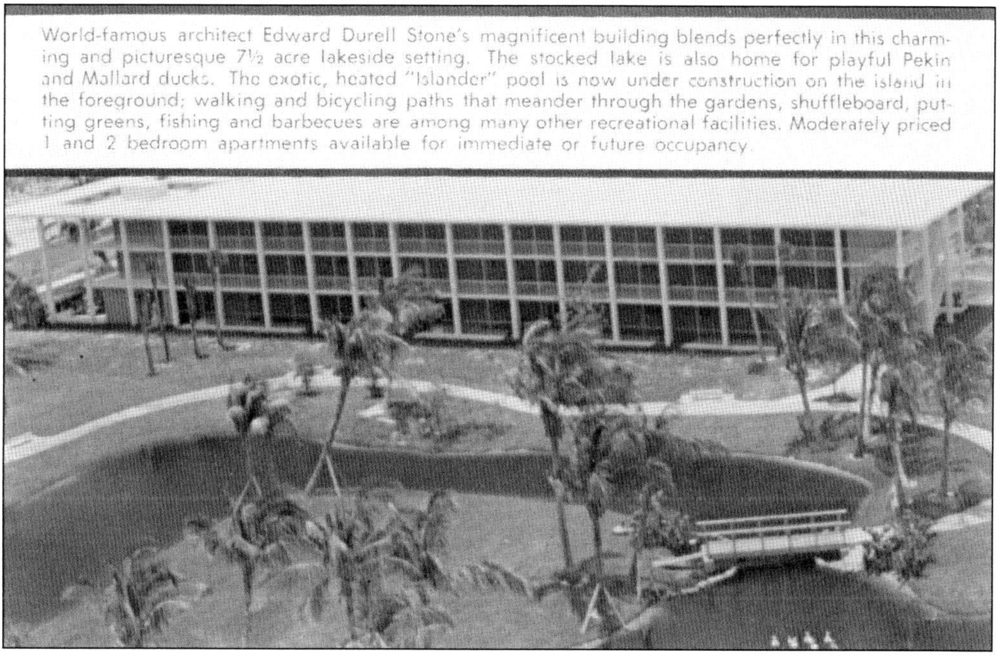

Rarely does a postcard for a business carry this much copy on the front, but this one, advertising "famous architect Edward Durrell Stone's magnificent building," certainly does. Published by Deerfield Lake Condominium Apartments, located at 177 Southeast Second Avenue, this late 1960s or early 1970s postcard offers "4 different apartments priced from $8,990 with excellent condominium financing." Prices currently range from $125,000 upward.

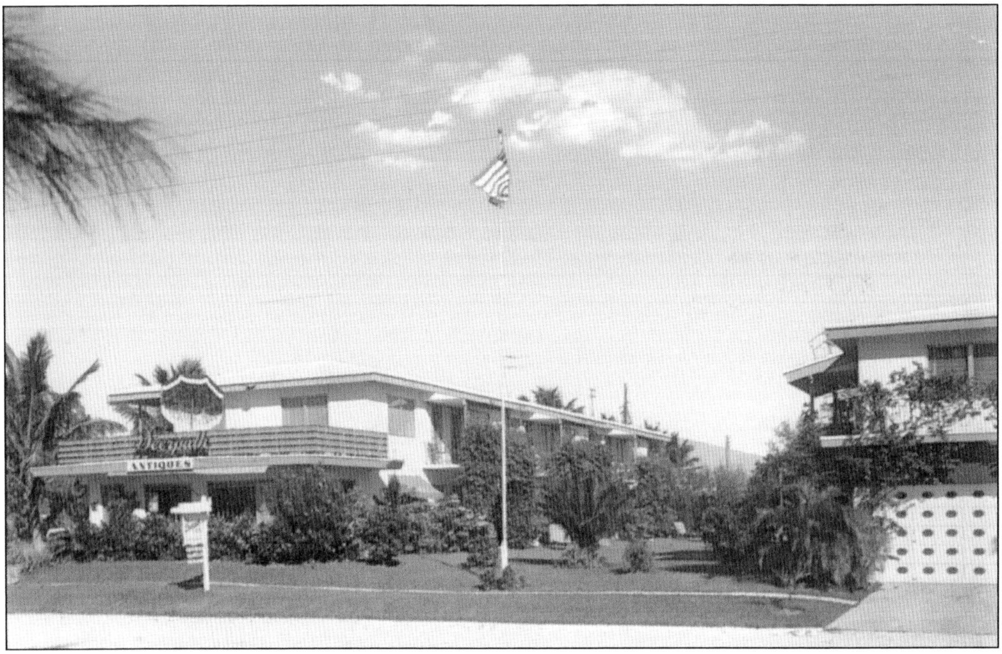

George Ockay owned the Deerpath apartment motel and offered "New Ultra-Modern Apartments in the Heart of the Gold Coast." This hostelry was on State Road A1A at 714 Southeast Twentieth Avenue. The photograph was taken and the card was made in 1963 or 1964.

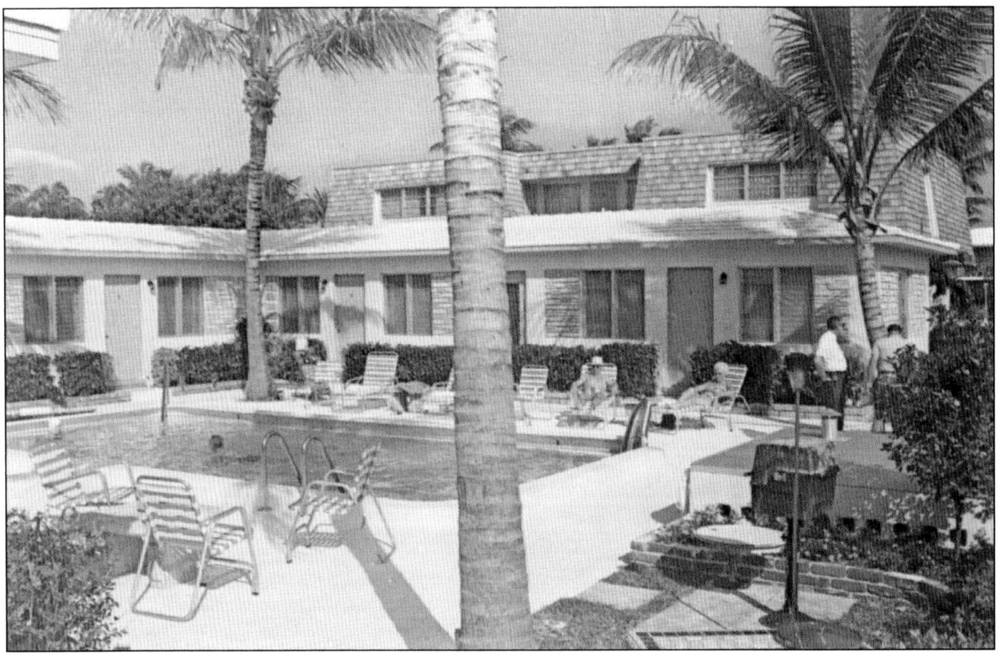

This postcard advertising the Shore Road Inn, located at 460 South A1A, featured this unique poolside view complete with swimmers and sunbathers. Color TV was a feature, as were "restaurants nearby."

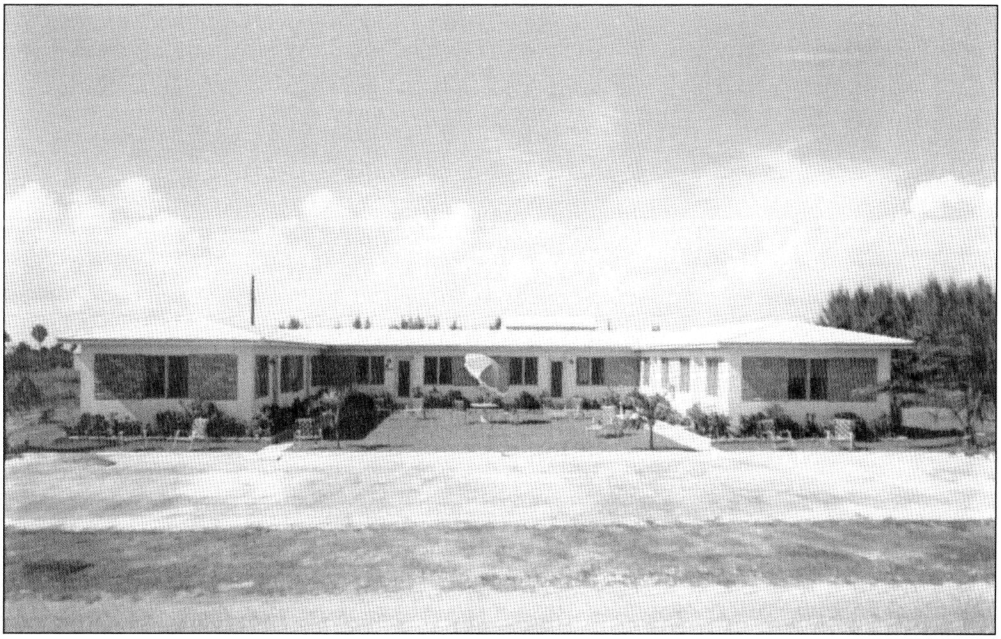

Owners Ruth and Harvey Copp were not shy about claiming that their Beverly Arms Apartments, "located on Route A1A," had the ocean in front and the Intracoastal Waterway in the back. "World's finest fishing, bathing and golf" is also noted on the back of this card—without offering any more specificity about the locations.

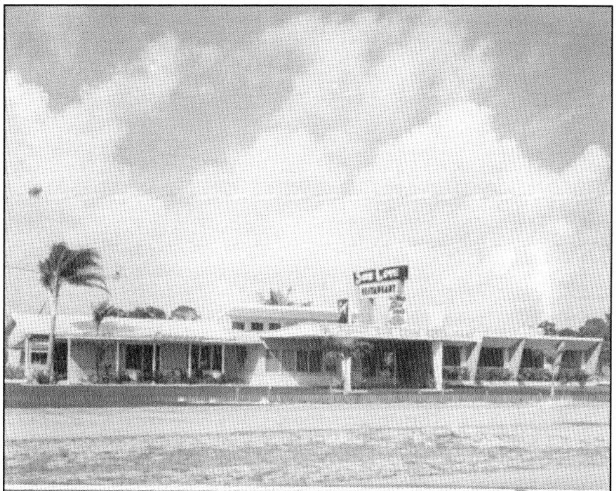

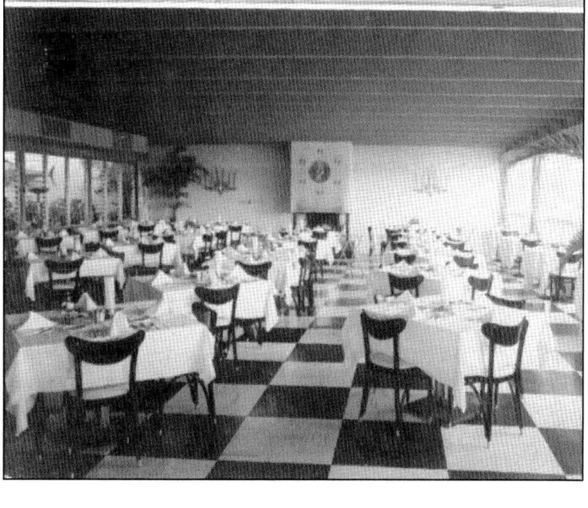

Mac Feggan's Sun Cove Restaurant–Cocktail Lounge was on Federal Highway, although the card is *sans* address. It does state, though, that the eatery was "Famous for Key Lime Pie—Flaming Foods and Charcoal Broiled Specialties."

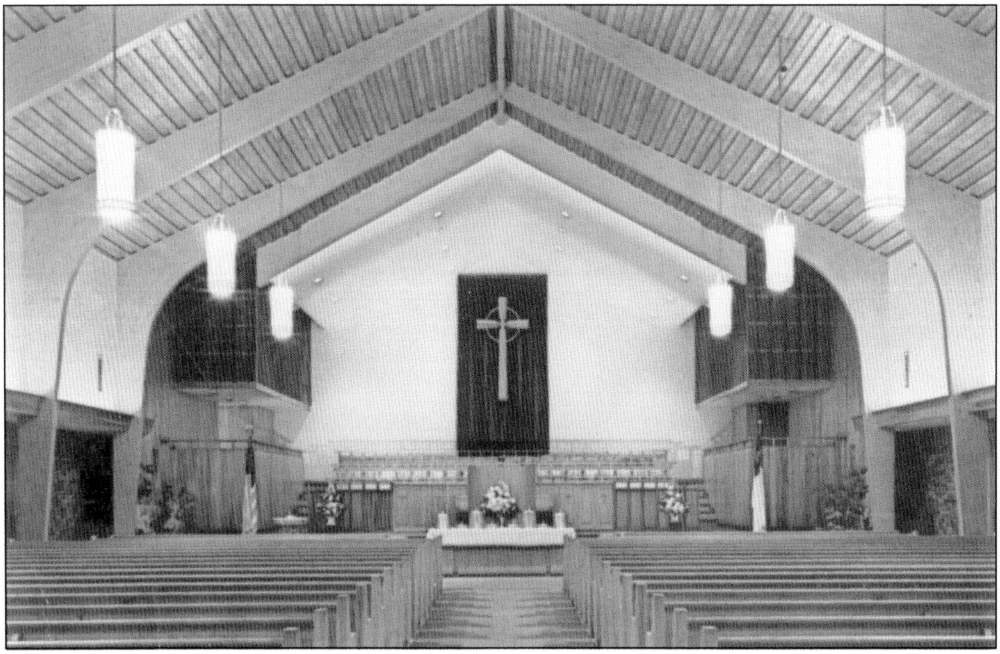

Community Presbyterian Church is located on Southeast Fifth Street on State Road A1A. This sanctuary was dedicated on May 19, 1963. The church remains in the same location but with a different street address—1420 Southeast Fourth Street in Deerfield Beach.

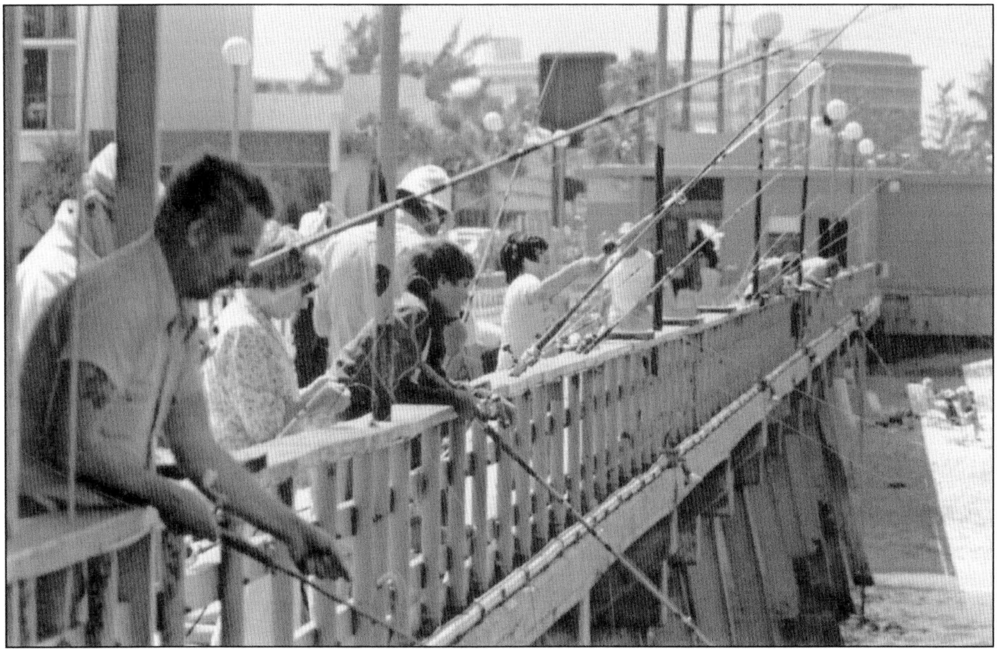

This is the Deerfield Beach Municipal Pier. In 1976, at the time this postcard was published, the pier was open 24 hours a day and had a coffee shop. According to the card, Pres. Gerald Ford visited the pier on February 28, 1976.

Nine

Towns and Cities of West Broward County

Like Miami-Dade County to the south and Palm Beach County to the north, Broward County is made up of a plethora of not only incorporated villages, towns, and cities but also unincorporated areas and communities.

While the bulk of the population lives on the east side of the county (at one time, there was a west side in the geographic area, but it had a minimal population and few businesses), the South Florida population explosion has caused a migration to areas west of the towns and cities along the Broward County Atlantic Coast seaboard. A number of new municipalities came into existence beginning in the early 1950s, and their increases in size—both in terms of land mass and numbers of people—have been nothing other than exponential.

For the purpose of understanding what "West Broward" includes, the term as used in this book refers in general to any village, town, city, or unincorporated community west of the State Road Seven/US Route 441 corridor. The western Broward municipalities include Coconut Creek, Cooper City, Coral Springs, Davie, Lauderhill, Lauderdale Lakes, Miramar, North Lauderdale, Parkland, Pembroke Park, Pembroke Pines, Plantation, Southwest Ranches, Sunrise, Tamarac, West Park, and Weston.

While the author has made every effort to obtain postcards from each of the named West Broward locales, the search, in several cases, has been frustrating and, regretfully, fruitless. Readers are therefore asked for their indulgence in the event that, for various reasons (including the possibility that no postcards may ever have been produced for that specific place on the map), no views or images of any particular place are included. The author assures readers that it has not been for lack of effort.

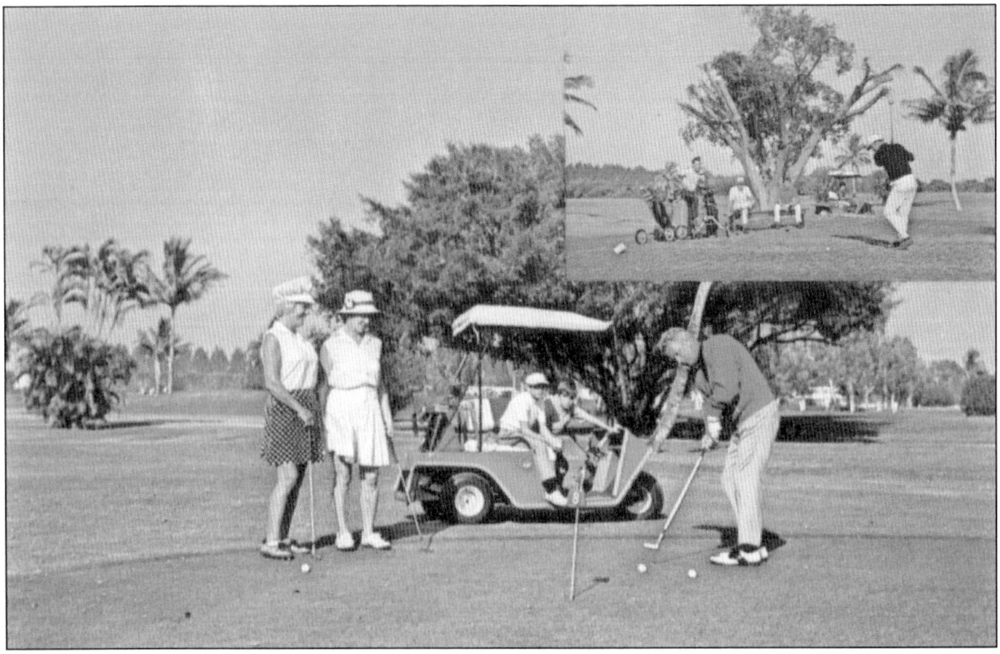

Cooper Colony Country Club developed over the years into a 3,820-yard, par-60 golf course complete with all expected amenities. Located at 5050 Southwest Ninetieth Avenue, it billed itself, on the back of this postcard, as "South Florida's Finest Semi-Private Par 60 Executive Golf Course."

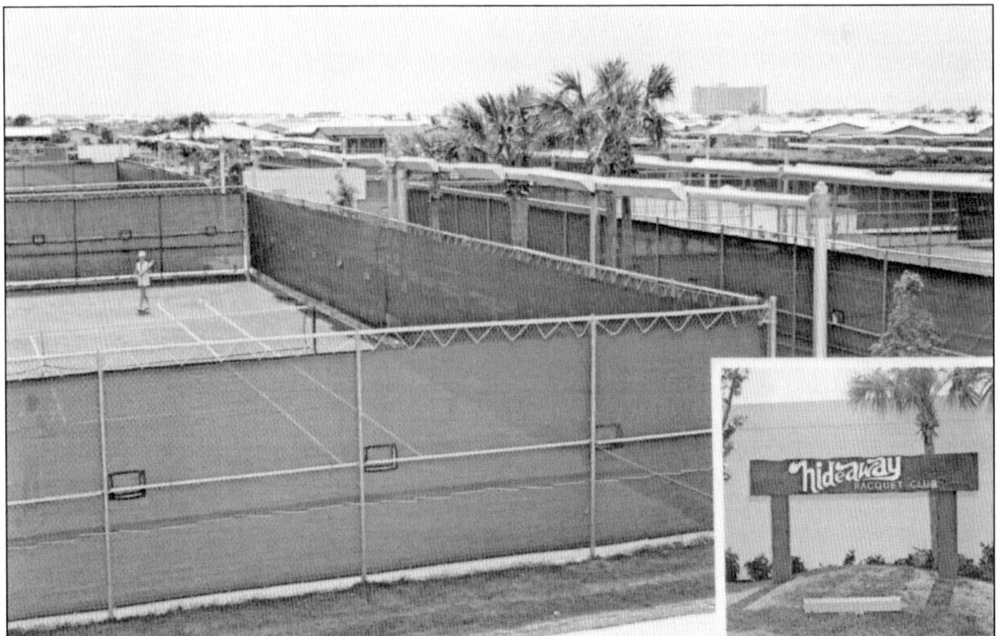

Hideaway Racquet Club was located at 10200 Wiles Road just west of University Drive. For a number of reasons, including competition and management issues, the club is no longer in operation.

The screw pine tree is native to Madagascar. This and the following postcard offer examples of the flora on display at Flamingo Groves, the original name of what is now known as Flamingo Gardens. Founded in 1927 by Floyd L. Wray and his wife, Jane, the Gardens are now a major botanical attraction.

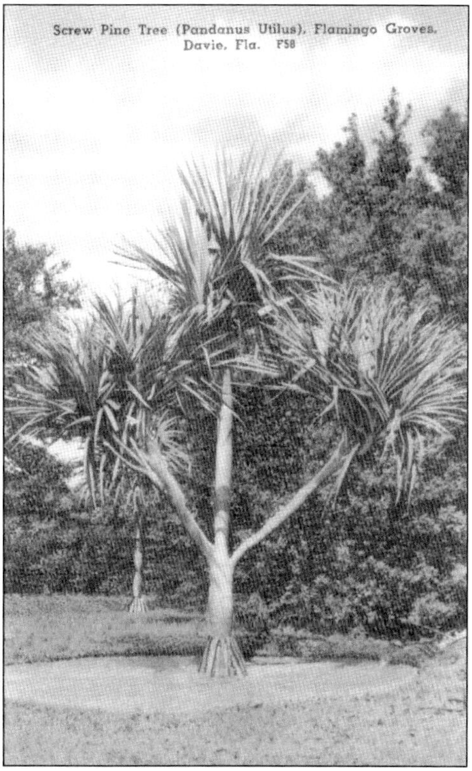

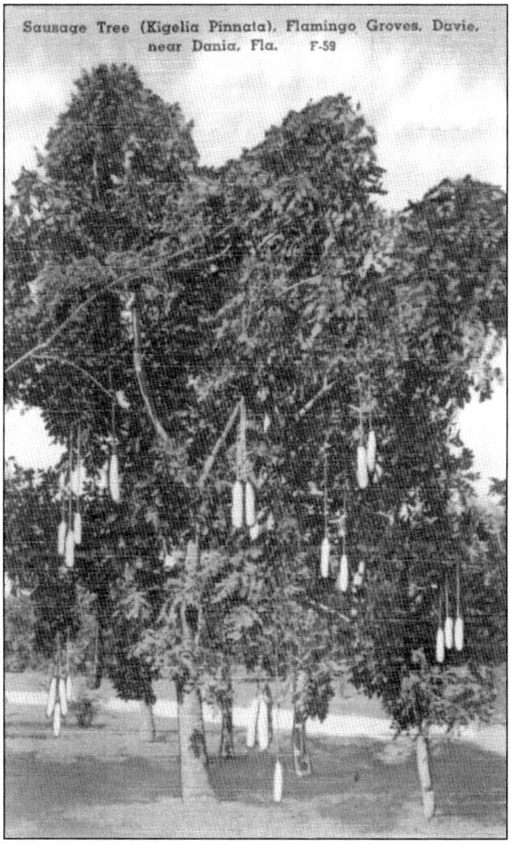

The Sausage Tree at Flamingo Groves is the subject of this postcard. At the time of its founding and well into the 1950s, the Groves were considered to be "out in the boonies." Today, at 750 South Flamingo Road (between Griffin Road and Interstate 595), they are right in the center of a megalopolis that stretches from Homestead in Miami-Dade County north to Stuart in Martin County, the next county north of Palm Beach County.

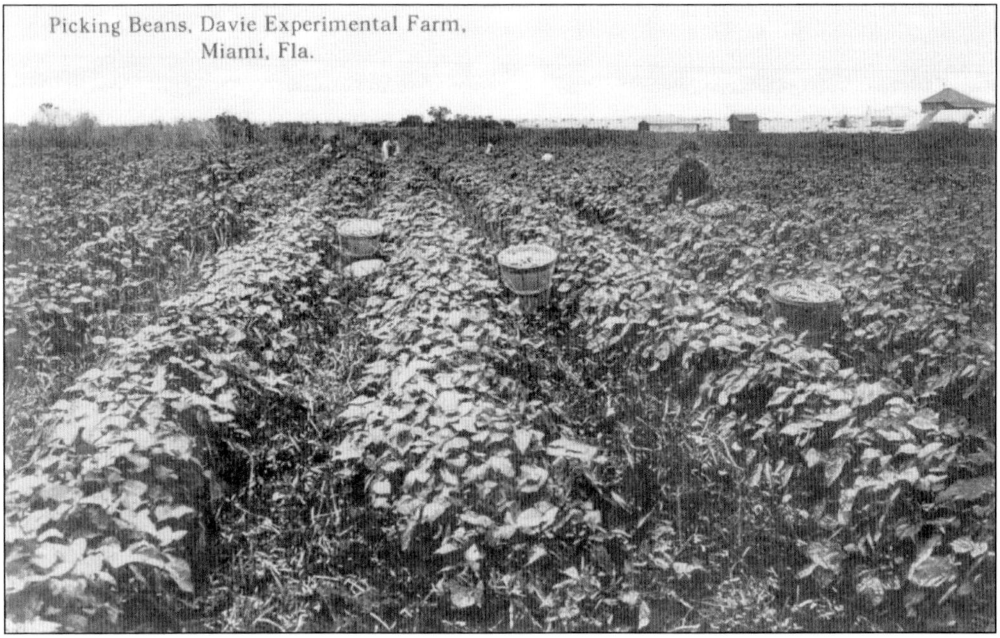

Although this early 20th century postcard shows the location of the Davie Experimental Farm as Miami, that was not its actual location. Before the farm had the name "Davie" (named for a local pioneer who bought much of the land on which the town would later be built), the area was called Zona. It was part of Dade (later Miami-Dade) County until 1915, when Broward County was created. In 1925, the Town of Davie was formally incorporated.

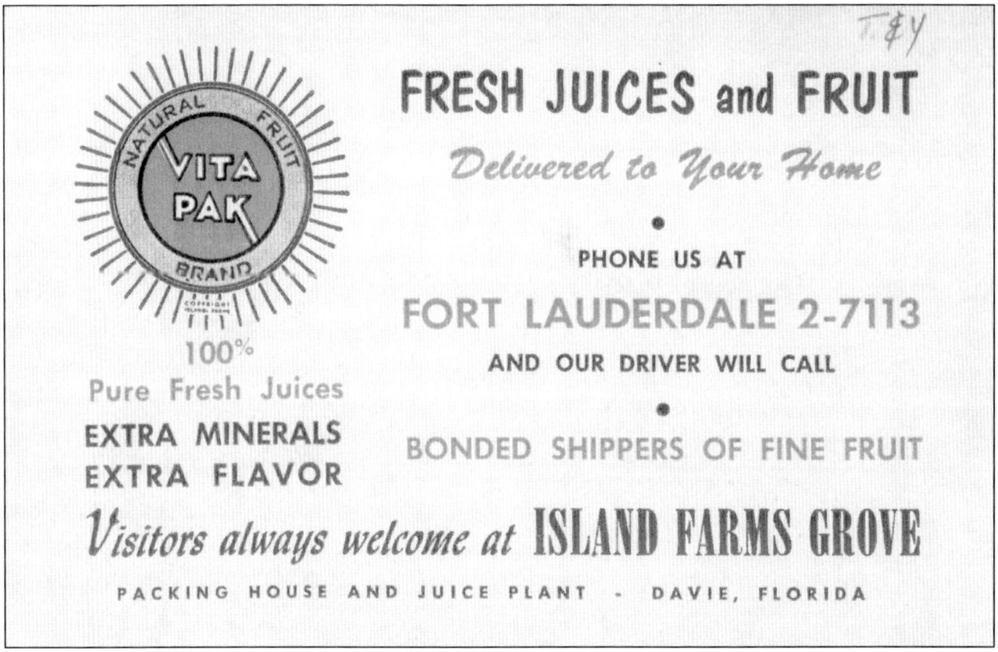

Island Farms maintained its packing house and juice plant in Davie. The phone number of its Island Farms Grove was shown as Fort Lauderdale 2-7113. They also shipped fruit nationwide.

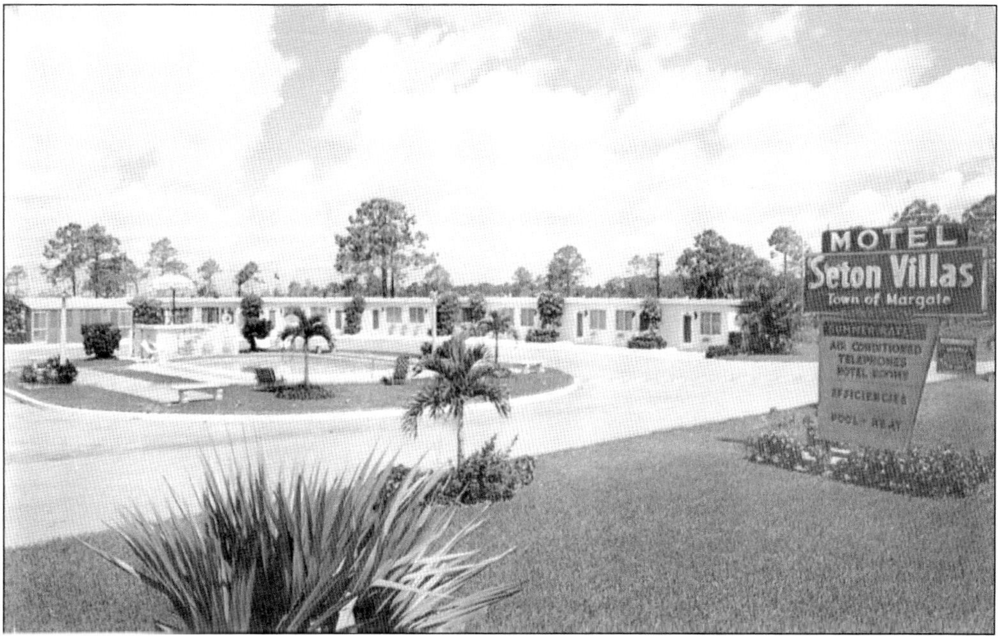

Seton Villas Motel was "Five Miles West of Pompano Beach" and had a Pompano Beach phone number, as Margate did not yet have its own exchange. Interestingly, as the reader might note, the sign says "Town of Margate" below the motel's name.

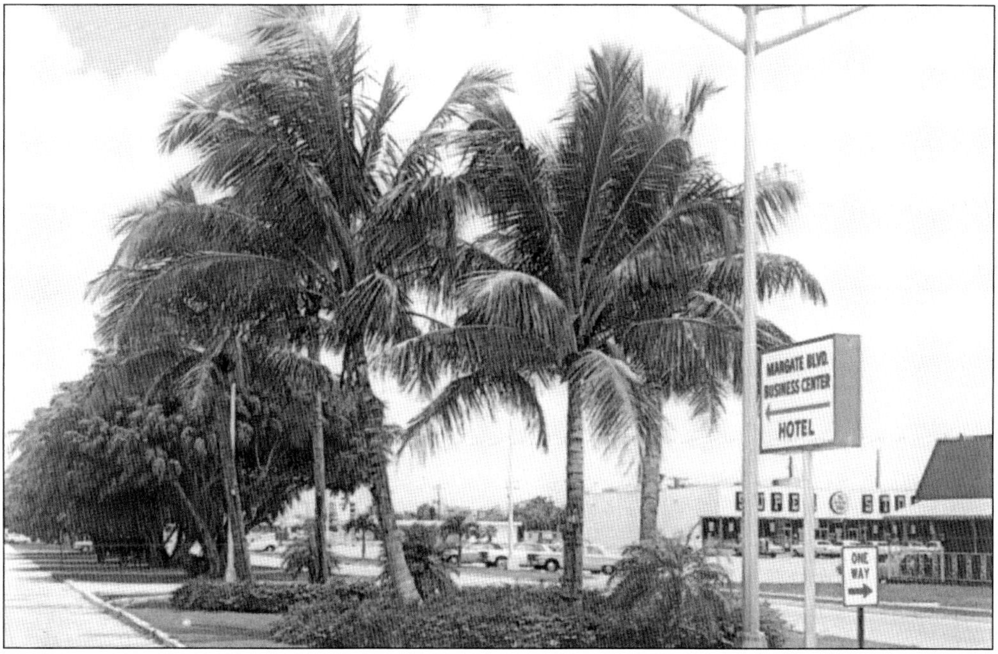

Margate Boulevard is pictured here around 1978. The pole sign points toward the "Margate Boulevard Business District." In the background is a shopping center with a Super Store visible on the left (behind the sign) and a 7-11 in the next block, with the sign almost directly at center.

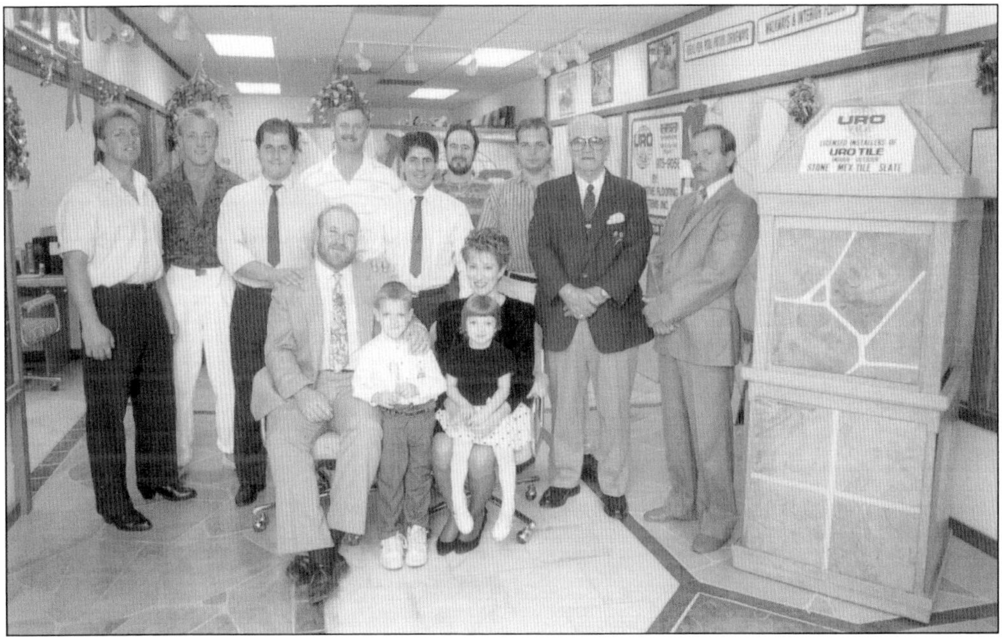

The owners, management, and staff of Uro Tile pose in the company's showroom at 6508 West Atlantic Boulevard, directly west of Pompano Beach. The company, which held the Uro Tile franchise, is now located in Boca Raton.

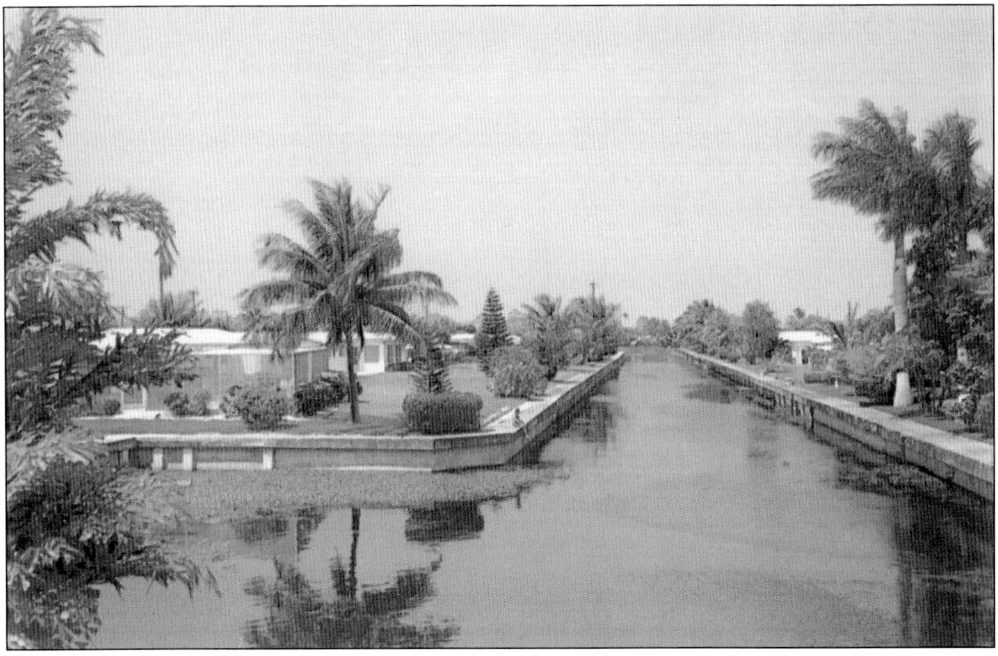

This 1980s postcard does not give an exact location for this view. The caption on the back reads, "residences along a beautiful waterway," with the next line stating, "where living is fun."

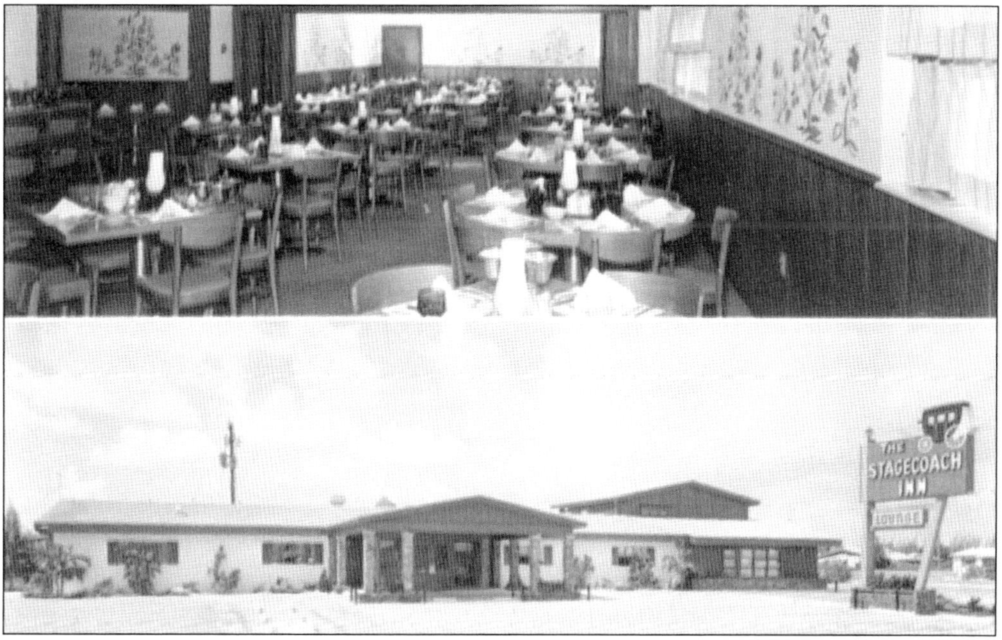

Popular for years, The Stagecoach Inn was located at 4520 West Hallandale Beach Boulevard. Families were welcome, and there was music in the lounge.

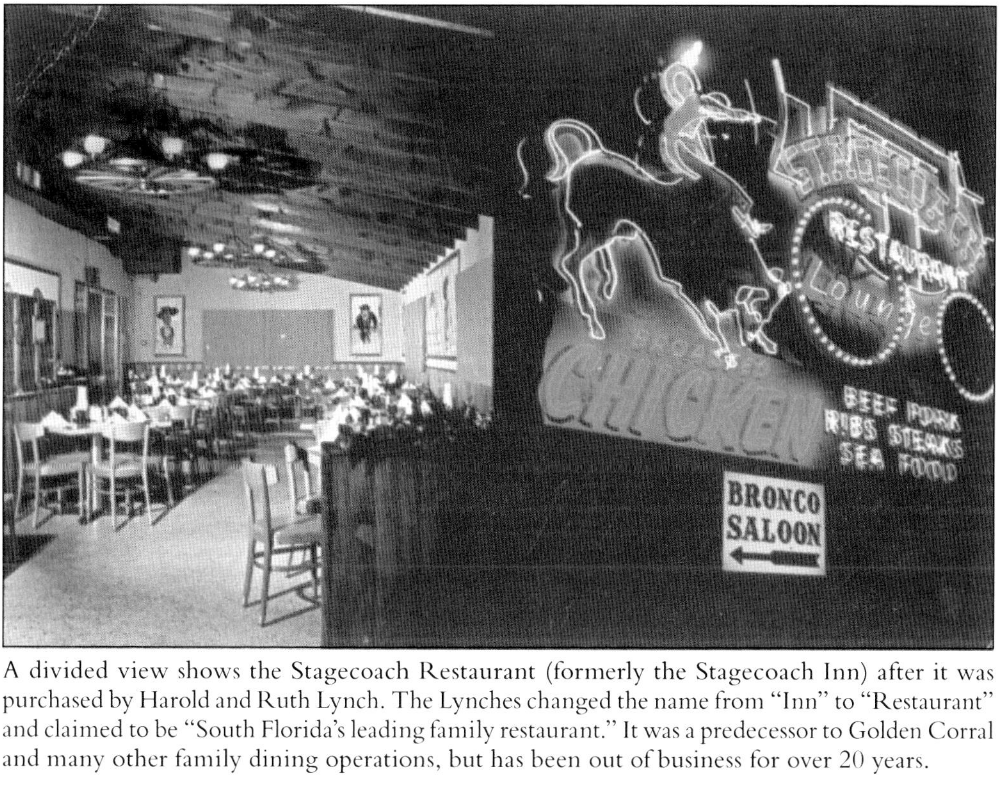

A divided view shows the Stagecoach Restaurant (formerly the Stagecoach Inn) after it was purchased by Harold and Ruth Lynch. The Lynches changed the name from "Inn" to "Restaurant" and claimed to be "South Florida's leading family restaurant." It was a predecessor to Golden Corral and many other family dining operations, but has been out of business for over 20 years.

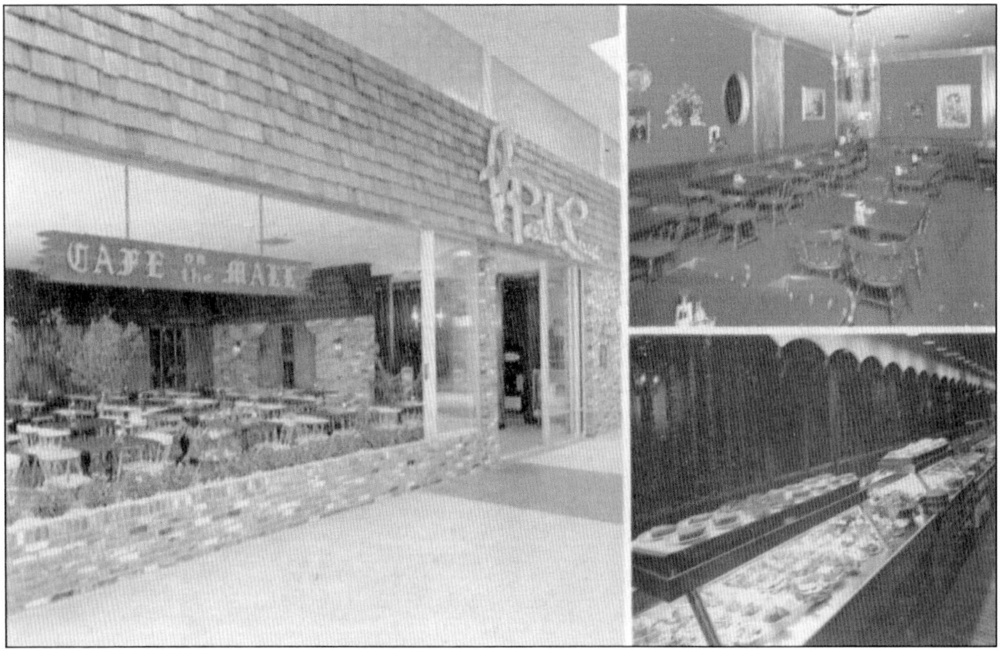

Park Lane Cafeterias was one of several South Florida chain operations but, along with Polly Davis, seemed to be a step above in terms of food quality and service. This is their cafeteria and café on the mall in Lauderhill. The operation, the card states, had "the charm of an Old English Café, featuring prime ribs."

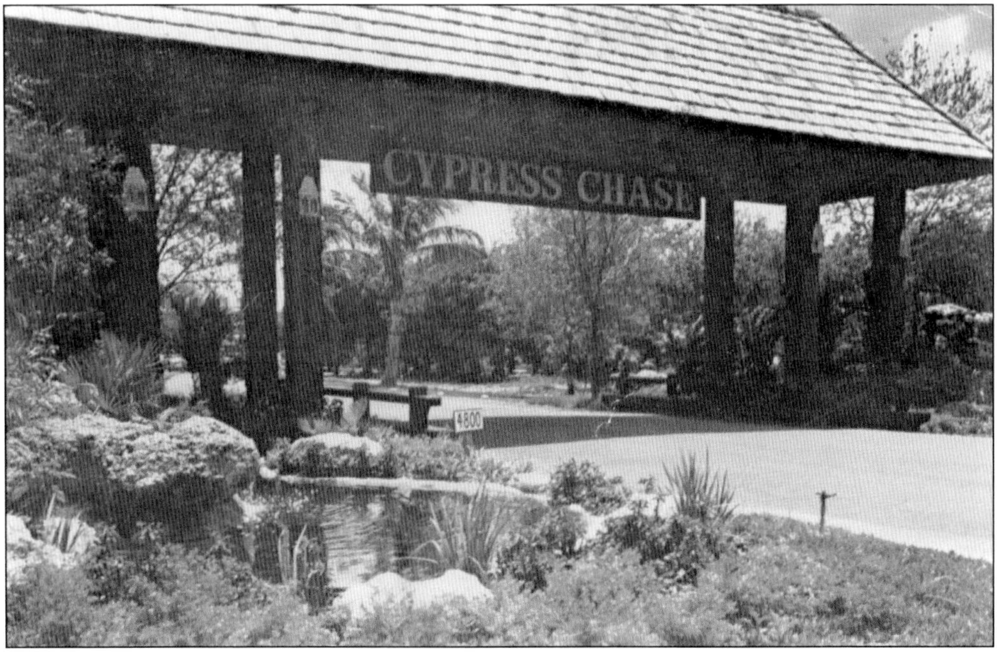

Cypress Chase billed itself as "the Garden Condominium" and was located at Northwest Forty-Seventh Terrace and Northwest Forty-Eighth Avenue. This 1972 postcard shows the rock garden and the entrance pavilion.

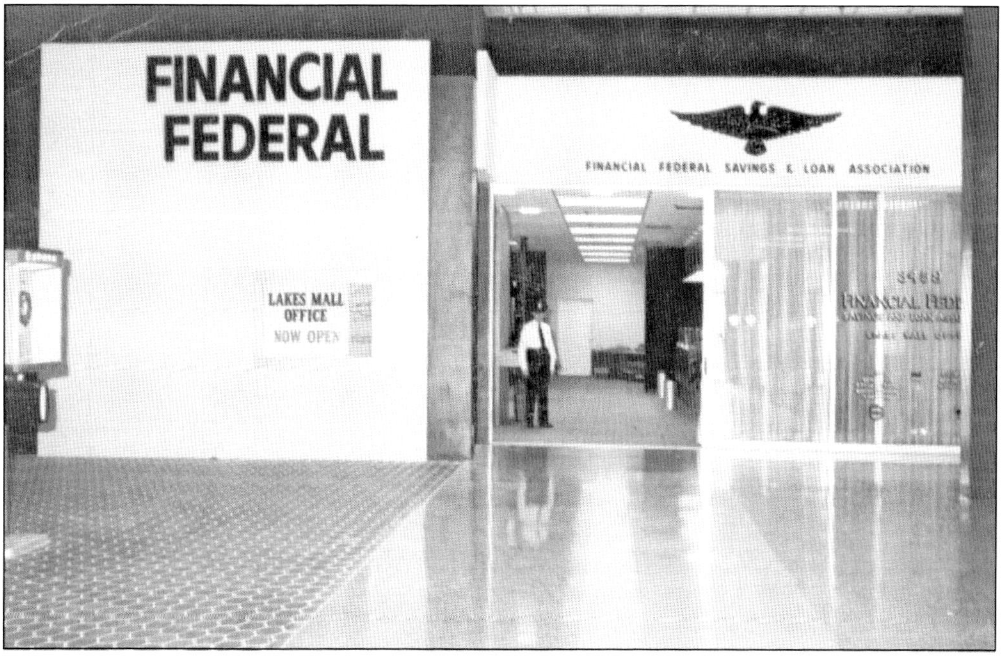

Financial Federal began as Miami Beach Federal in the late 1930s. The Lauderdale Lakes office, located in the Lakes Mall, is shown here. Following a name change in the early 1970s, the bank branched out, reaching much of South Florida. It was eventually taken over by Bank of America. This office was located at 3459 North State Road Seven (US Route 441).

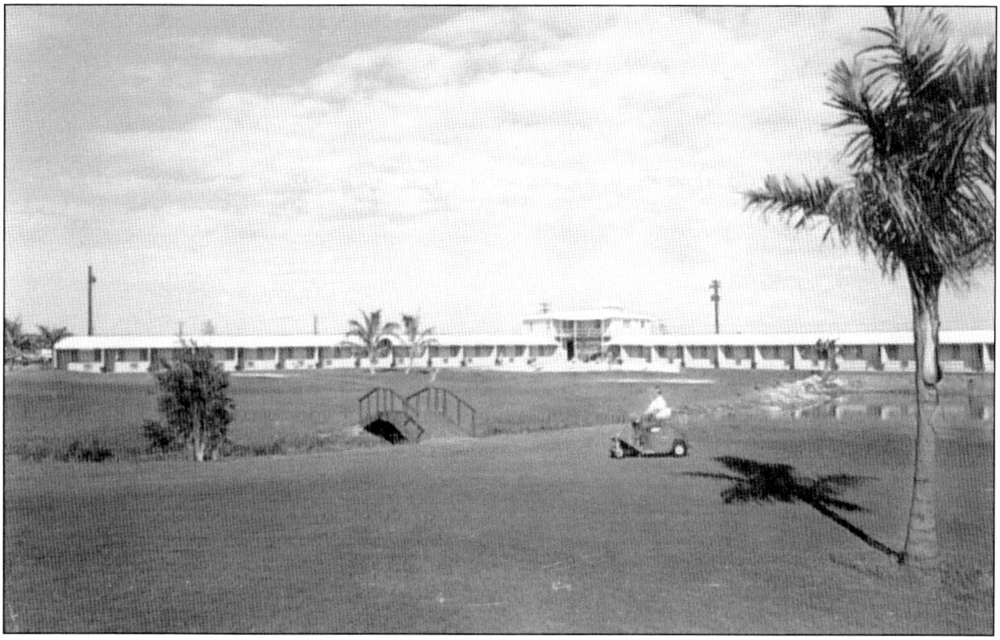

This view of the Lauderdale Lakes Golf Motor Lodge shows the 18th green. The club, located at 3700 West Oakland Park Boulevard, is now called Lauderdale Lakes Country Club and Golf Motor Lodge and is much changed since this postcard was originally produced in 1962.

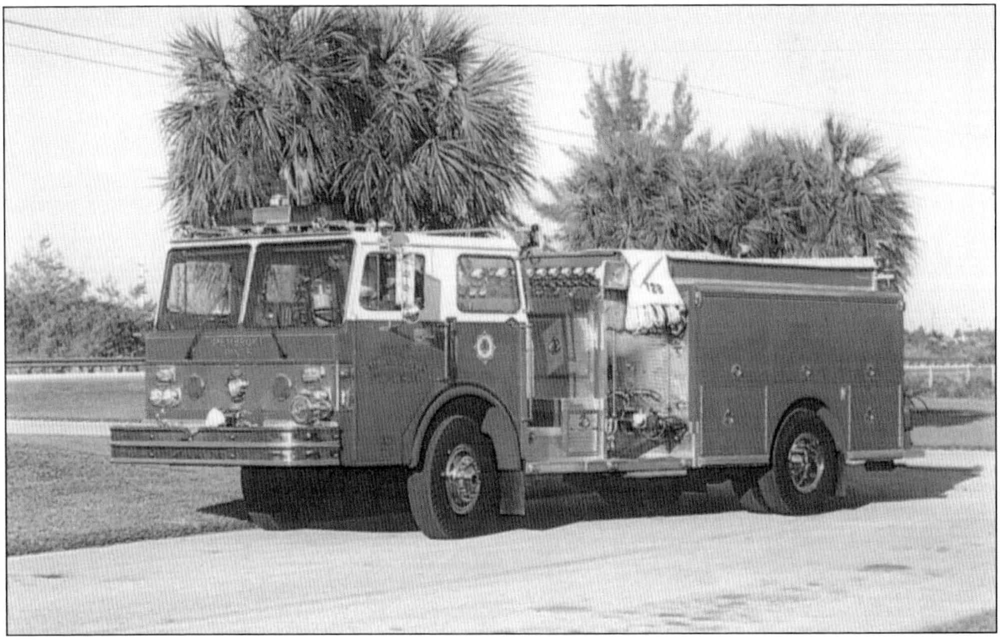

In 1983, the Pembroke Pines Fire Department purchased one of the first Indiana Fire Apparatus units put on a Spartan chassis. That information and much more appears on the back of this very rare crossover collectible, a marvelous piece for any collector of fire department or South Florida local memorabilia.

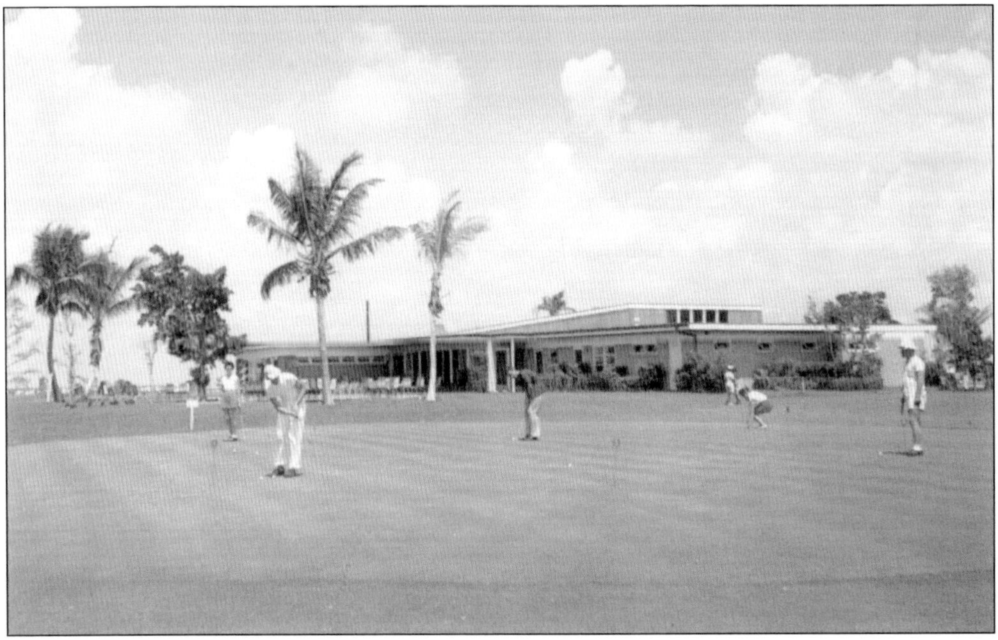

The address for the Plantation Golf Club at the time this postcard was made was simply "end of West Broward Boulevard." It is certainly possible that the Jacaranda Golf Club, now located at 9200 West Broward Boulevard, might once have been the Plantation Golf Club. The original club boasted of "one of the South's finest golf courses with 18 holes and 6,621 yards," as well as a modern clubhouse and all golf amenities.

At least in South Florida, the buffet-style all-you-care-to-eat restaurants seem to be fading away. However, in the 1970s and 1980s, King's Plate Smorgasbord and Buffet, located at 300 South State Road Seven (US Route 441) offered diners "a delightful dining experience/famous for delicious food." Of course, diners were welcomed to "eat as much as you wish."

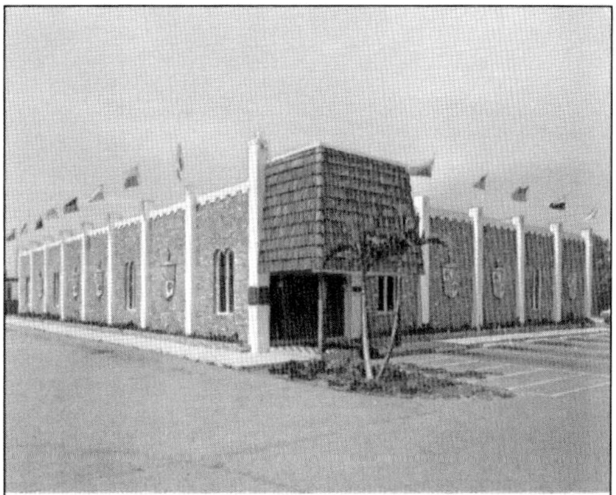

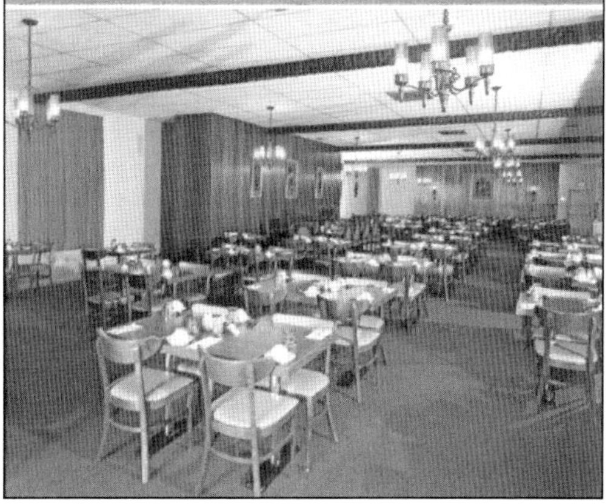

Covenant Village, located at 9201 West Broward Boulevard, is directly across that very busy street from Jacaranda Golf Club. Covenant Village is a high-quality adult-living facility that offers various levels of care and fine dining in the dining room with a snack bar available to residents throughout the day and evening.

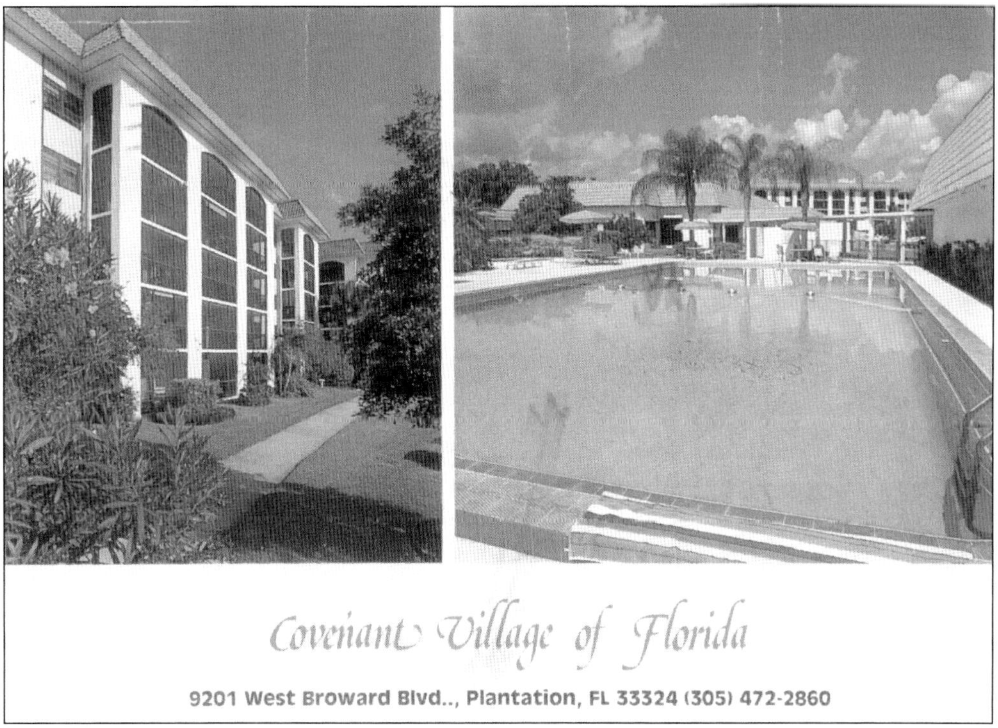

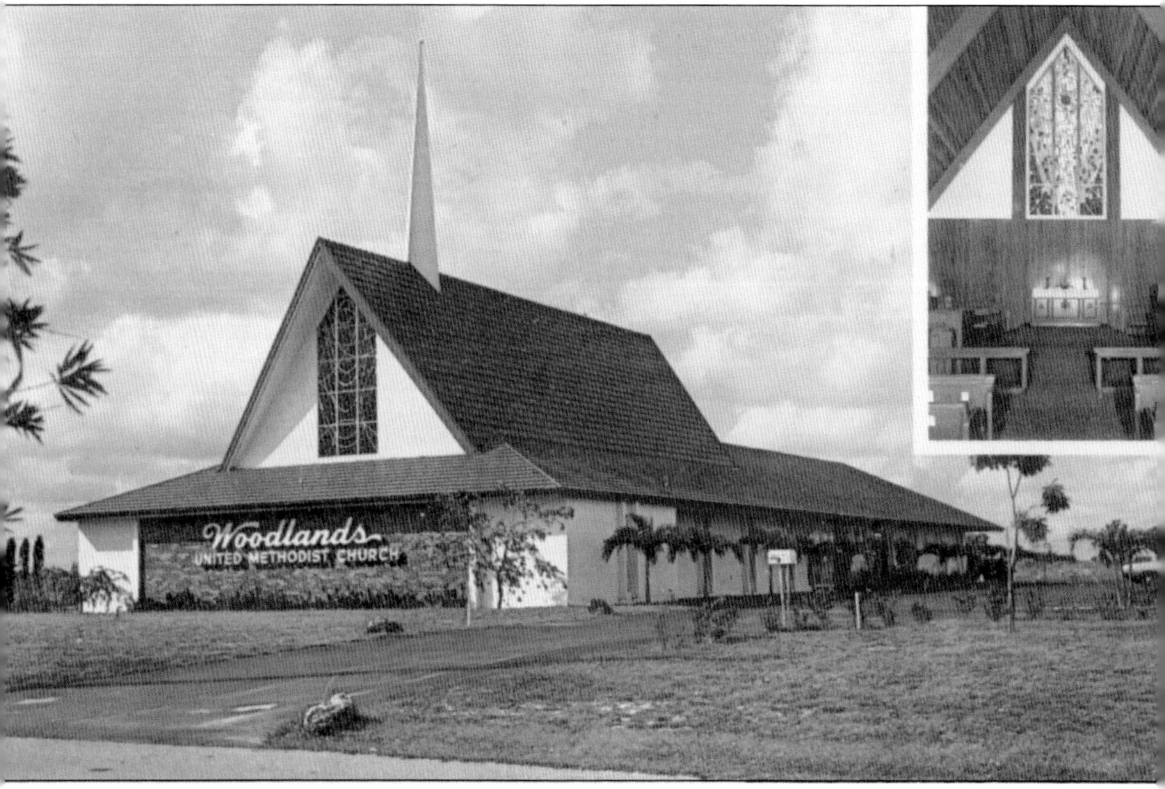

Woodlands United Methodist Church issued this chrome postcard upon the church's opening in 1972. Still ministering to a growing flock, the church remains in the same location—6901 Northwest 70th Avenue.

Ten

Fantasy Lands and Tourist Attractions

While Dade County became known as a business and tourism mecca, and Palm Beach County provided similar facilities for commerce and guest accommodation, Broward County (the smallest of the three) evolved a bit differently. Although there were certainly numerous beachfront and mainland businesses, along with tourist courts, cabins, and other accommodations for visitors, Broward, for whatever reason, hosted an inordinate number of unique tourist attractions, particularly in the pre-Disney era.

From Beatty's Jungle Zoo, modeled after much larger zoos in major cities but complete with "big cat" training, to the utterly fascinating Creatureland, Pioneer City, Storyland, and others, Broward County was truly a grand place to enjoy off-beat and one-of-a-kind attractions rarely found anywhere else!

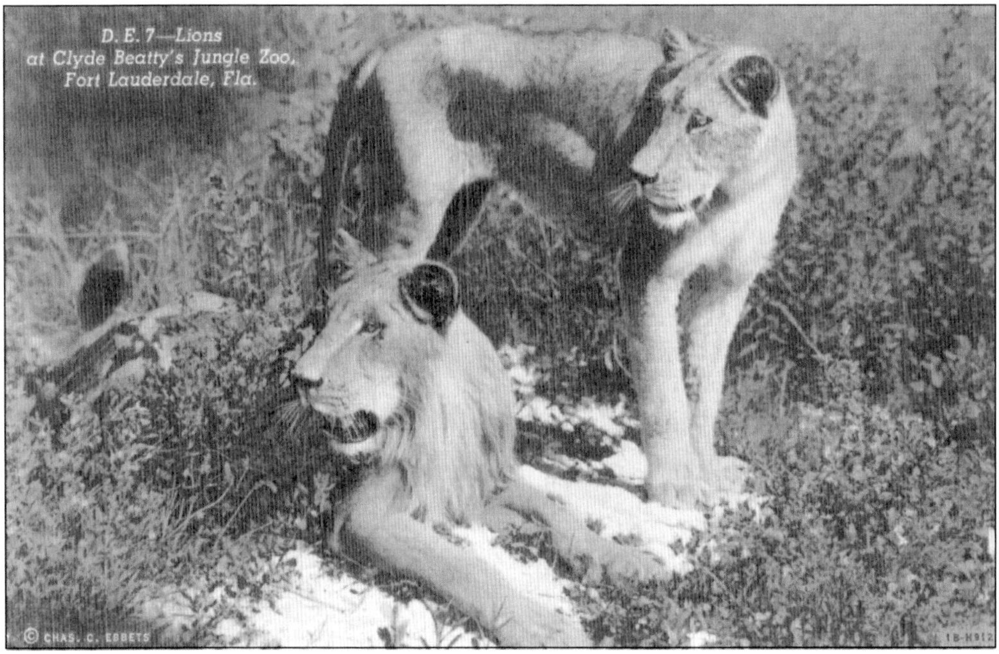

Barely—if at all—remembered, the great big cat trainer Clyde Beatty, who was once a partner with the Cole brothers in the circus bearing their names, maintained his Jungle Zoo on Federal Highway in Fort Lauderdale. Sometime in the early 1950s, the business was moved to North Miami and then closed. Except for several very rare brochures and a smattering of photographs and postcards, no evidence remains of the short existence of Beatty's Jungle Zoo in Fort Lauderdale.

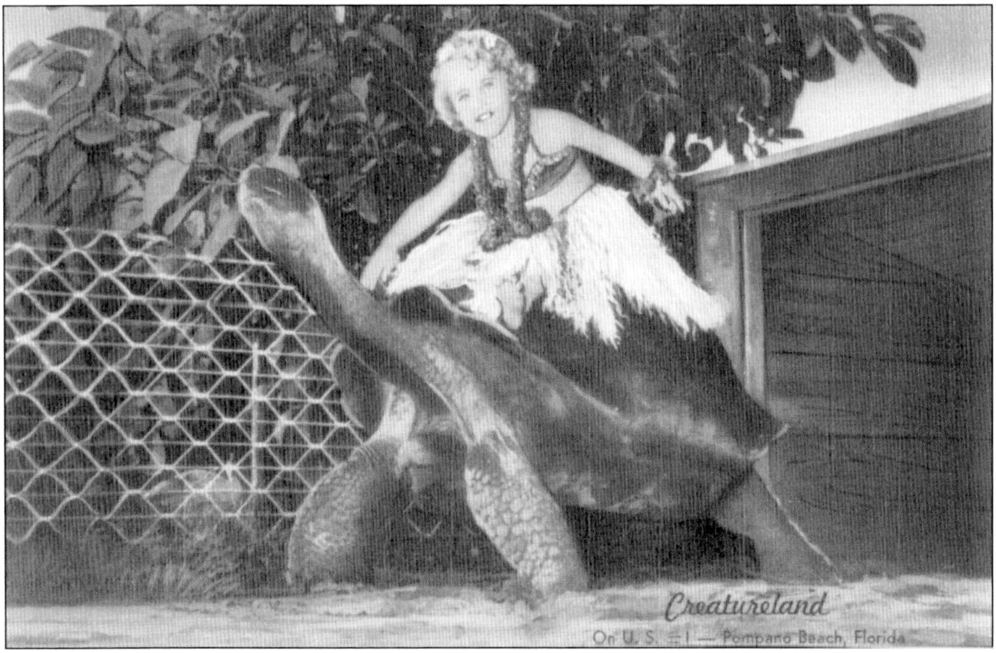

Creatureland was at some unknown point in the past located on US Route 1 in Pompano Beach. This linen postcard is likely from the late 1940s or early 1950s. The back of the card states that "little Jonnie Shadoin is on the back of the giant Galapagos Tortoise."

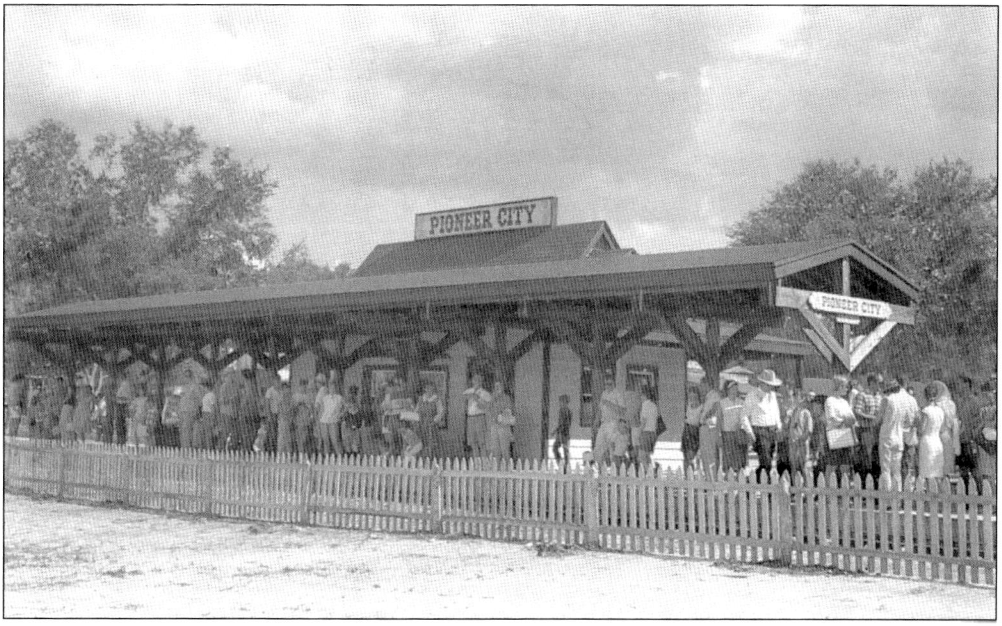

Photography studio magnate Myron M. "Mike" Weiss Sr. opened Pioneer City on Memorial Day weekend 1966 as a model of the Old West town of Dodge City, complete with a range of businesses that would have been found there around the turn of the 20th century. Unfortunately for Weiss, the area was inundated with 21 inches of rain during the first month of operation. Other problems, including paltry attendance numbers—mostly due to the attraction's location in western Broward County, which then had no expressway access—led to the park's closing in February 1968.

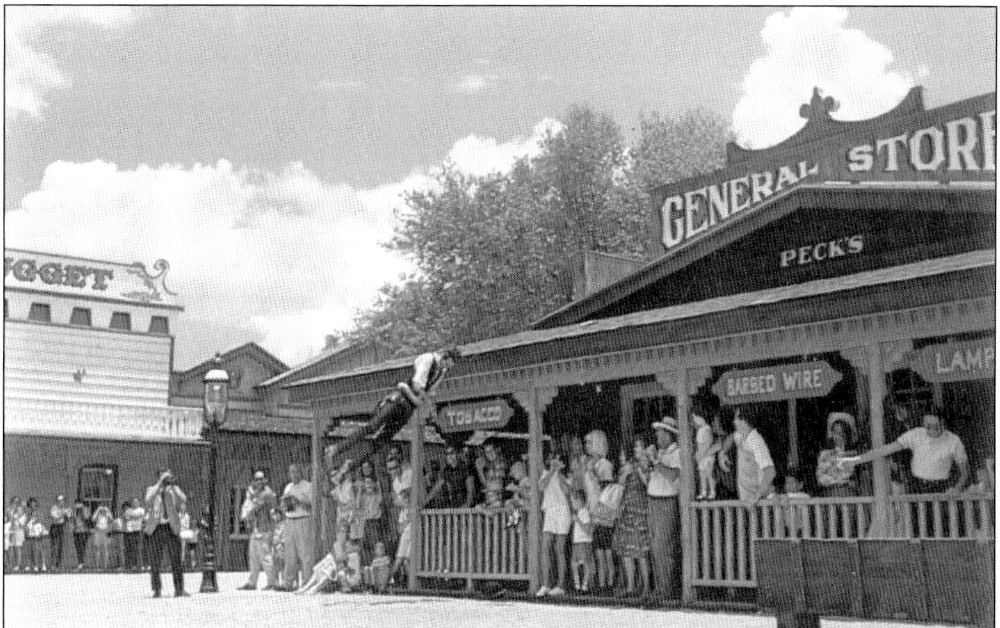

Daily gunfights took place outside of Peck's General Store in Pioneer City. One of the gunfighter stunt men is visible well off the ground at center (left of the "tobacco" sign).

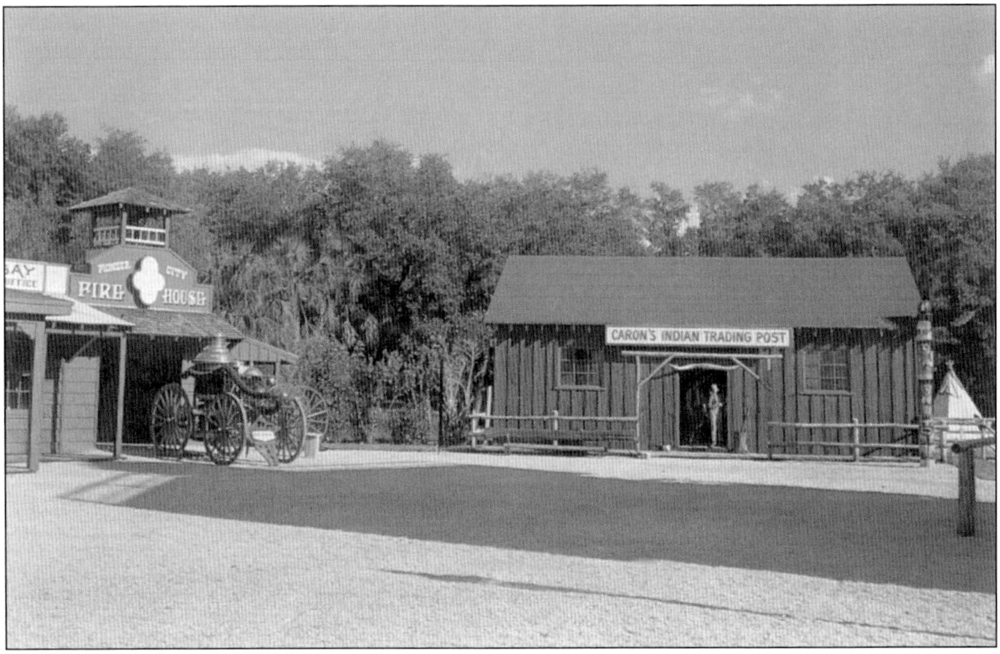

This Pioneer City postcard features the corner of the assay office at far left, the fire house with a pumper in front, and Canon's Indian Trading Post at right. Located 15 miles west of Fort Lauderdale on a two-lane road, the attraction was difficult to access, which contributed to the park's demise.

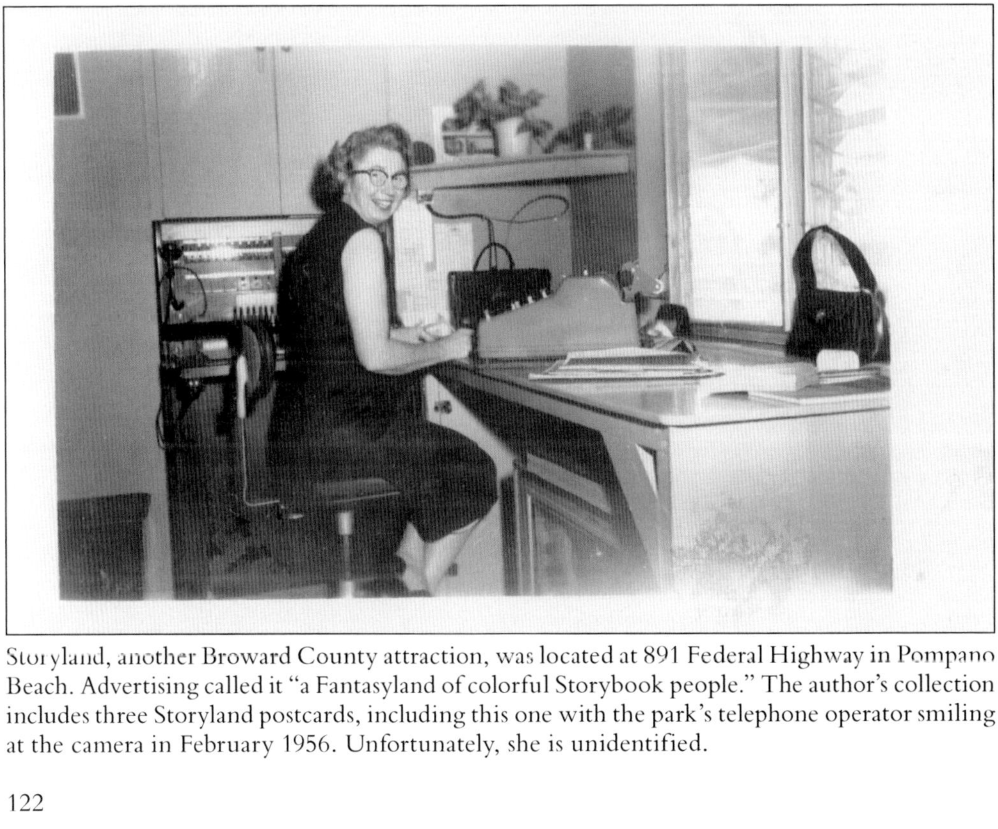

Storyland, another Broward County attraction, was located at 891 Federal Highway in Pompano Beach. Advertising called it "a Fantasyland of colorful Storybook people." The author's collection includes three Storyland postcards, including this one with the park's telephone operator smiling at the camera in February 1956. Unfortunately, she is unidentified.

The same woman from the previous postcard is shown "on television" in this postcard dated "Dec, 1956" in ink on the back. "A new T. V. Star—Fatty Davis" is written below the date. Note the Storyland logo at the bottom.

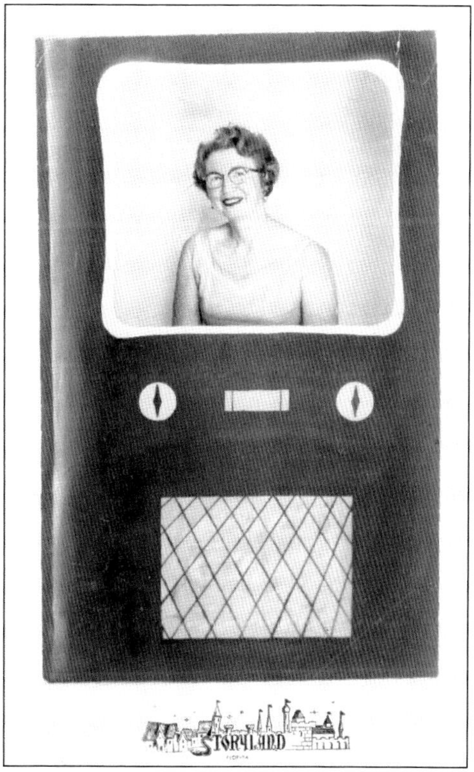

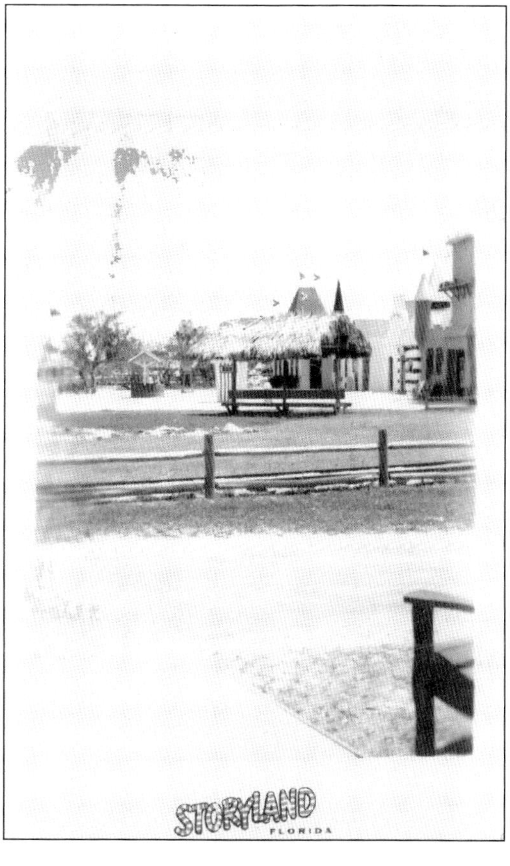

This card offers an early view of Storyland and was mailed to Geneva, New York, in September 1956. A different Storyland logo appears at the bottom of this postcard.

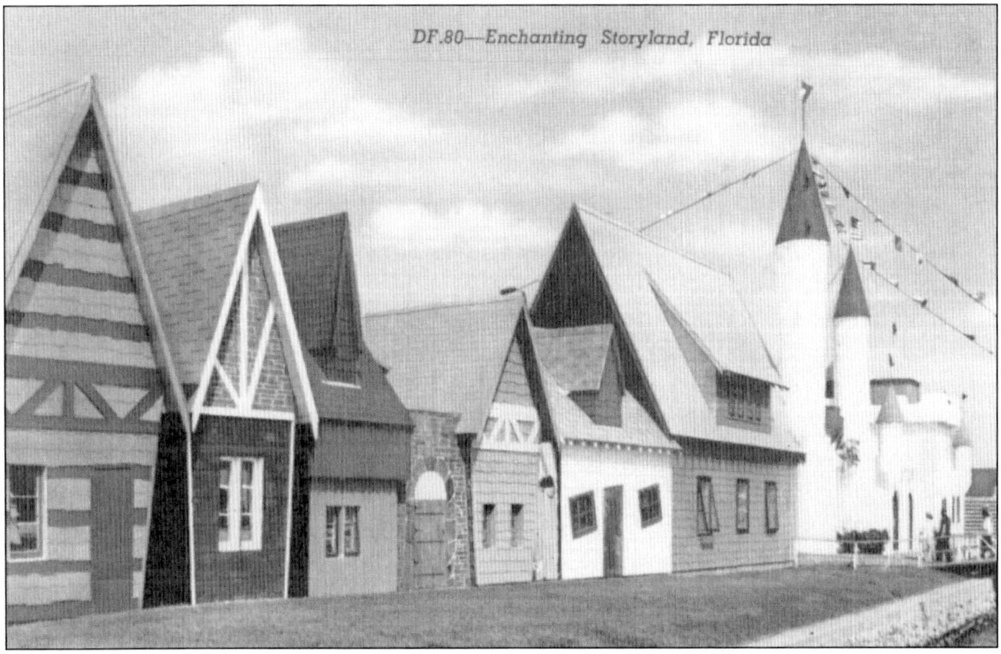

Storyland was a fairy tale–themed, child-oriented park that opened on the day after Thanksgiving in November 1955. Unfortunately, unlike the Disney parks, it failed to appeal to the entire family. This linen-finish postcard shows the castle and several buildings, possibly homes.

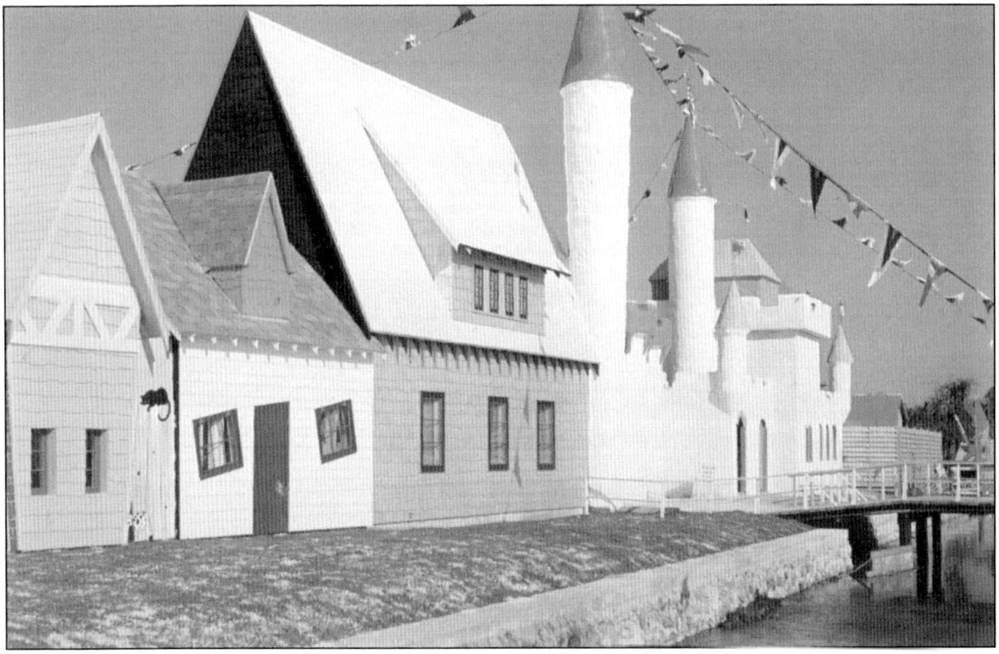

A later, chrome-finish Storyland postcard is similar to the linen-finish card in the previous image, but this one shows the moat more clearly. Additionally, it appears as if several of the buildings have been renovated and enlarged.

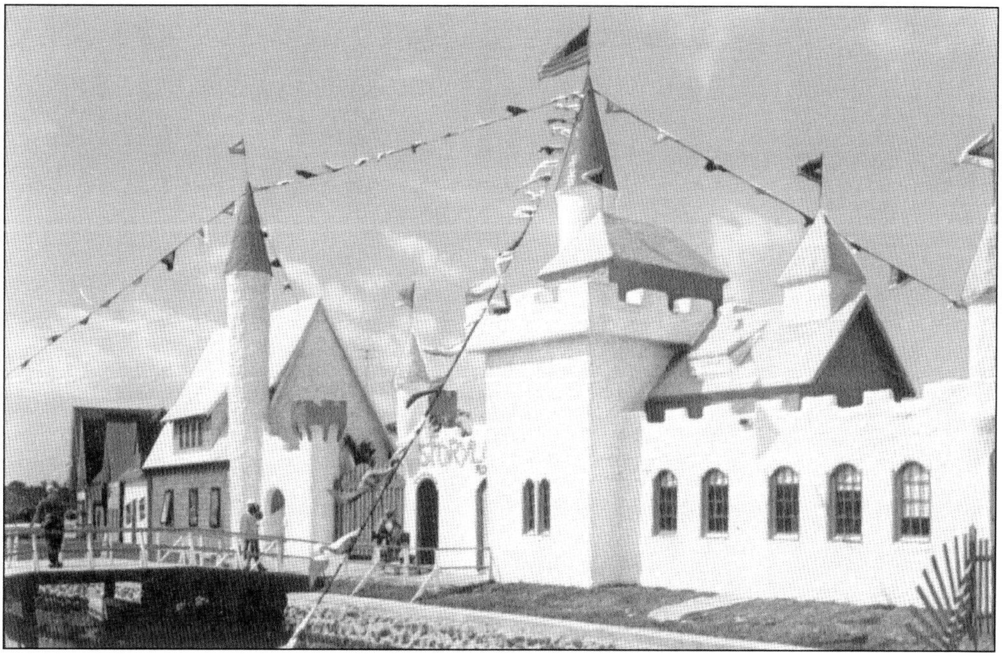

This photograph of Storyland was taken from the opposite direction of the two cards on the previous page and shows the bridge over the moat. The full length of the castle is evident in this chrome postcard.

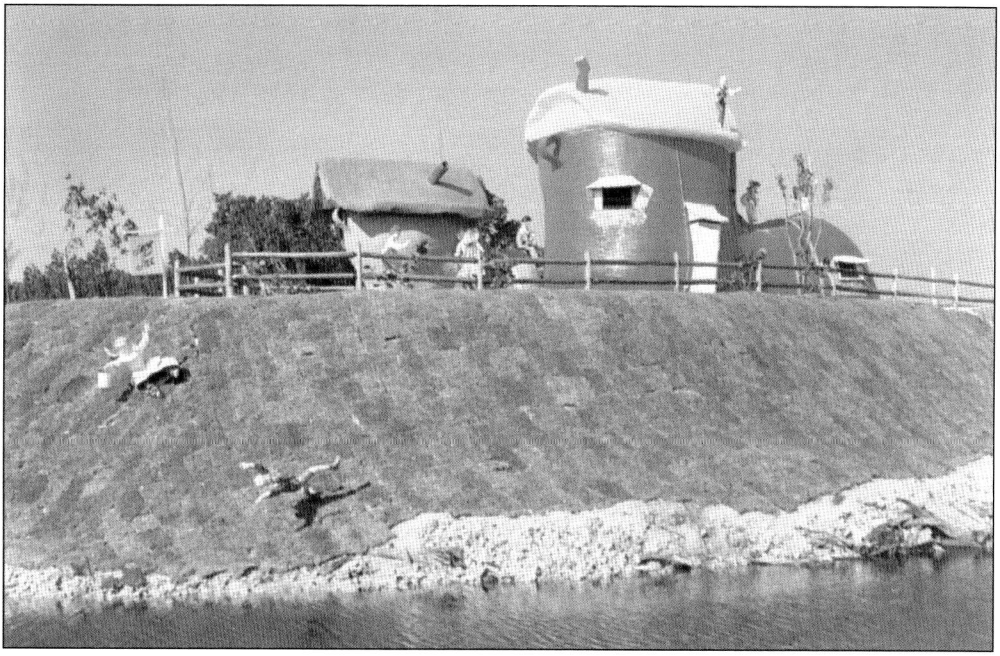

Jack and Jill are tumbling down the Storyland Hill, and the old lady who lived in a shoe was probably out shopping when this postcard was made. Storyland was a wonderful place, but its appeal was simply too limited.

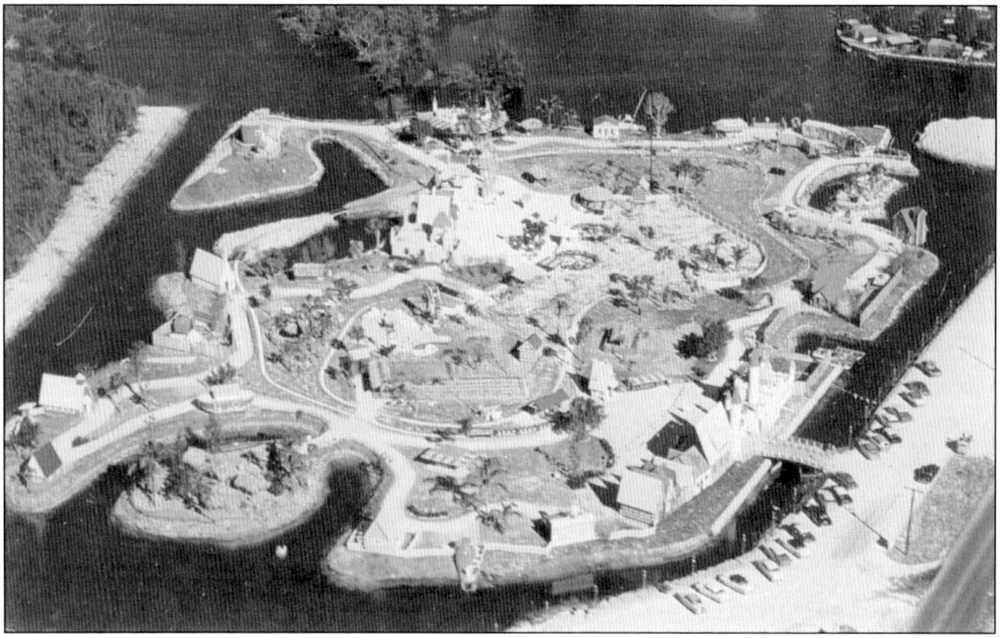

This aerial view, likely taken from a helicopter by McFadden Air Photographs, shows the entire Storyland layout. When the first group of children who had initially enjoyed the park got a little older, it began to run into trouble. Storyland closed in early 1961, changed hands, was reopened, and was back on the block by 1964. Due mostly to the damage caused by Hurricane Cleo, it finally closed for good and was torn down in 1964.

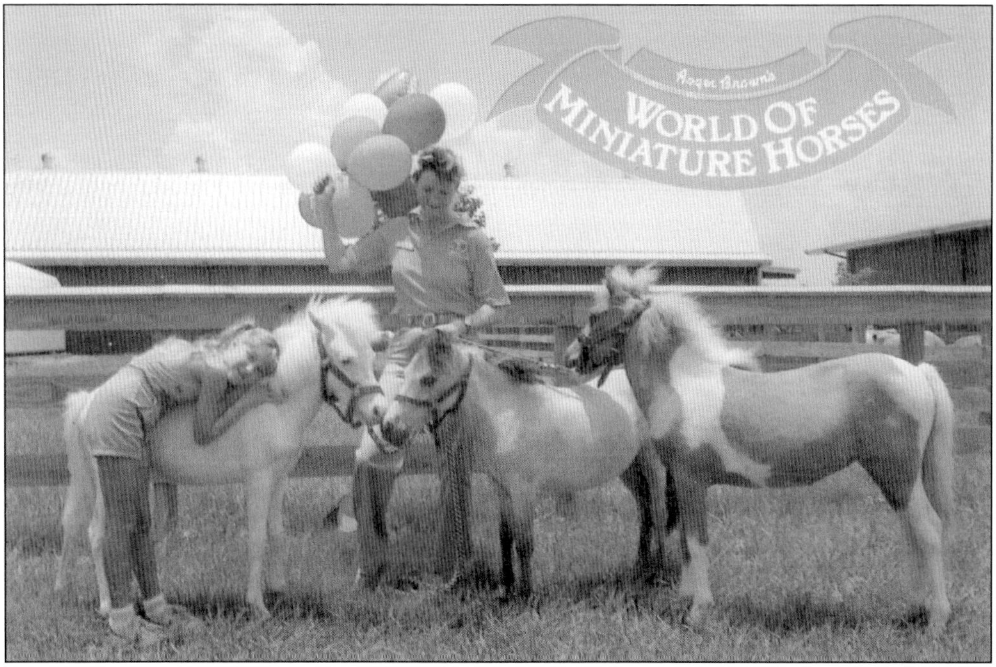

Roger Brown's World of Miniature Horses was located at 1000 Northwest Thirty-First Avenue (then called the Atlantic Avenue Extension) west of Pompano Beach. With its picturesque, farm-like setting, it was a paradise for horse lovers and equestrians.

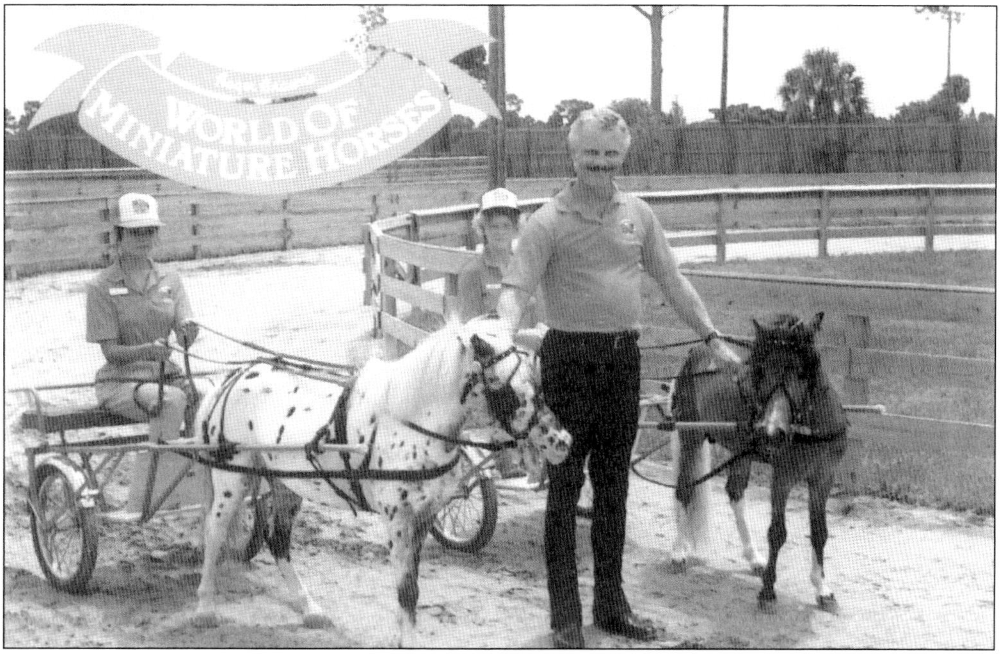

World of Miniature Horses was owned by Roger Brown, who is shown here with two of his beautiful charges. The attraction included animal displays and performances.

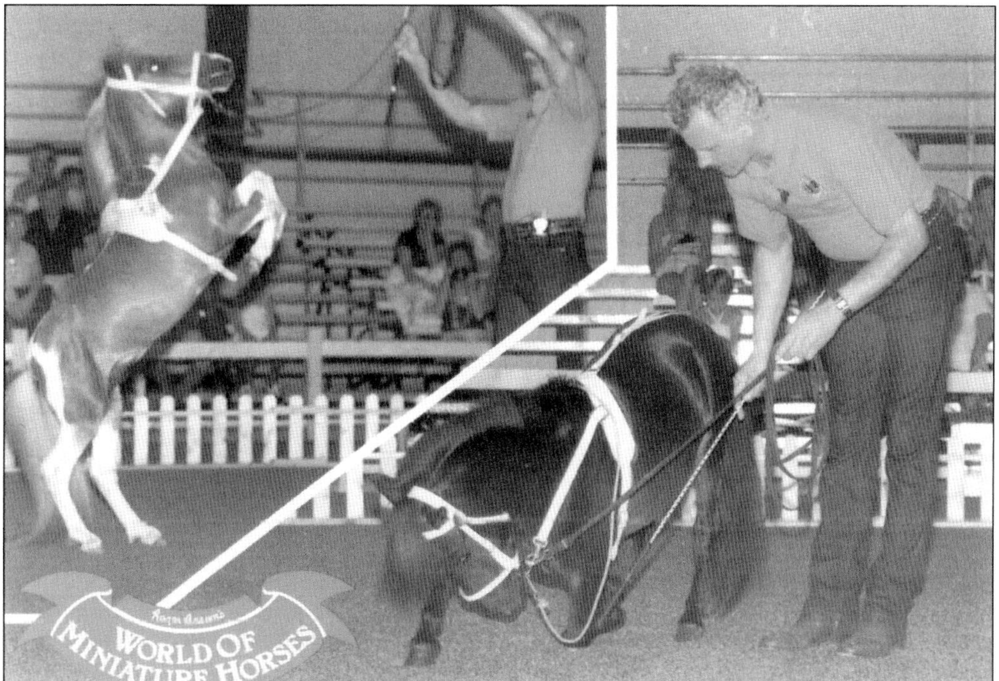

Roger Brown opened the World of Miniature Horses in 1982. Although he was well-meaning and had a good heart, he was not prepared for the changes that would overtake South Florida in the tourist attractions and entertainment businesses and, sadly, his "World" closed for good in 1984 and completely disappeared within a year.